Crochet YOUR OWN Cat

12 Life-Size Amigurumi Kitties to Make and Love!

Mieko Shindo

Contents

Introduction

Cats are such mysterious and charming creatures—one minute, they are completely independent, with their own lives to live, and the next, they're curled up in your lap demanding attention. Petting a cat, or even just being in their presence, makes us humans feel relaxed and at ease. Cats are magical creatures that have the power to heal us just by being there.

I started this project with the hope of creating amigurumi that expresses the illusive charm of the cat; capturing a cat's trademark characteristics, from their lithe, agile bodies to their distinctive fur colors and patterns and their absorbing gazes. I was so grateful to have the help and feedback of many cat lovers.

If you're new to amigurumi, I suggest starting with one of the smaller projects, such as a kitten. This will allow you to develop your skills before moving on to one of the larger designs. Feel free to change the colors, markings, and other elements to recreate a special feline in your life.

I hope that these crochet cats provide you with a little bit of the joy and companionship of their real life counterparts!

Mieko Shindo

Norwegian Forest

A long-haired breed from Norway, these cats are characterized by their powerful, strong bodies, thick fur, triangular ears, and adorable eyes that look as if they're wearing eye shadow.

INSTRUCTIONS • PAGE 70

British Shorthair

This British breed boasts an impressive blue-gray fur color. They have stocky bodies and thick coats, so make sure to graft plenty of yarn to create a rounded shape.

INSTRUCTIONS • PAGE 78

Ragdoll (SEE PAGE 16)

Mandalay

The Mandalay cat is an exotic breed related to the Burmese cat. It is known for its jet-black coat color. Since it is a short-haired breed, the key is not to graft the yarn, but to fluff up the crocheted areas with a slicker grooming brush.

INSTRUCTIONS • PAGE 93

Tabby

Tabby is not a breed of cat, but rather a coat pattern found among many domestic cats around the world. To capture the distinctive striped pattern, use a few different shades of brown yarn when grafting the fur.

INSTRUCTIONS • PAGE 62

MEOW
Mandalay (SEE PAGE 10)
Somali (SEE PAGE 31)

Norwegian Forest (SEE PAGE 7)

Ragdoll

Ragdolls are known for their beautiful, luxurious fur and striking blue eyes. If you can't find blue eye buttons, paint clear ones with nail polish to capture this breed's characteristic eye color. These cats have an affectionate, docile nature, so give the body a rounded shape to suggest their cuddly disposition.

INSTRUCTIONS • PAGE 80

Calico

Calico cats are domestic cats with mostly white fur and large patches of orange and black. Calico cats are usually female, so here is a mother with her kitten. Have fun arranging different fur patterns.

INSTRUCTIONS • PAGE 83 (ADULT) • PAGE 86 (KITTEN)

Persian (SEE PAGE 27)

Tuxedo (SEE PAGE 28)

Macmillan
MORE THAN SOMEWHAT

American Shorthair

As its name suggests, this cat breed is from the United States and is characterized by its short hair. A beautiful marbled pattern and short, thick legs are the hallmarks of this breed.

INSTRUCTIONS • PAGE 100

INSTRUCTIONS • PAGE 113 (KITTEN)

Persian

The Persian is the king of long-haired cats. Graft plenty of white yarn to create a distinctive and charming flat face.

MEOW

INSTRUCTIONS • PAGE 107 (ADULT)

Tuxedo

Tuxedo is a coloration pattern that can occur in many different cat breeds, but usually presents in a striking black and white combination.

INSTRUCTIONS • PAGE 119

YES?

Somali

The Somali boasts abundant long hair featuring rich bands of color. With their patches of white fur at the neck, clear eyes, and bushy tails, they are nicknamed "fox cats."

INSTRUCTIONS • PAGE 126

Persian (Kitten) (SEE PAGE 27)

Calico (Kitten) (SEE PAGE 18)

Tools and Materials

1. **Grooming scissors:** Use to trim yarn into shape after grafting. Designed specifically for grooming, these scissors can be purchased online or at a pet supply store.
2. **Yarn scissors:** Use to cut or trim yarn to length required.
3. **Needle felting claw:** Use to press the yarn into small areas, such as around the eyes. This tool is made by Clover.
4. **Slicker brush:** This tool is normally used for grooming real pets. In this book, it is used to loosen grafted yarn.
5. **Yarn threader:** Use to thread tapestry needles with yarn. This tool is made by Clover.
6. **Craft glue:** Use to glue whiskers and safety eyes and noses in place.
7. **Crochet hooks:** Use to crochet the different body parts for the cats. You'll need sizes US C-2 (2.5 mm) and US 7 (4.5 mm) hooks to crochet the designs in this book, plus US B-1 (2.25 mm) and US G-6 (4 mm) hooks for crocheting the kittens. The hooks pictured here are from the Amour collection by Clover.
8. **Water soluble marker:** Use to mark the grafting areas. The lines disappear in time or with water.
9. **Sewing needle (fine):** Use to embroider the details around the face.
10. **Tapestry needle:** Use a needle with a large eye designed for yarn or thick thread to attach body parts and graft yarn.
11. **Felting needle:** This type of needle is sold as a refill to be used with a needle felting pen. In this book, the needle is used on its own when grafting yarn.
12. **Sewing pins:** Use to fix body parts in position.
13. **Stitch markers:** Use when crocheting the body. Insert into crochet stitches for counting rows and rounds.

1 **Armature wire for needle felting:** Insert into amigurumi legs, ears, and tails to enable movement. This plastic armature is made by Hamanaka, but you can also use wire.

2 **Needle felting whiskers:** Use black and clear needle felting whiskers for cat whiskers.

3 **Polyester stuffing:** Use to stuff the amigurumi.

4 **Yarn:** Both acrylic and acrylic/mohair blend yarns are used to create these cats. In this book, 2-4 strands of yarn are used together as one strand. Hamanaka Piccolo (sport weight acrylic) and Hamanaka Mohair (light-fingering weight acrylic/mohair blend) yarn were used throughout the book.

Note: Hamanaka Piccolo is a thin sport weight yarn from Japan that is more like a thicker 4 ply. KnitPicks Brava Sport is an alternative option that is readily available in the US and UK.

Eyes & Noses

Plastic toy safety eyes and noses are available in a variety of different sizes, shapes, and colors. They come with a washer that is used to secure them in place on the inside of the stuffed animal.

1 **Cat eyes:** 15 mm and 18 mm are used in this book.

2 **Crystal eyes:** 18 mm are used in this book.

3 **Safety nose:** A 12 mm triangular black plastic safety nose was used for the Mandalay on page 10.

4 **Clear cat eyes and crystal eyes:** For custom colored eyes, 15 mm cat eyes and crystal eyes are painted as shown below.

How to Create Custom Colored Eyes

If you cannot find eyes in a specific color, you can paint clear eyes to create a custom look. Simply apply acrylic paint or nail polish to the back of the clear area to achieve your desired look.

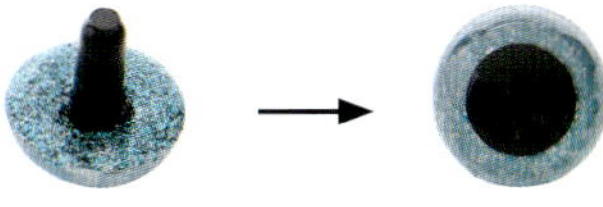

Health and Safety Note: Toy safety eyes and noses are not suitable for children under the age of three as they pose a choking hazard. For safety reasons, if your cat is intended to be used as a child's toy, use a tapestry needle and yarn to embroider the eyes and nose instead. If you are using toy safety eyes and noses, make sure to follow the manufacturer's instructions.

Getting Started

The following instructions outline the basic construction steps for all the cats in this book. Refer to pages 37–61 for more detailed tutorials on crocheting and assembling the cats and pages 62–133 for project instructions for each type of cat.

Basic Construction Steps

1. Crochet each body part. Instructions are provided in both written and chart format. Always leave a 12" (30 cm) yarn tail when you finish crocheting a body part. These will be used to sew the body parts together when assembling the stuffed animal.

Note: Some of the outer ears will be crocheted over armature wire.

2. Fill the body and the head and chest piece with polyester stuffing.

Note: Make sure to attach the eye buttons to the head before stuffing; otherwise, you won't be able to attach the washers to the backs. Attach toy safety eyes and noses following the manufacturer's instructions, or embroider them with yarn if the cat is intended as a child's toy (see healthy and safety note on page 35).

3. Close the body and the head and chest before sewing them together (see page 51).

4. Attach armature wire to the body where the front legs will be added. Wrap the wires with yarn and polyester stuffing to shape the legs (see page 51).

5. Slide the crocheted front legs over the wire and close.

6. Fill the narrow area of the back legs with polyester stuffing and attach to the body (see page 52).

7. Attach the tail in the same way as the front legs (see page 53).

8. Use polyester stuffing to fill the mouth before attaching it to the head (see page 53).

9. Sew the base of the nose to the mouth, then sew the sides of the nose to the face and the top of the nose to the forehead (see page 54). The crocheted nose should be positioned slightly over the eyes.

10. Attach the ears to the head (see page 55).

11. If necessary, draw the grafting pattern on the body using water-soluble marker and then graft the fur (see page 57). Do not graft yarn to the ears, toes, or stomach area, unless otherwise noted. For areas of cats without grafting, style the fur by brushing with the slicker brush.

12. Stab the base of the grafted yarn with a felting needle to secure it in place.

13. Trim into shape with scissors as you loosen the grafted yarn with the slicker brush.

14. Continue brushing with the slicker brush, trimming, and adjusting the shape with the felting needle.

15. Embroider the nose, mouth, and eyelids (see pages 60–61).

16. Glue the whiskers in place (see page 56).

1. Crochet the Body Parts

Here we introduce the basic techniques used for crocheting each body part. Refer to the individual project instructions, but use these photos for additional guidance. The photos use the Tabby on page 62 as an example, but the same techniques apply to all cats, unless otherwise noted.

Anatomy of a Crochet Cat

US vs UK Crochet Terminology

US and UK crochet terms have different meanings, so it's important to check which style was used to write the pattern. Note that this book uses US crochet terms. The chart below highlights the differences in terminology that apply in this book.

US	UK
single crochet (sc)	double crochet (dc)
half double crochet (hdc)	half treble crochet (htr)
double crochet (dc)	treble crochet (tr)
half double crochet cluster (hdc-cl)	half treble crochet cluster (htr-cl)
single crochet 2 stitches together (sc2tog)	double crochet 2 stitches together (dc2tog)
double crochet 3 stitches together (dc3tog)	treble crochet 3 stitches together (tr3tog)
double crochet 4 stitches together (dc4tog)	treble crochet 4 stitches together (tr4tog)

Abbreviations

beg	beginning
ch	chain
dc	double crochet
g	grams
hdc	half double crochet
rnd	round
sc	single crochet
slst	slip stitch
st(s)	stitch(es)
tog	together
yd(s)	yard(s)

BEFORE YOU BEGIN

Prepare Your Yarn: Unless otherwise noted, align 4 strands of yarn (2 strands of sport weight acrylic and 2 strands of light-fingering weight acrylic/mohair blend) and wind into a ball. For the inner ears, mouth, and nose, use 2 strands of yarn (1 strand of sport weight acrylic and 1 strand of light-fingering weight acrylic/mohair blend).

Measure Your Gauge: Crochet a swatch and make sure you have the following gauge:

Adult Cats: 13 stitches × 15 rows = 4" (10 cm) using a US 7 (4.5 mm) crochet hook

Kittens: 14 stitches × 16 rows = 4" (10 cm) using a G-6 (4 mm) crochet hook

MAKE A MAGIC RING

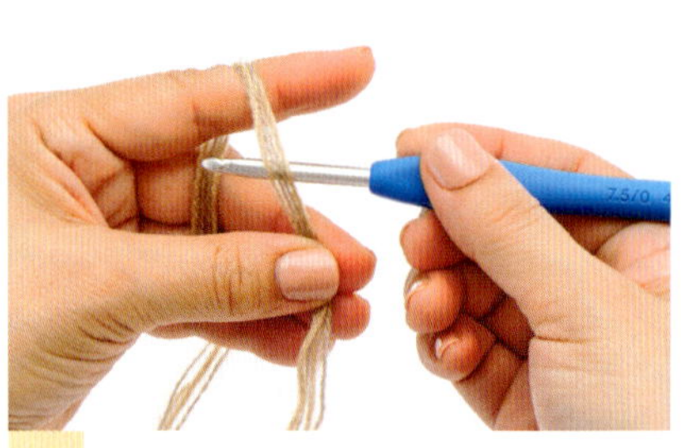

01 Set the hook behind the yarn and bring the hook toward the front in a counterclockwise direction.

02 The yarn is wrapped around the hook, making a loop.

03 The yarn that was under the thumb in step 2 is crossed as shown in the photo above.

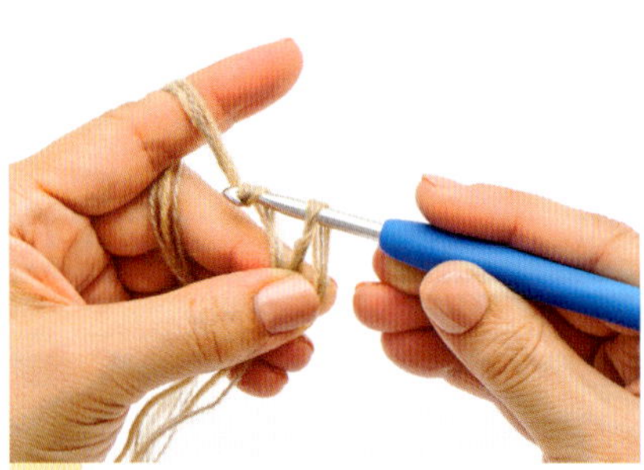

04 Hold the yarns where they cross and wrap the yarn around the hook.

05 Pull the yarn through the loop on the hook to secure the magic ring.

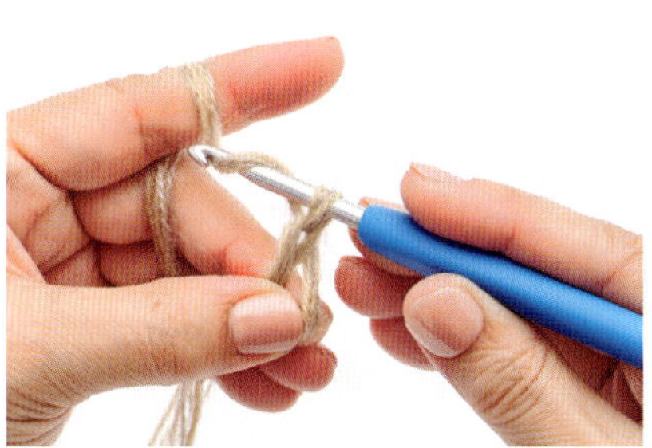

01 Yarn over the hook and pull through again (chain stitch).

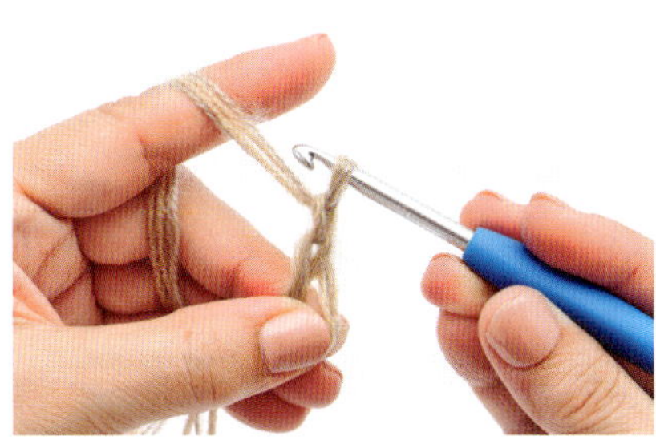

02 The first chain of the round is complete.

03 Insert the hook into the center of the magic ring again.

04 Yarn over and pull loop through.

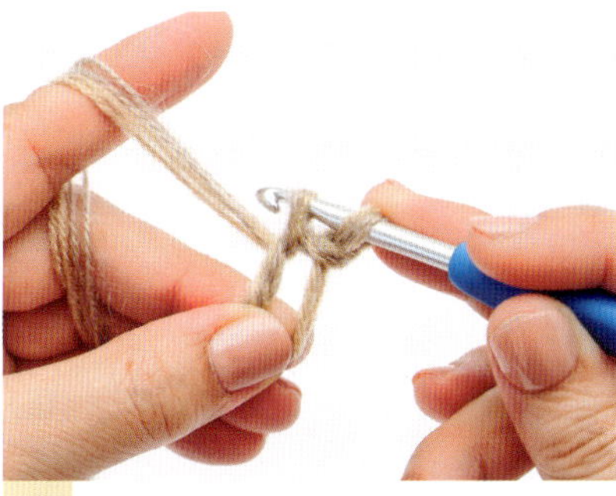

05 There are two loops on the hook.

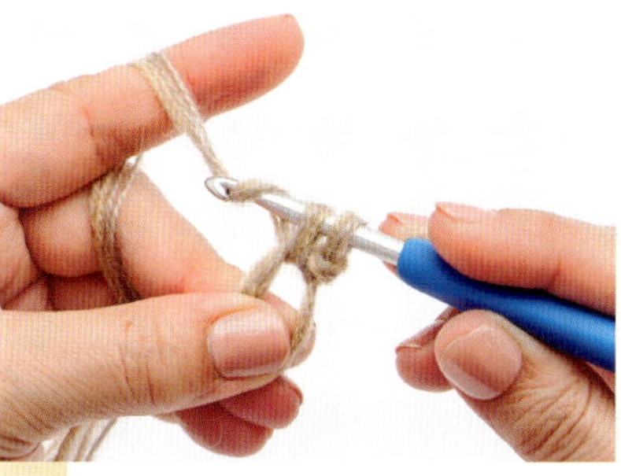

06 Yarn over and pull through two loops.

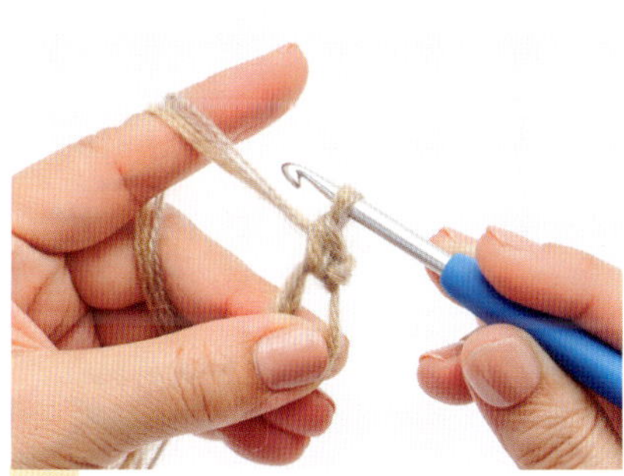

07 The first single crochet is complete. This is noted with an × symbol in the crochet charts.

08 Insert a stitch marker into the first single crochet stitch of the first round. This will serve as a guide so that you will know where the second round starts.

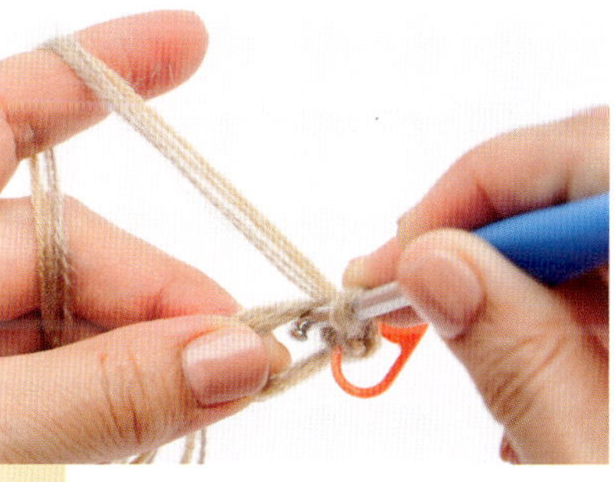

09 Repeat steps 3-7 seven more times to make eight single crochet stitches in total.

10 The first round of eight single crochet stitches is complete.

11 Remove the hook temporarily. Pull the end of yarn to close the magic ring. Hold on to the stitches and don't let them unravel.

12 The ring is now closed, and the stitches are now a circle shape.

13 Insert the hook back into the working loop. Insert the hook into the first single crochet (under top loops of the stitch), or under the beginning chain 1 (if directed in your pattern).

14 Yarn over and pull loop through all loops (to make a slip stitch) to close the round. Remove marker. The first round is complete.

CROCHET THE PAWS

Ⓣ = Cluster stitch variation with two half double crochet

01 Starting with a magic ring, work 8 single crochet stitches. For the second round, make two single crochets (inserting a stitch marker into the first stitch to mark the start of the round).

02 Yarn over and insert hook in the next stitch.

03 Yarn over and pull through, leaving the loop longer.

04 Repeat steps 2 and 3 in the same stitch; five loops remain on the hook.

05 Yarn over and pull through four loops; two loops remain on the hook.

06 Yarn over and pull through the last two loops.

07 The cluster stitch variation with two half double crochet is completed.

08 Repeat the cluster stitches in the next three stitches.

09 Work two single crochet stitches to complete the round.

CROCHET THE LEGS

Note: For the Tabby, you will change yarn frequently when crocheting the legs. The following guide shows how to work the color change for each round. Refer to individual project instructions for each type of cat.

01 On the last stitch of the round, work single crochet stitch halfway (leaving two loops on hook).

02 Drop old color and pick up new color yarn.

03 Pull new yarn through the last two loops to complete the single crochet stitch.

04 Insert hook under the top loops of the first single crochet stitch, yarn over and pull through all loops to join the round.

05 Before the chain stitch for the next round, bring the yarn end toward the front to avoid loosening the yarn. Leave the original yarn as it is.

06 Make a single crochet stitch and insert a stitch marker to mark the start of the round.

07 Work one round and work the last single crochet stitch halfway as before.

08 Change to the next yarn and pull through two loops to complete the single crochet stitch.

09 Make next round in same way.

CROCHET THE EARS

Ŧ = Double crochet T = Half double crochet

Note: The outer ear is crocheted first, then the inner ear is crocheted separately and the two are sewn together. These instructions are for the right ear. The left ear has a different crochet chart, so please refer to the individual project instructions.

01 For chain stitch, count the first stitch as one chain, and don't pull it too tight or it will be difficult to see.

02 Make six chain stitches.

03 Make three more chain stitches to count as a turning stitch.

04 Yarn over and insert the hook in the 5th chain stitch from the hook, through one side of the chain.

05 Yarn over and pull through, yarn over again, then pull through two loops.

06 Yarn over again and pull through the remaining two loops.

07 The double crochet stitch is complete.

08 Make another double crochet stitch in the next chain stitch.

09 Yarn over and insert hook in the next stitch.

10 Yarn over again and pull through (three loops on hook), yarn over again and pull through all three loops.

11 The half double crochet stitch is complete.

12 Make a single crochet stitch in the next chain stitch.

13 Make three single crochet stitches in the end stitch. Turn around to work along the other side of the chain stitches.

14 Yarn over and insert hook in the opposite side of the chain stitch and make a half double crochet.

15 Make a half double crochet in the next stitch.

16 Make a double crochet in the next two stitches.

17 Make two double crochets in the last stitch. The first row of the ear is complete.

18 After the first row, make one chain stitch as a turning stitch for the next row. Turn work to the other side. This is the beginning of the second row.

19 Cut a 6" (15 cm) long piece of armature wire. Fold it in half and align with the working edge of the ear.

20 When you insert the hook under the top loops of each single crochet stitch, place it under the armature wire as well.

21 One round of single crochet is completed. This is the reverse side of the ear.

22 At the end of the crochet, fasten off. Leave 12" (30 cm) of yarn to attach the other parts. Turn right side out to complete.

23 Make the inner ear using one strand of sport weight acrylic and one strand of light-fingering weight acrylic/mohair blend. The inner ear will follow the same pattern as the outer ear, but is crocheted with a smaller hook.

24 Sew the outer and inner ear together, picking up the inside of the chain stitches. Weave in the tail end from inner ear.

25 The right ear is finished. Follow the same process to make the left ear. Note that the left ear has a different crochet chart, so refer to the individual project instructions.

CROCHET THE NOSE

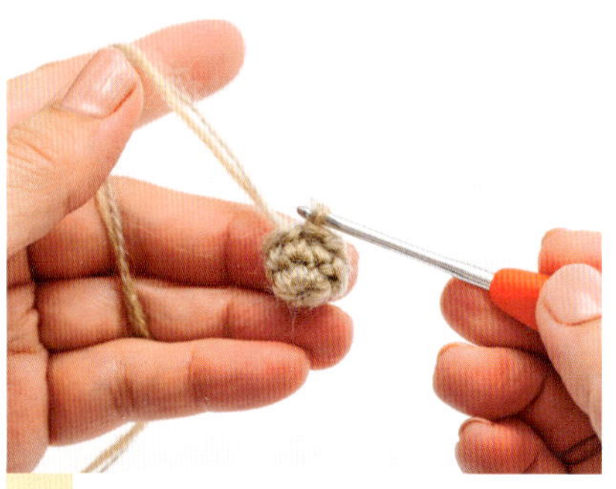

01 Using one strand of sport weight acrylic and one strand of light-fingering weight acrylic/mohair blend, make two rounds with five single crochet stitches.

02 Without making a turning stitch, make the first stitch with slip stitch.

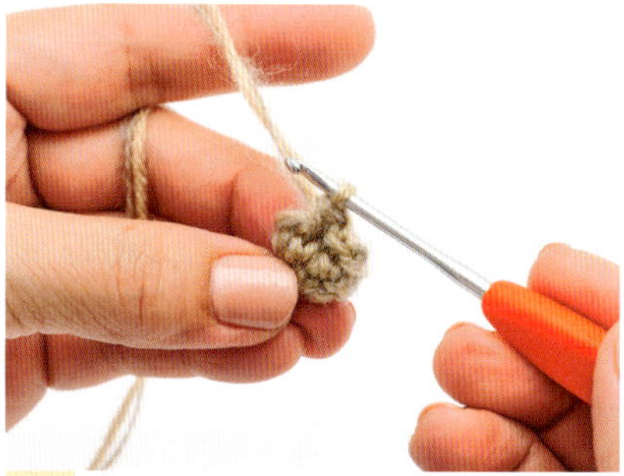

03 Using the second stitch as a turning stitch, make one single crochet stitch.

04 In the same way, make three more single crochet (the last stitch of the previous row is unworked).

05 Draw the fourth single crochet stitch to make a large loop.

06 Pass the yarn ball into the loop.

07 Pull the yarn (noted by the • in the crochet chart).

08 Insert the hook under the loop of first stitch at the third round.

09 Pass the yarn across to start the fourth round.

10 At the end of the round, repeat steps 5 to 7. After each subsequent round, also follow steps 5 to 7.

11 Leave a 12" (30 cm) yarn tail for sewing the nose to the head, then cut the yarn to finish.

CROCHET THE MOUTH

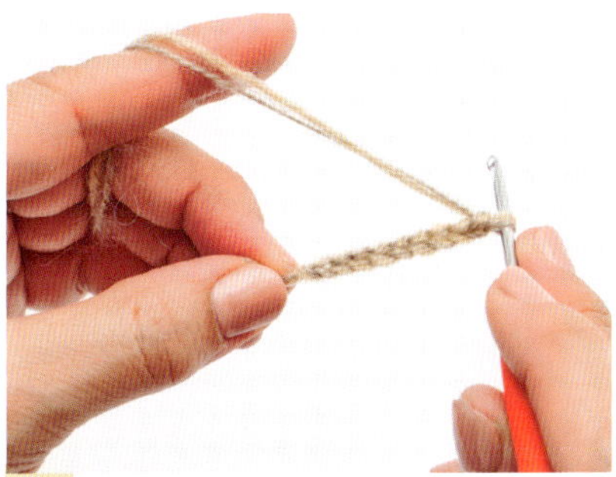

01 Make nine chain stitches.

02 Make one chain stitch as a turning stitch, then make one single crochet in the ninth chain stitch, through top loop only, and one half double crochet in the next chain.

03 Make two double crochet stitches.

04 Make one single crochet stitch.

05 Make two double crochet stitches and one half double crochet stitch.

06 Make three single crochet stitches at the last stitch. Turn and work the other side to match, working two single crochets in last stitch.

07 The first round is complete.

08 Make four single crochet stitches for the second round.

09 Insert the hook at the fifth (central) stitch.

10 Yarn over and pull through all loops (slip stitch).

11 Work in single crochet around, with a slip stitch in central stitch on opposite side, completing the second round.

12 Make top area with single crochet stitches for the third round.

13 Make 12 single crochet stitches.

14 Make two chain stitches.

15 Then make an incomplete double crochet stitch in the next stitch.

16 Make incomplete double crochet stitch in the next stitch, then skip one stitch.

17 Then make incomplete double crochet stitch in the next two stitches.

18 Yarn over and pull through five loops at once.

19 Make one chain stitch to complete the dc4tog (shown as a slip stitch on charts).

20 Make two chain stitches.

21 Make single crochet to the end of the row. The third round is complete.

22 Use the reverse side as the right side for the mouth and assemble.

2. Assemble

Next, you'll sew the body parts together to assemble the foundation before grafting the fur.

ASSEMBLY OVERVIEW 1

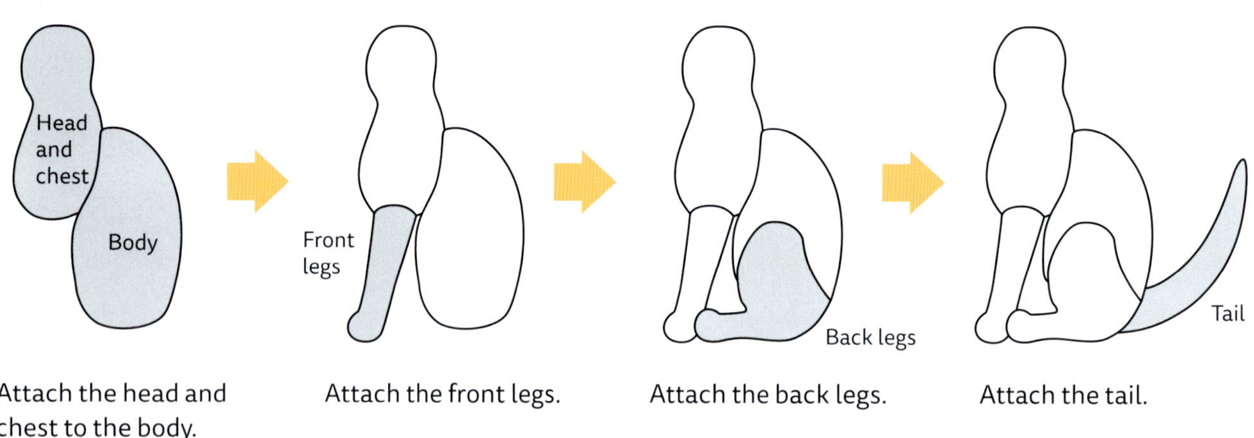

Attach the head and chest to the body.

Attach the front legs.

Attach the back legs.

Attach the tail.

ASSEMBLY OVERVIEW 2

Use this diagram as a reference when assembling the Tabby, Norwegian Forest, British Shorthair, Ragdoll, and Calico (adult).

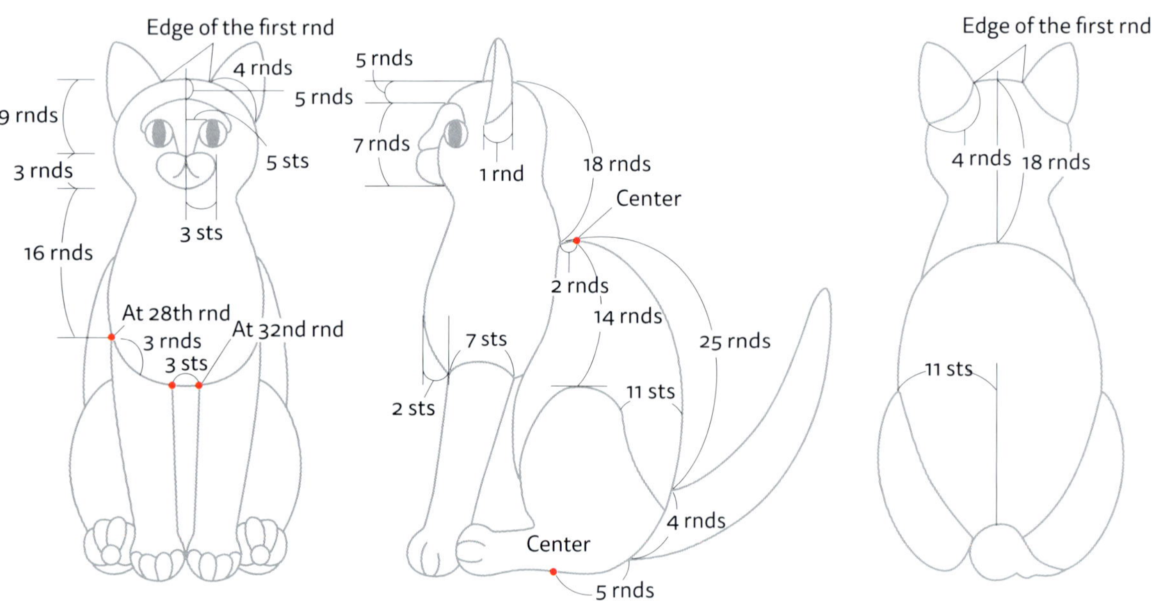

ATTACH THE HEAD AND CHEST TO THE BODY

01 Align the center back of the head and chest with the center of the body. Start by sewing the oval-shaped top of the body to the head and chest (the stitches have been loosened for visual clarity in the photo).

02 Using mattress stitch (often called ladder stitch), stitch the two body parts together all the way around.

ATTACH THE FRONT LEGS

01 Prepare a piece of armature wire four times the length of the leg. Make a double loop with a diameter of ⅝" (1.5 cm) at the center. Insert the wire into the base of the body where the front leg will attach and fold the ends as shown.

02 Use a needle to wrap yarn around the loops.

03 Tightly wrap the yarn along the length of the wire. This will form a foundation for the paw and leg.

04 Next, wrap the leg with polyester stuffing to give it more shape. Then wrap more yarn around the leg to hold the stuffing in place.

05 Slide the crocheted front leg over the wire and sew to the body using mattress stitch.

ATTACH THE BACK LEGS

Stuff the thin area of the back leg only (up to the seventh round) with polyester stuffing before attaching it to the body.

01 Align the back leg with the body at the desired location. Using a tapestry needle threaded with the yarn tail from the back leg, insert the needle under one stitch on the body.

02 Next, insert the needle under one stitch on the outer layer of the back leg.

03 Continue this process to attach the back leg to the body using mattress stitch. Make sure to tuck the inner layer of the back leg inside as you sew so it is hidden.

04 Use the same process to attach the curved portion of the back leg to the body, applying pressure as you sew.

Note: Refer to page 99 for instructions on attaching the back legs of the Mandalay Cat.

ATTACH THE TAIL

01 Fold a 24" (60 cm) long piece of armature wire in half. Insert into the base of the body at the position to attach the tail, crossing the ends as shown.

02 Wrap the wire with polyester stuffing, adjusting the shape of the tail as desired. Wrap yarn around the tail to hold the polyester stuffing in place.

03 Slide the crocheted tail over the wire. Thread the yarn tail from the crocheted tail onto a tapestry needle. You'll use this to sew the base of the tail to the body using mattress stitch.

04 Use mattress stitch to secure the tail to the body on all sides.

ATTACH THE FACIAL FEATURES

01 Pin the nose and mouth to the head following the placement noted in the individual project instructions. Use polyester stuffing to fill the mouth before pinning it to the head.

02 Thread the yarn tail from the mouth onto a tapestry needle. You'll use this to sew the mouth to the head using mattress stitch.

03 When sewing the mouth to the head, insert the needle under the closest stitch on the head.

04 Use mattress stitch to secure the mouth to the head on all sides.

05 Next, you'll sew the nose to the head. Align the tip of the nose on top of the mouth.

06 Make 2 or 3 stitches to secure the tip of the nose to the mouth.

07 Sew the nose to the head from the tip to the fourth row on one side.

08 Insert the needle behind the nose and draw it out on the other side.

09 Follow the same process to sew the nose to the head from the tip to the fourth row on the other side. Leave the areas near the eyes unsewn.

10 Make one stitch to attach the top corner of the nose to the head.

11 Insert the needle under one single crochet stitch (vertical yarn) on the nose.

12 Continue using mattress stitch to attach the nose to the forehead.

13 Completed view once the nose has been attached to the head. Make sure that the crocheted fabric is positioned slightly over the eye buttons.

14 Use pink yarn to embroider the tip of the nose with satin stitch. Make 4 or 5 stitches so that the crocheted base is not visible underneath the pink yarn.

15 Use a felting needle to secure the embroidered stitches in place.

ATTACH THE EARS

01 Pin each ear to the head following the placement noted in the individual project instructions. Insert the armature wire protruding from the base of the ear into the head.

02 Thread the yarn tail from the ear onto a tapestry needle. Use mattress stitch to sew the outer ear (back of the ear) to the head.

03 Follow the same process to sew the inner ear (front of the ear) to the head.

ATTACH THE WHISKERS

Note: Graft the fur before embroidering the remaining facial features (see page 60) and attaching the whiskers.

01 Insert a toothpick into the spot where a whisker is to be placed.

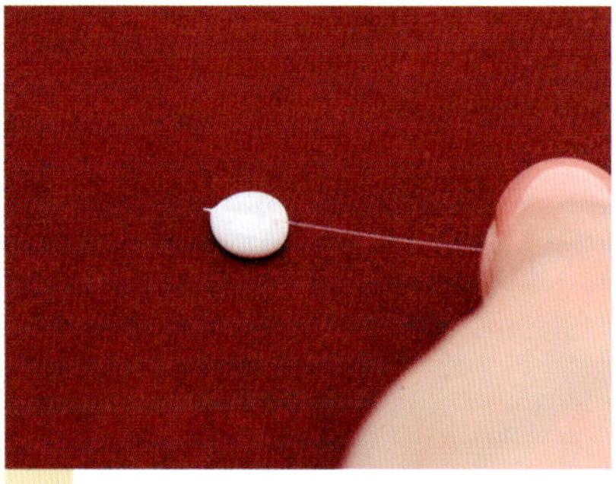

02 Dip the tip of a whisker into a dab of glue so that about ⅜" (1 cm) is covered with glue.

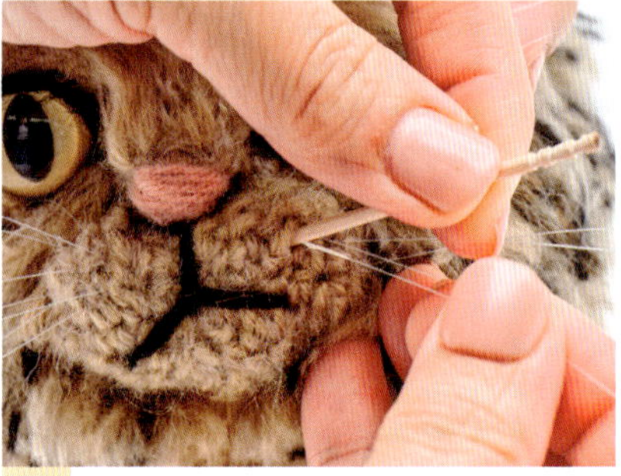

03 Wiggle the toothpick to widen the hole in the crocheted fabric. Insert the glued tip of the whisker into the hole.

04 Remove the toothpick. Use your finger to apply pressure while the glue sets.

WHISKER PLACEMENT GUIDE

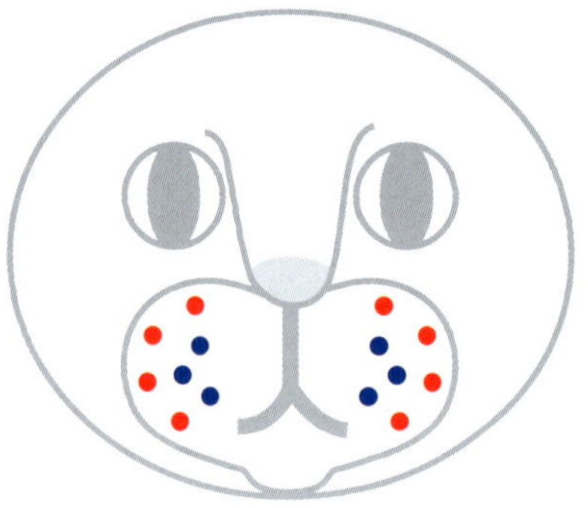

- Outside = 4 whiskers
- Inside = 3 whiskers

Note: If you brush the whiskers before attaching them to the face, it will create a slightly curved natural shape.

3. Graft the Fur

GRAFTING PLACEMENT GUIDE

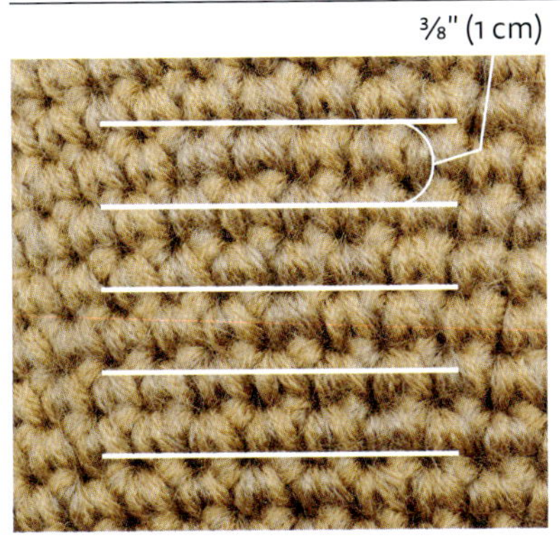

Space the tufts of yarn ⅜" (1 cm) apart vertically. After grafting between single crochet rows, next graft the row above. Each subsequent row of grafting is staggered between the stitches of the rows (and for each row to the face).

Position the tufts of grafting yarn between the stitches or between the rows, scooping up one stitch at a time.

Use a water-soluble marker or pencil to draw the grafting pattern directly on the crocheted body (refer to the individual project instructions for grafting diagram). Don't worry about lines being perfect as the grafted yarn will blend together once it's attached.

GRAFT THE BODY

01 Thread a tapestry needle with grafting yarn (refer to individual project instructions for specific yarns). Fold the yarn in half so it is doubled. There are eight strands.

Note: Wind the different yarns together to create a ball to use for grafting. This will make the grafting process quicker and easier.

02 Start at the base of the tail and graft upward. First, insert the needle under one stitch. Pull the yarn through the stitch, leaving the length noted in the individual project instructions. Next, insert the needle back through the same stitch, creating a backstitch.

03 Cut the yarn so that the length matches the length left in step 2. Follow the same process to graft a tuft of yarn to the adjacent stitch.

04 Follow the same process to graft the rest of the row.

05 Use a felting needle to poke the tufts of grafting yarn at the base. This will tangle the fibers and ensure that the tufts of yarn are attached securely.

06 Use a slicker brush to loosen the twist on the tufts of grafting yarn. Then use the felting needle again to tangle the fur together.

07 For the second row, insert the needle above the grafted stitch on the previous row. It will appear slightly offset (staggered) compared to the previous row.

08 Completed view once the second row has been grafted. Repeat steps 5-6 to loosen the fibers for the second row.

09 Continue grafting fur along the center back, starting at the bottom and working upward.

10 Use the slicker brush and felting needle to loosen the fibers and shape the fur as you work.

11 Change the grafting yarn according to the pattern (refer to the individual project instructions).

12 Graft the fur on the side of the body from the center toward the outside. Just like with the tail, start at the bottom and work upward.

13 Completed view once two patterned areas next to the tail have been grafted. Follow the same process to graft the yarn to the rest of the body. Use the slicker brush to smooth the yarn out and trim any excess yarn.

HOW TO HANDLE AREAS WITHOUT GRAFTING

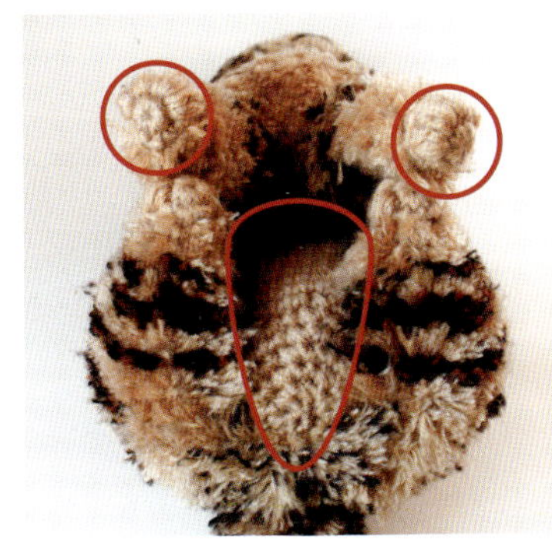

The ears, the bottom of the paws, the upper area of the stomach where the front legs meet, and the underside of the cat do not need to be grafted as they are not visible.

Note: If you don't like seeing the crocheted surface, use a slicker brush to make the yarn a bit more fuzzy or graft short yarns to these areas.

GRAFT THE FACE

01 Graft fur to the face one row at a time, starting at the nose and working upward.

02 Graft ⅝" (1.5 cm) long pieces of yarn to the second row of the nose.

03 Use a felting needle to poke the tufts of grafting yarn at the base. This will tangle the fibers and ensure that the tufts of yarn are attached securely. Hold the fur up as you work so that it flows toward the forehead.

04 Use a slicker brush to loosen the twist on the tufts of grafting yarn.

05 Graft a second row of tufts to the nose.

06 Use a felting needle and slicker brush alternately to loosen the fibers and shape the fur as you work. Trim yarn as necessary.

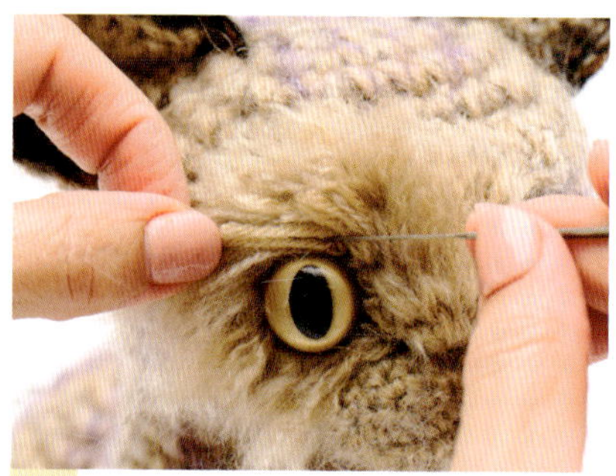

07 Next, graft tufts of fur to the crocheted surface of the eyelid, then repeat steps 3 and 4 to adjust and shape the fur.

08 To create the striped pattern on the forehead, you'll need to attach tufts of yarn in vertical rows.

09 Graft tufts of yarn to the forehead in vertical rows to fill the striped pattern drawn in marker. Trim the yarn to the required length.

10 Use a felting needle to poke the tufts of grafting yarn at the base following the outline of the drawn pattern.

11 Follow this process to fill the forehead with tufts of grafting yarn, creating the different colored stripes by changing yarn colors.

12 View once fur has been grafted to half of the forehead.

EMBROIDER THE FACIAL FEATURES

01 Insert a tapestry needle threaded with a doubled strand of sport weight acrylic yarn under one stitch at the inner corner of the eye.

02 Pull the yarn through, leaving a ⅝" (1.5 cm) yarn tail.

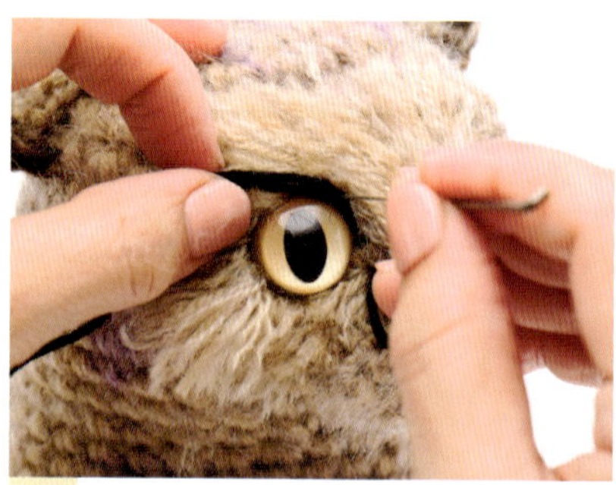

03 Arrange the yarn along the curved outline of the eye button, using a felting needle to adjust the placement.

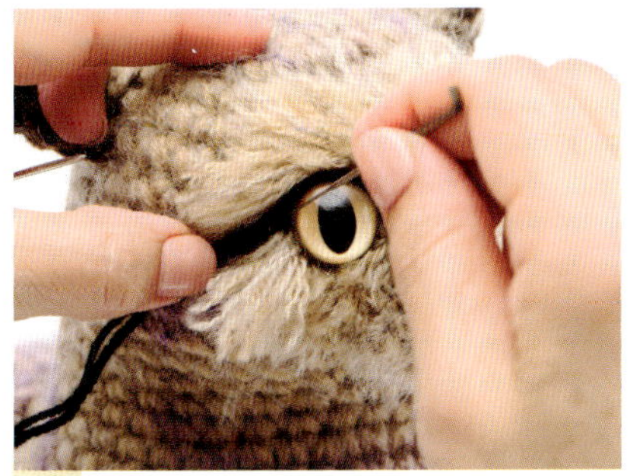

04 Poke the yarn with the felting needle to secure it in place along the curve of the eye button.

05 Insert the tapestry needle under one stitch at the outer corner of the eye and pull the yarn through.

06 Trim the excess yarn at the length noted in the individual project instructions.

07 Use a felting needle to poke the yarn tail at the outer corner of the eye and secure it in place on the face.

08 Use your fingers to adjust the placement of the yarn. Poke with the felting needle to secure in place.

09 Completed view. Glue the eye button in place.

07 Use one strand of sport weight acrylic yarn to embroider the mouth as noted in the diagram at right.

Odd Numbers: Draw the needle out
Even Numbers: Insert the needle

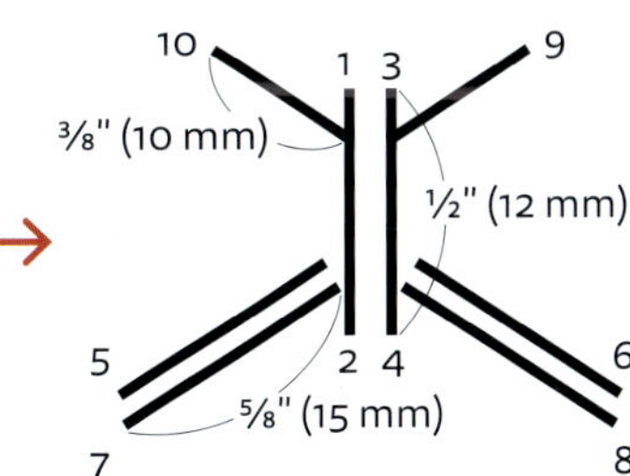

Note: Embroider underneath the satin stitch nose (9 and 10) for the Tabby, American Shorthair, and Somali only.

Tabby

SHOWN ON PAGE 12

TOOLS & MATERIALS

- US 7 (4.5 mm) crochet hook
- US C-2 (2.5 mm) crochet hook
- Sport weight acrylic yarn
  - 630 yds (576 m) in dark beige
  - 119 yds (108 m) in dark brown
  - 119 yds (108 m) in black
- Light-fingering weight acrylic/mohair blend yarn
  - 700 yds (640 m) in sand beige
  - 132 yds (120 m) in dark brown
  - 132 yds (120 m) in black
- About 12" (30 cm) of sport weight acrylic yarn in pink for embroidering the nose
- About 36" (90 cm) of sport weight acrylic yarn in black for embroidering the eyes and mouth [24" (60 cm) for eyes and 12" (30 cm) for mouth]
- Pair of 18 mm cat eye buttons in gold
- 2¾" (7 cm) long clear whiskers
- Polyester fiber fill toy stuffing (about 70 g)
- 2 yds (1.9 m) of armature wire
  - Cut two 6" (15 cm) long pieces for the ears
  - Cut two 20" (50 cm) long pieces for the front legs
  - Cut one 24" (60 cm) long piece for the tail
- Stitch marker
- Yarn needle
- Felting needle
- Slicker brush

CONSTRUCTION STEPS

1. Crochet the body, head and chest, front legs, back legs, tail, nose, mouth, and ears following the instructions on pages 63–68 (also see pages 37–49).
2. Stuff as required and assemble the body parts following the instructions on pages 50–56. Make sure to attach the eye buttons to the head before stuffing (refer to page 36).
3. Graft yarn as noted in the diagrams on page 69. Loosen the yarn and trim the fur into shape. Embroider the facial features. Refer to pages 57–61 for general grafting instructions and use these photos as a reference.

FINISHED SIZE

Height: 13" (33 cm)
Length: 8" (20 cm)
Tail: 8" (20 cm)

Front

Back

Side

YARN COMBINATION CHART

	Area	Yarn Used	Yarn Color	Strands	Total Strands	Yarn	Hook Size
Crocheting the Foundation	• Head and chest • Body	Sport weight acrylic	Dark beige	2	4	A	US 7 (4.5 mm)
		Light-fingering weight acrylic/mohair blend	Sand beige	2			
	• Front legs • Back legs • Tail	Sport weight acrylic	Dark brown	1	4	B (Yarn B will alternate with Yarn A to create the striped pattern)	US 7 (4.5 mm)
		Sport weight acrylic	Black	1			
		Light-fingering weight acrylic/mohair blend	Dark brown	1			
		Light-fingering weight acrylic/mohair blend	Black	1			
	• Outer ears	Sport weight acrylic	Dark brown	1	4	E	US 7 (4.5 mm)
		Sport weight acrylic	Black	1			
		Light-fingering weight acrylic/mohair blend	Dark brown	1			
		Light-fingering weight acrylic/mohair blend	Sand beige	1			
	• Inner ears • Nose • Mouth	Sport weight acrylic	Dark beige	1	2	D	US C-2 (2.5 mm)
		Light-fingering weight acrylic/mohair blend	Sand beige	1			
Grafting the Fur						A, B*	
		Sport weight acrylic	Dark beige	1	4	C	
		Sport weight acrylic	Black	1			
		Light-fingering weight acrylic/mohair blend	Sand beige	2			

*Graft using same yarn used to crochet the foundation

CROCHET INSTRUCTIONS

Head & Chest (make 1)

With Yarn A and US 7 hook, ch4.
Rnd 1: skip first ch, sc1 in next ch, sc1 in next ch, sc3 in last ch, rotate and work along opposite side of chain, sc1 in next ch, sc2 in next ch, slst in skipped ch at beg of round [8]
Place stitch marker in first st of rnd 1 and move it up after each round
Rnd 2: ch1, sc2 in each st to end, slst in beg ch1 [16]
Rnd 3: ch1, sc1, sc2 in next st, sc2, sc2 in next st, sc1, (sc2 in next st) twice, sc1, sc2 in next st, sc2, sc2 in next st, sc1, (sc2 in next st) twice, slst in beg ch1 [24]
Rnd 4: ch1, sc2 in next st, sc6, sc2 in next st, sc4, sc2 in next st, sc6, sc2 in next st, sc4, slst in beg ch1 [28]
Rnd 5: ch1, sc10, sc2 in next st, sc2, sc2 in next st, sc10, sc2 in next st, sc2, sc2 in next st, slst in beg ch1 [32]
Rnd 6: ch1, sc10, sc2 in next st, sc4, sc2 in next st, sc10, sc2 in next st, sc4, sc2 in next st, slst in beg ch1 [36]
Rnds 7-11: ch1, sc1 in each st, slst in beg ch1 (5 rnds)
Rnd 12: ch1, sc18, (sc2tog, sc2) twice, sc2tog, sc8, slst in beg ch1 [33]

Crochet Symbol Key

★ = magic ring
0 = ch st
• = slst
∧ = ∧ = sc2tog
∨ = ∨ = sc2 in next st
∨ = sc3 in next st
∨ = sc5 in next st
• = make a knot (see page 46)

Rnd 13: ch1, sc3, sc2 in next st, sc4, sc2 in next st, sc7, (sc2tog, sc1) 3 times, sc2tog, sc6, slst in beg ch1 [31]
Rnds 14-15: ch1, sc1 in each st, slst in beg ch1 (2 rnds)
Rnd 16: ch1, sc18, (sc2 in next st, sc2) twice, sc2 in next st, sc6, slst in beg ch1 [34]
Rnd 17: ch1, sc3, sc2 in next st, sc6, sc2 in next st, sc7, sc2 in next st, sc8, sc2 in next st, sc6, slst in beg ch1 [38]
Rnds 18-19: ch1, sc1 in each st, slst in beg ch1 (2 rnds)
Rnd 20: ch1, sc20, sc2 in next st, sc10, sc2 in next st, sc6, slst in beg ch1 [40]
Rnd 21: ch1, sc20, sc2 in next st, sc12, sc2 in next st, sc6, slst in beg ch1 [42]
Rnds 22-27: ch1, sc1 in each st, slst in beg ch1 (6 rnds)
Rnd 28: ch1, (sc5, sc2tog) 6 times, slst in beg ch1 [36]
Rnd 29: ch1, (sc4, sc2tog) 6 times, slst in beg ch1 [30]
Begin to fill with toy stuffing.
Rnd 30: ch1, (sc3, sc2tog) 6 times, slst in beg ch1 [24]
Rnd 31: ch1, (sc2, sc2tog) 6 times, slst in beg ch1 [18]
Rnd 32: ch1, (sc1, sc2tog) 6 times, slst in beg ch1 [12]
Add more toy stuffing before final rnd.
Rnd 33: ch1, (sc2tog) 6 times, slst in beg ch1 [6]
Fasten off.

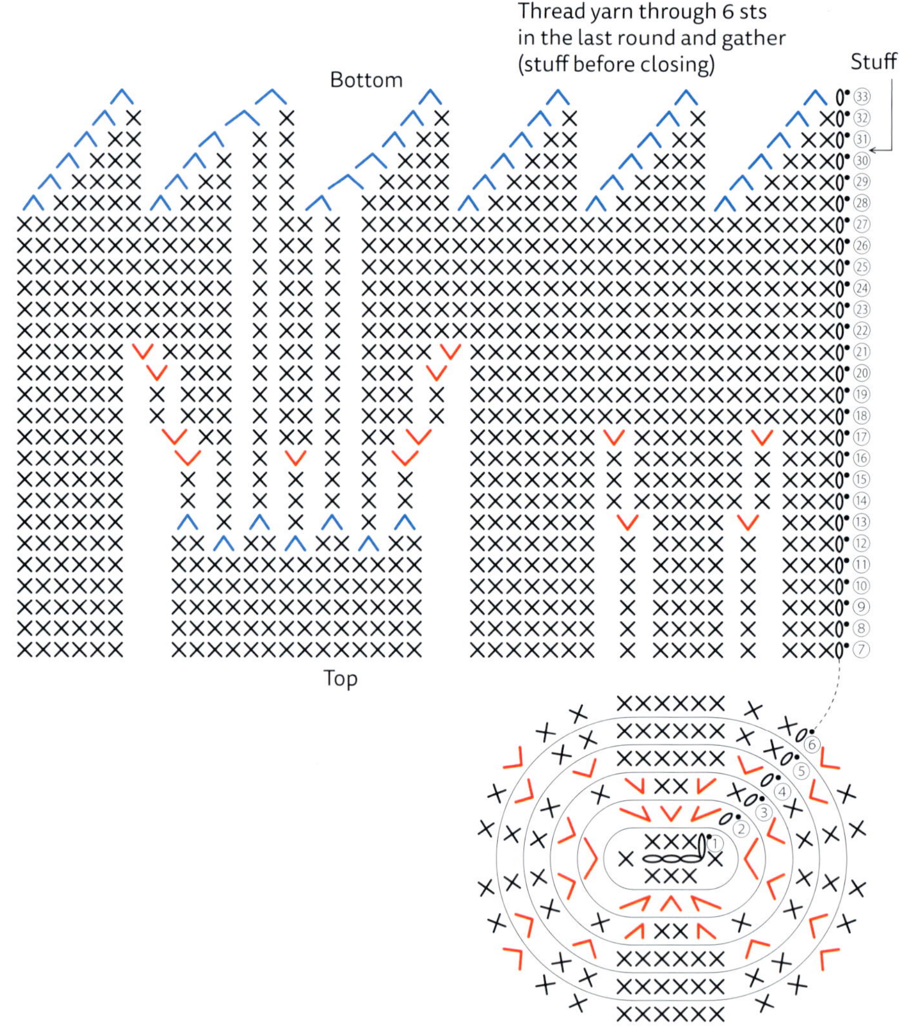

Body (make 1)

With Yarn A and US 7 hook, ch6.

Rnd 1: skip first ch, sc1 in next ch, sc1 in next 3 ch, sc3 in last ch, rotate and work along opposite side of chain, sc1 in next 3 ch, sc2 in next ch, slst in skipped ch at beg of round [12]

Place stitch marker in first st of rnd 1 and move it up after each round

Rnd 2: ch1, sc2 in next st, sc3, (sc2 in next st) 3 times, sc3, (sc2 in next st) twice, slst in beg ch1 [18]

Rnd 3: ch1, sc1, sc2 in next st, sc4, (sc2 in next st, sc1) twice, sc2 in next st, sc4, sc2 in next st, sc1, sc2 in next st, slst in beg ch1 [24]

Rnd 4: ch1, sc2, sc2 in next st, sc5, (sc2 in next st, sc2) twice, sc2 in next st, sc5, sc2 in next st, sc2, sc2 in next st, slst in beg ch1 [30]

Rnd 5: ch1, sc3, sc2 in next st, sc6, (sc2 in next st, sc3) twice, sc2 in next st, sc6, sc2 in next st, sc3, sc2 in next st, slst in beg ch1 [36]

Rnd 6: ch1, sc4, sc2 in next st, sc7, (sc2 in next st, sc4) twice, sc2 in next st, sc7, sc2 in next st, sc4, sc2 in next st, slst in beg ch1 [42]

Rnds 7-10: ch1, sc1 in each st, slst in beg ch1 (4 rnds)

Rnd 11: ch1, sc17, sc2 in next st, sc7, sc2 in next st, sc5, sc2 in next st, sc7, sc2 in next st, sc2, slst in beg ch1 [46]

Rnds 12-13: ch1, sc1 in each st, slst in beg ch1 (2 rnds)

Rnd 14: ch1, sc17, sc2 in next st, sc8, sc2 in next st, sc7, sc2 in next st, sc8, sc2 in next st, sc2, slst in beg ch1 [50]

Rnds 15-24: ch1, sc1 in each st, slst in beg ch1 (10 rnds)

Rnd 25: ch1, sc17, sc2tog, sc8, sc2tog, sc7, sc2tog, sc8, sc2tog, sc2, slst in beginning ch1 [46]

Rnd 26: ch1, sc1 in each st, slst in beg ch1

Rnd 27: ch1, sc17, sc2tog, sc7, sc2tog, sc5, sc2tog, sc7, sc2tog, sc2, slst in beginning ch1 [42]

Rnd 28: as rnd 26

Rnd 29: ch1, (sc5, sc2tog) 6 times, slst in beg ch1 [36]

Rnd 30: ch1, (sc4, sc2tog) 6 times, slst in beg ch1 [30]

Begin to fill Body with toy stuffing.

Rnd 31: ch1, (sc3, sc2tog) 6 times, slst in beg ch1 [24]

Rnd 32: ch1, (sc2, sc2tog) 6 times, slst in beg ch1 [18]

Rnd 33: ch1, (sc1, sc2tog) 6 times, slst in beg ch1 [12]

Add more toy stuffing to body before final rnd.

Rnd 34: ch1, (sc2tog) 6 times, slst in beg ch1 [6]

Fasten off.

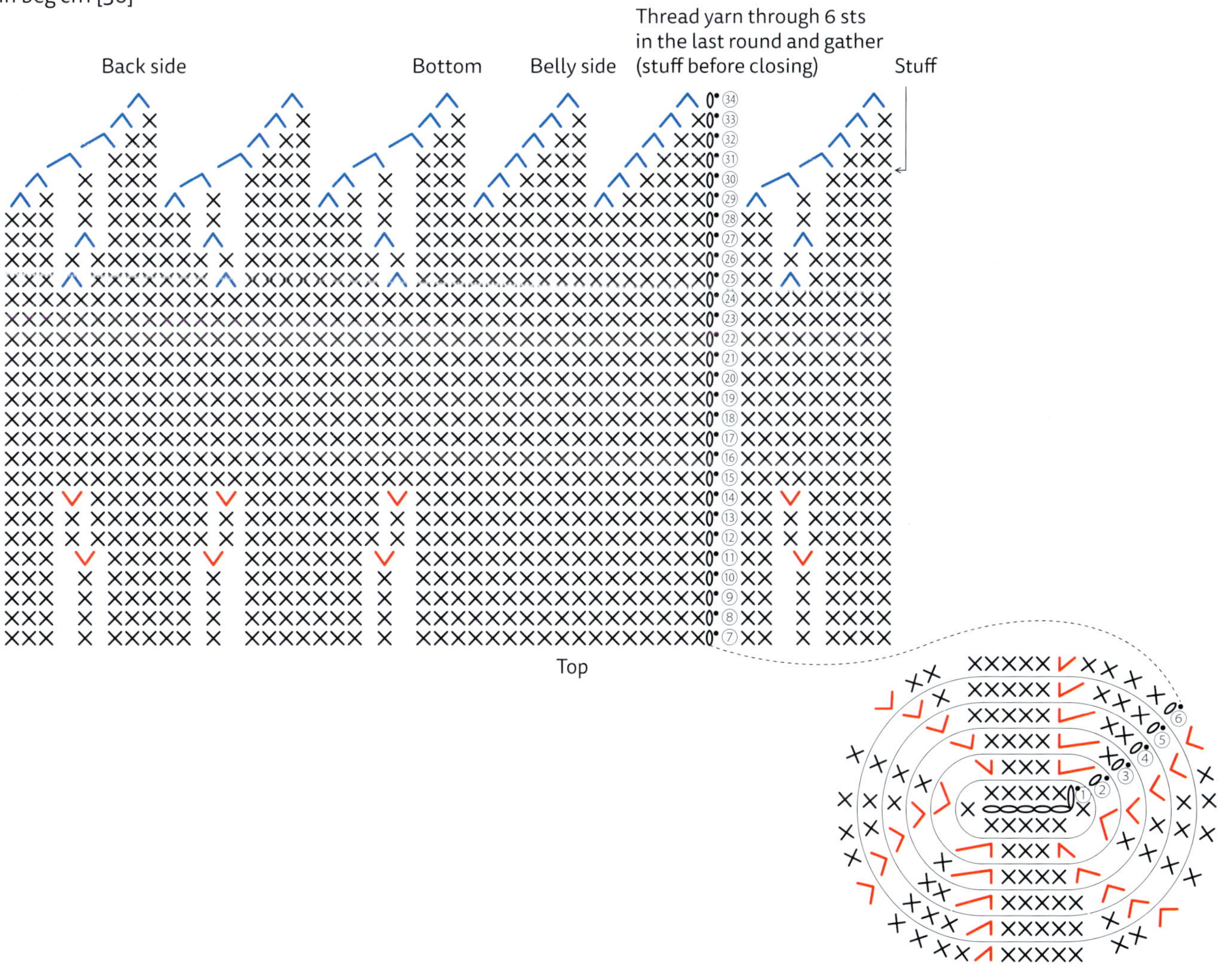

Back side

Bottom

Belly side

Thread yarn through 6 sts in the last round and gather (stuff before closing)

Stuff

Top

Front Legs

Left (make 1)

With Yarn A and US 7 hook, make a magic ring.
Rnd 1: ch1 (does not count as a st throughout), sc8 in magic ring, slst in beg ch1 [8]
Place stitch marker in first st of rnd 1 and move it up after each round
Rnd 2: ch1, sc2, (hdc-cl in next st) 4 times, sc2, slst in beg ch1
Rnds 3-7: ch1, sc1 in each st, slst in beg ch1 (5 rnds)
Rnd 8: ch1, sc2, sc2 in next st, sc5, slst in beg ch1 [9]
Rnd 9: change to Yarn B, ch1, sc3, sc2 in next st, sc5, slst in beg ch1 [10]
Rnd 10: change to Yarn A, ch1, sc4, sc2 in next st, sc5, slst in beg ch1 [11]
Rnd 11: ch1, sc4, sc2 in next st, sc6, slst in beg ch1 [12]
Rnd 12: change to Yarn B, ch1, sc4, sc2 in next st, sc7, slst in beg ch1 [13]
Rnd 13: change to Yarn A, ch1, sc4, sc2 in next st, sc8, slst in beg ch1 [14]
Rnd 14: ch1, sc4, sc2 in next st, sc9, slst in beg ch1 [15]
Rnd 15: change to Yarn B, ch1, sc4, hdc2 in next st, hdc1, sc9, slst in beg ch1 [16]
Rnd 16: ch1, sc4, hdc2 in next st, hdc1, sc10, slst in beg ch1 [17]
Rnd 17: change to Yarn A, ch1, sc1 in each st, slst in beg ch1. Fasten off.

Right (make 1)

With Yarn A and US 7 hook, make a magic ring.
Rnd 1: ch1 (does not count as a st throughout), sc8 in magic ring, slst in beg ch1 [8]
Place stitch marker in first st of rnd 1 and move it up after each round
Rnd 2: ch1, sc2, (hdc-cl in next st) 4 times, sc2, slst in beg ch1
Rnds 3-7: ch1, sc1 in each st, slst in beg ch1 (5 rnds)
Rnd 8: ch1, sc5, sc2 in next st, sc2, slst in beg ch1 [9]
Rnd 9: change to Yarn B, ch1, sc6, sc2 in next st, sc2, slst in beg ch1 [10]
Rnd 10: change to Yarn A, ch1, sc7, sc2 in next st, sc2, slst in beg ch1 [11]
Rnd 11: ch1, sc8, sc2 in next st, sc2, slst in beg ch1 [12]
Rnd 12: change to Yarn B, ch1, sc9, sc2 in next st, sc2, slst in beg ch1 [13]
Rnd 13: change to Yarn A, ch1, sc10, sc2 in next st, sc2, slst in beg ch1 [14]
Rnd 14: ch1, sc11, sc2 in next st, sc2, slst in beg ch1 [15]
Rnd 15: change to Yarn B, ch1, sc11, hdc1, hdc2 in next st, sc2, slst in beg ch1 [16]
Rnd 16: ch1, sc12, hdc1, hdc2 in next st, sc2, slst in beg ch1 [17]
Rnd 17: change to Yarn A, ch1, sc1 in each st, slst in beg ch1. Fasten off.

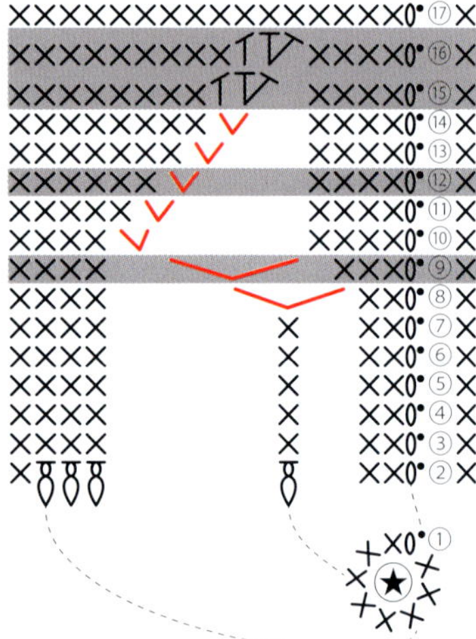

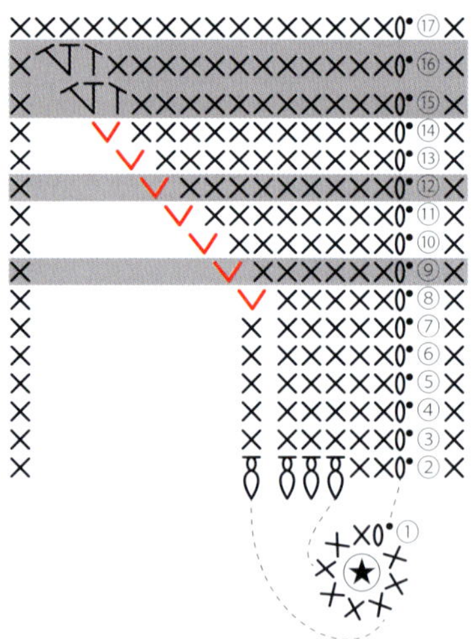

Back Legs (make 2)

With Yarn A and US 7 hook, make a magic ring.

Rnd 1: ch1 (does not count as a st throughout), sc8 in magic ring, slst in beg ch1 [8]

Place stitch marker in first st of rnd 1 and move it up after each round

Rnd 2: ch1, sc2, (hdc-cl in next st) 4 times, sc2, slst in beg ch1

Rnds 3-4: ch1, sc1 in each st, slst in beg ch1 (2 rnds)

Rnd 5: change to Yarn B, ch1, sc1 in each st, slst in beg ch1

Rnd 6: change to Yarn A, ch1, sc7, sc2 in next st, slst in beg ch1 [9]

Rnd 7: change to Yarn B, ch1, sc1 in each st, slst in beg ch1

Rnd 8: change to Yarn A, ch1, sc1, (sc2 in next st) twice, sc3 in next st, sc5 in next st, sc3 in next st, (sc2 in next st) twice, sc1, slst in beg ch1 [21]

Rnd 9: change to Yarn B, ch1, sc10, sc5 in next st, sc10, slst in beg ch1 [25]

Rnd 10: change to Yarn A, ch1, sc12, sc5 in next st, sc12, slst in beg ch1 [29]

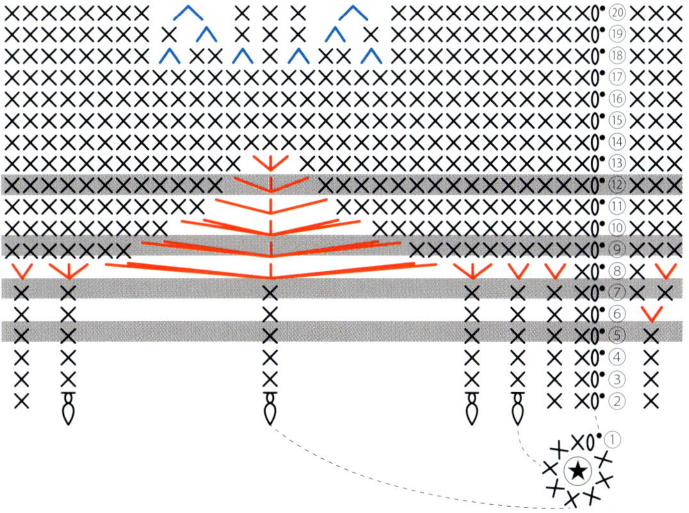

Rnd 11: ch1, sc14, sc3 in next st, sc14, slst in beg ch1 [31]

Rnd 12: change to Yarn B, ch1, sc15, sc3 in next st, sc15, slst in beg ch1 [33]

Rnd 13: change to Yarn A, ch1, sc16, sc3 in next st, sc16, slst in beg ch1 [35]

Rnds 14-17: ch1, sc1 in each st, slst in beg ch1 (4 rnds)

Rnd 18: ch1, sc11, sc2tog, sc2, sc2tog, sc1, sc2tog, sc2, sc2tog, sc11, slst in beg ch1 [31]

Rnd 19: ch1, sc12, sc2tog, sc3, sc2tog, sc12, slst in beg ch1 [29]

Rnd 20: ch1, sc11, sc2tog, sc3, sc2tog, sc11, slst in beg ch1 [27]

Fasten off.

Tail (make 1)

With Yarn B and US 7 hook, make a magic ring.

Rnd 1: ch1 (does not count as a st throughout), sc5 in magic ring, slst in beg ch1 [5]

Place stitch marker in first st of rnd 1 and move it up after each round

Rnd 2: ch1, sc4, sc2 in last st, slst in beg ch1 [6]

Rnd 3: ch1, sc5, sc2 in last st, slst in beg ch1 [7]

Rnd 4: ch1, sc6, sc2 in last st, slst in beg ch1 [8]

Rnd 5: ch1, sc1 in each st, slst in beg ch1

Rnd 6: change to Yarn A, ch1, sc1 in each st, slst in beg ch1

Rnd 7: change to Yarn B, ch1, sc1 in each st, slst in beg ch1

Rnd 8: ch1, sc7, sc2 in last st, slst in beg ch1 [9]

Rnd 9: change to Yarn A, ch1, sc1 in each st, slst in beg ch1

Rnd 10: change to Yarn B, ch1, sc8, sc2 in last st, slst in beg ch1 [10]

Rnd 11: change to Yarn A, ch1, sc1 in each st, slst in beg ch1

Rnd 12: change to Yarn B, ch1, sc9, sc2 in last st, slst in beg ch1 [11]

Rnd 13: change to Yarn A, ch1, sc1 in each st, slst in beg ch1

Rnd 14: change to Yarn B, ch1, sc1 in each st, slst in beg ch1

Rnds 15-18: Rep rnds 13-14, twice

Rnd 19: as rnd 13

Rnd 20: change to Yarn B, ch1, sc10, sc2 in last st, slst in beg ch1 [12]

Rnds 21-22: as rnds 13-14

Rnd 23: as rnd 13

Fasten off.

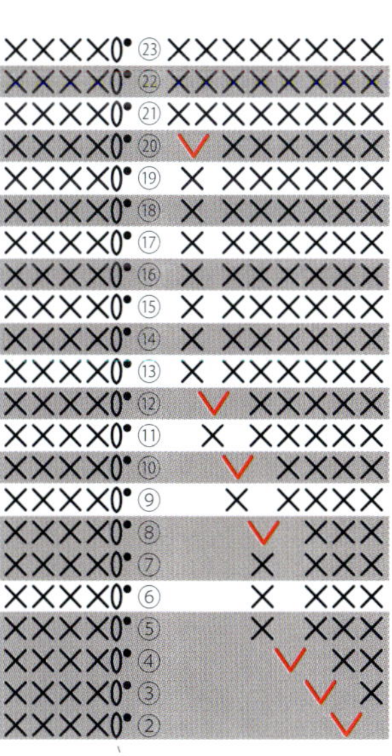

Nose (make 1)

With Yarn D and US C-2 hook, make a magic ring.
Rnd 1: ch1 (does not count as a st throughout), sc6 in magic ring, slst in beg ch1 [6]
Place stitch marker in first st of rnd 1 and move it up after each round
Rnd 2: ch1, sc1 in each st, slst in beg ch1
Slst in next 2 sts, then continue in rows.
Row 3: ch1, sc1 in next 4 sts, lengthen loop from hook and pass yarn through, pull tight to make a knot, do not turn [4]
Row 4: pass yarn across back of work, pull through beg ch1 of prev row, and rep row 3.
Row 5: pass yarn across back of work, pull through beg ch1 of prev row, ch1, sc2 in first st, sc2, sc2 in last st, lengthen loop from hook and pass yarn through, pull tight to make a knot, do not turn [6]
Row 6: pass yarn across back of work, pull through beg ch1 of prev row, ch3 (counts as dc), dc2 in first st, sc4, dc3 in last st, lengthen loop from hook and pass yarn through, pull tight to make a knot, do not turn [10]
Row 7: pass yarn across back of work, pull through top of beg ch3 of prev row, (ch3, dc2) in same st (beg ch3 counts as dc), sc8, dc3 in last st, lengthen loop from hook and pass yarn through, pull tight to make a knot [14]
Fasten off.

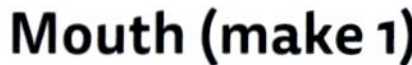

Mouth (make 1)

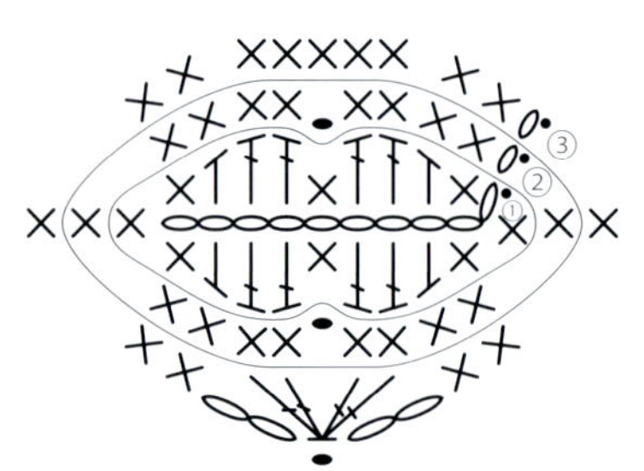

With Yarn D and US C-2 hook, ch10.
Rnd 1: skip first ch, sc1 in next ch, hdc1, dc2, sc1, dc2, hdc1, sc3 in last ch, rotate and work along opposite side of chain, hdc1, dc2, sc1, dc2, hdc1, sc2 in last ch, slst in skipped ch at beg of rnd [20]
Place stitch marker in first st of rnd 1 and move it up after each round
Rnd 2: ch1, sc4, slst in next st, sc9, slst in next st, sc5, slst in beg ch1
Rnd 3: ch1, sc12, ch2, dc4tog over next 4 sc (and skipping the slst), ch2, sc3, slst in beg ch1 [20]
Fasten off. Use the wrong side as the right side.

Ears

Right Ear (make 1 each of outer and inner ear)

Outer Ear

With Yarn E and US 7 hook, ch9, leaving a 12" (30 cm) tail of yarn.
Work in rows.
Row 1: dc1 in fifth ch from hook (counts as 2dc), dc1, hdc1, sc1, sc3 in last chain, rotate and work along opposite side of chain stitches, hdc2, dc2, 2dc in next ch, turn [14]
Cut a 6" (15 cm) long piece of armature wire, fold in half, position the folded area at the corner of the ear, and crochet next rnd over the wire to trap it into the sts.
Row 2: ch1 (does not count as a st throughout), sc7, sc2 in next st, sc6 [15]
Fasten off.

Inner Ear

Make inner ear in the same way with Yarn D and US C-2 hook, omitting wire.

Left Ear (make 1 each of outer and inner ear)

Outer Ear

With Yarn E and US 7 hook, ch9, leaving a 12" (30 cm) tail of yarn.
Work in rows.
Row 1: dc1 in fourth ch from hook (counts as 2dc), dc2, hdc2, sc3 in last chain, rotate and work along opposite side of chain stitches, sc1, hdc1, dc3, turn [14]
Cut a 6" (15 cm) long piece of armature wire, fold in half, position the folded area at the corner of the ear, and crochet next rnd over the wire to trap it into the sts.
Row 2: ch1 (does not count as a st throughout), sc6, sc2 in next st, sc7 [15]
Fasten off.

Inner Ear

Make inner ear in the same way with Yarn D and US C-2 hook, omitting wire.

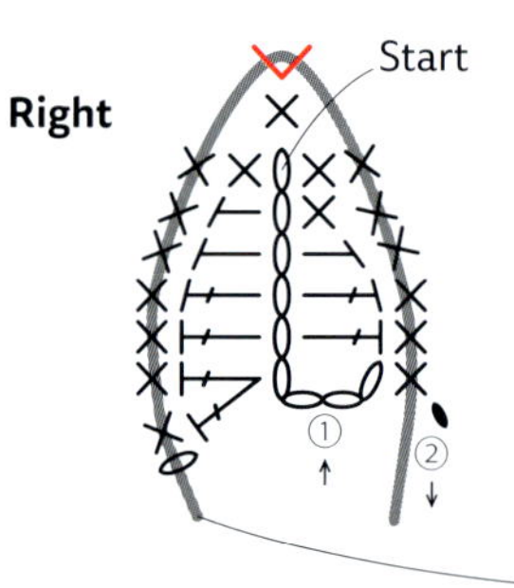

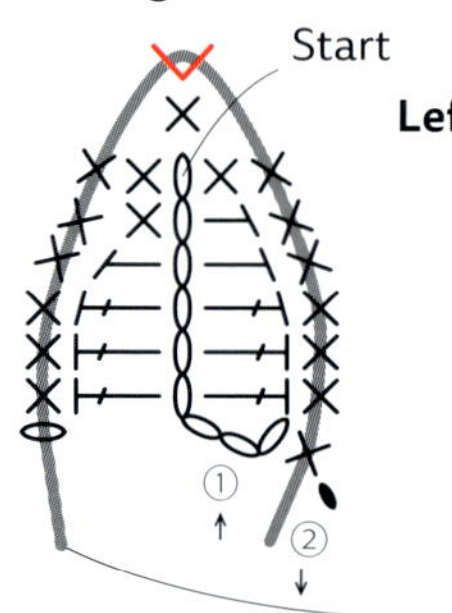

Align a 6" (15 cm) long piece of armature wire with the corner of the ear and crochet around the wire (for outer ear only)

GRAFTING

Placement Key

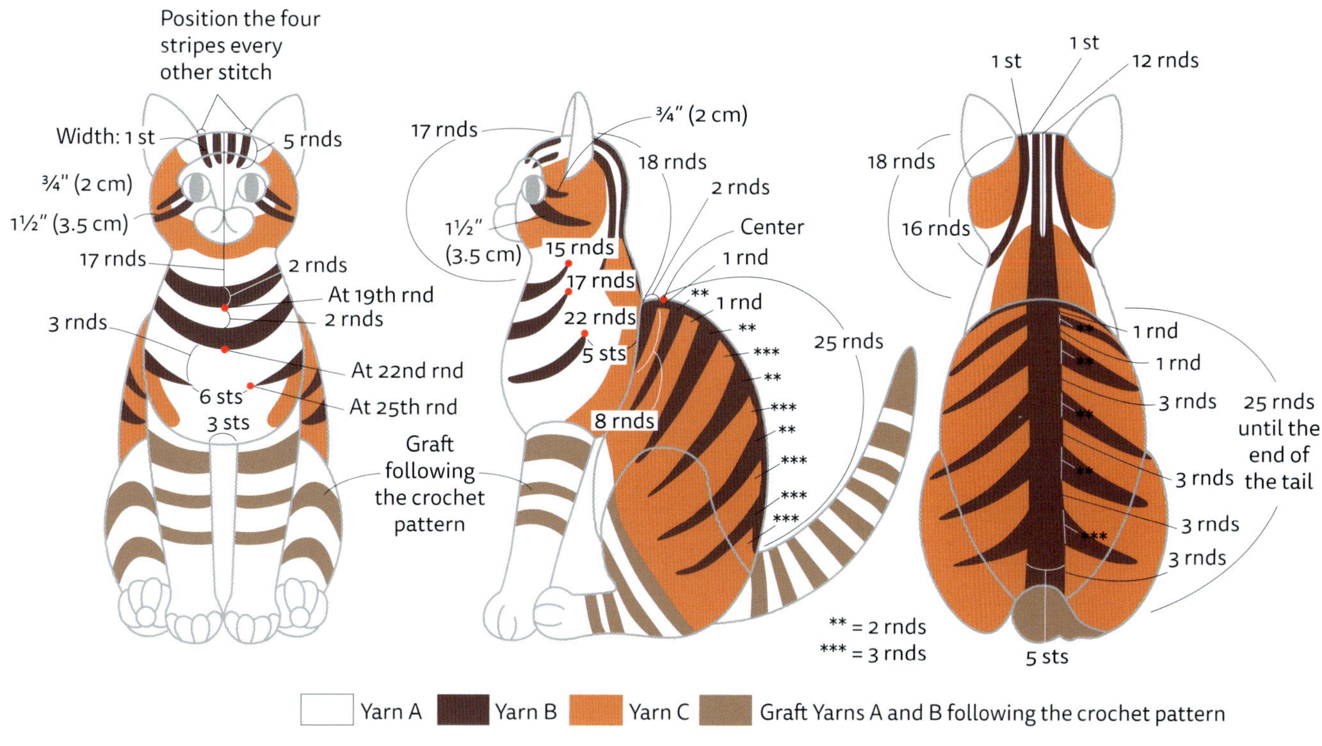

Yarn Length Key

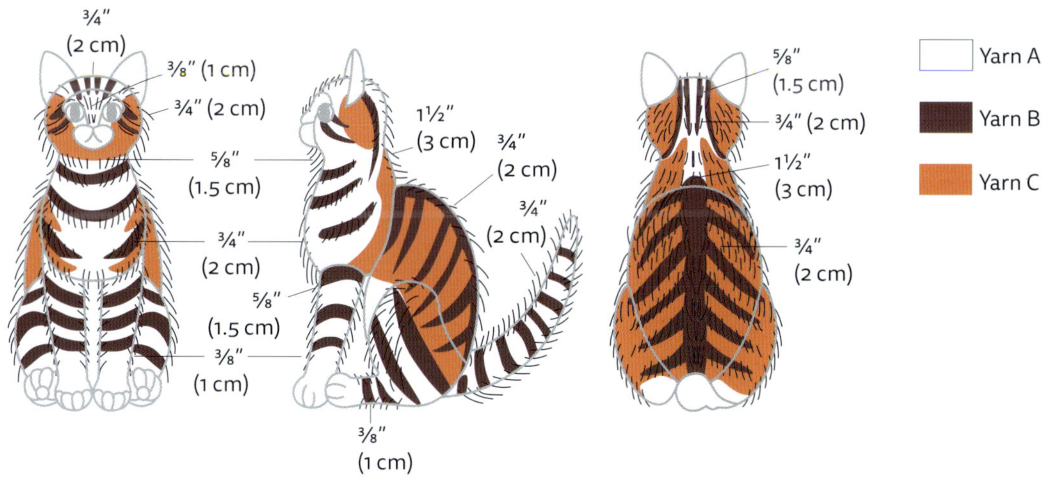

TIPS

- Do not graft the ears, toes, or stomach area.
- Brush the back of the ears with a slicker brush to make them fuzzy.
- Cover the eye buttons slightly with fur to create cat-like almond-shaped eyes.

Norwegian Forest

SHOWN ON PAGE 7

TOOLS & MATERIALS

- US 7 (4.5 mm) crochet hook
- US C-2 (2.5 mm) crochet hook
- Sport weight acrylic yarn
  - 433 yds (396 m) in white
  - 158 yds (144 m) in light beige
  - 591 yds (540 m) in brown
  - 20 yds (18 m) in dark brown
- Light-fingering weight acrylic/mohair blend yarn
  - 482 yds (440 m) in white
  - 788 yds (720 m) in sand beige
- About 12″ (30 cm) of sport weight acrylic yarn in pink for embroidering the nose
- About 24″ (60 cm) of sport weight acrylic yarn in dark brown for embroidering the eyes
- About 12″ (30 cm) of sport weight acrylic in brown for embroidering the mouth
- Pair of 18 mm cat eye buttons in beige
- 2¾″ (7 cm) long clear whiskers
- Polyester fiber fill toy stuffing (about 70 g)
- 2 yds (1.9 m) of armature wire
  - Cut two 6″ (15 cm) long pieces for the ears
  - Cut two 20″ (50 cm) long pieces for the front legs
  - Cut one 24″ (60 cm) long piece for the tail
- Stitch marker
- Yarn needle
- Felting needle
- Slicker brush

CONSTRUCTION STEPS

1. Crochet the body, head and chest, front legs, back legs, tail, nose, mouth, and ears following the instructions on pages 71–76 (also see pages 37–49).
2. Stuff as required and assemble the body parts following the instructions on pages 50–56. Make sure to attach the eye buttons to the head before stuffing (refer to page 36).
3. Graft yarn as noted in the diagrams on page 77. Loosen the yarn and trim the fur into shape. Embroider the facial features. Refer to pages 57–61 for general grafting instructions and use these photos as a reference.

FINISHED SIZE

Height: 13″ (33 cm)
Length: 8″ (20 cm)
Tail: 8″ (20 cm)

Front

Back

Side

YARN COMBINATION CHART

	Area	Yarn Used	Yarn Color	Strands	Total Strands	Yarn	Hook Size
Crocheting the Foundation	• Body • Tail • Outer ears	Sport weight acrylic	Dark brown	2	4	A	US 7 (4.5 mm)
		Light-fingering weight acrylic/mohair blend	Sand beige	2			
	• Front legs	Sport weight acrylic	White	2	4	B	US 7 (4.5 mm)
		Light-fingering weight acrylic/mohair blend	White	2			
	• Head and chest • Back legs					Alternate A and B (refer to diagrams)	US 7 (4.5 mm)
	• Inner ears • Nose	Light-fingering weight acrylic/mohair blend	Sand beige	1*	2	E	US C-2 (2.5 mm)
	• Nose • Mouth	Sport weight acrylic	White	1	2	F	
		Light-fingering weight acrylic/mohair blend	White	1			
Grafting the Fur						A, B**	
		Sport weight acrylic	Light beige	2	4	C	
		Light-fingering weight acrylic/mohair blend	Sand beige	2			
	• Face	Sport weight acrylic	Dark brown	1*	2	D	

*Use a double strand of the same yarn

**Graft using the same yarn used to crochet the foundation

CROCHET INSTRUCTIONS

Body (make 1)

With Yarn A and US 7 hook, ch6.

Rnd 1: skip first ch, sc1 in in next ch, sc1 in next 3 ch, sc3 in last ch, rotate and work along opposite side of chain, sc1 in next 3 ch, sc2 in next ch, slst in skipped ch at beg of round [12]

Place stitch marker in first st of rnd 1 and move it up after each round

Rnd 2: ch1, sc2 in next st, sc3, (sc2 in next st) 3 times, sc3, (sc2 in next st) twice, slst in beg ch1 [18]

Rnd 3: ch1, sc1, sc2 in next st, sc4, (sc2 in next st, sc1) twice, sc2 in next st, sc4, sc2 in next st, sc1, sc2 in next st, slst in beg ch1 [24]

Rnd 4: ch1, sc2, sc2 in next st, sc5, (sc2 in next st, sc2) twice, sc2 in next st, sc5, sc2 in next st, sc2, sc2 in next st, slst in beg ch1 [30]

Rnd 5: ch1, sc3, sc2 in next st, sc6, (sc2 in next st, sc3) twice, sc2 in next st, sc6, sc2 in next st, sc3, sc2 in next st, slst in beg ch1 [36]

Rnd 6: ch1, sc4, sc2 in next st, sc7, (sc2 in next st, sc4) twice, sc2 in next st, sc7, sc2 in next st, sc4, sc2 in next st, slst in beg ch1 [42]

Rnds 7-10: ch1, sc1 in each st, slst in beg ch1 (4 rnds)

Join in Yarn B.

Rnd 11: in Yarn A ch1, sc8, in Yarn B sc6 in Yarn A sc3, sc2 in next st, sc7, sc2 in next st, sc5, sc2 in next st, sc7, sc2 in next st, sc2, slst in beg ch1 [46]

Rnds 12-13: in Yarn A sc5, in Yarn B sc12, in Yarn A sc29, slst in beg ch1 (2 rnds)

Crochet Symbol Key

- ★ = magic ring
- 0 = ch st
- • = slst
- ∧ = (symbol) = sc2tog
- ∨ = (symbol) = sc2 in next st
- (symbol) = sc3 in next st
- (symbol) = sc5 in next st
- • = make a knot (see page 46)

Rnd 14: in Yarn A ch1, sc5, in Yarn B sc12, in Yarn A sc2 in next st, sc8, sc2 in next st, sc7, sc2 in next st, sc8, sc2 in next st, sc2, slst in beg ch1 [50]
Rnds 15-18: in Yarn A sc4, in Yarn B sc14, in Yarn A sc32, slst in beg ch1 (4 rnds)
Rnds 19-20: in Yarn A sc3, in Yarn B sc16, in Yarn A sc31, slst in beg ch1 (2 rnds)
Rnds 21-24: in Yarn A sc4, in Yarn B sc14, in Yarn A sc32, slst in beg ch1 (4 rnds)
Rnd 25: in Yarn A ch1, sc5, in Yarn B sc12, in Yarn A sc2tog, sc8, sc2tog, sc7, sc2tog, sc8, sc2tog, sc2, slst in beginning ch1 [46]
Rnd 26: in Yarn A ch1, sc5, in Yarn B sc13, in Yarn A sc 28, slst in beg ch1
Rnd 27: in Yarn A ch1, sc5, in Yarn B sc12, in Yarn A sc2tog, sc7, sc2tog, sc5, sc2tog, sc7, sc2tog, sc2, slst in beginning ch1 [42]
Rnd 28: in Yarn A ch1, sc8, in Yarn B sc6, in Yarn A sc 28, slst in beg ch1
Continue in Yarn A only.
Rnd 29: ch1, (sc5, sc2tog) 6 times, slst in beg ch1 [36]
Rnd 30: ch1, (sc4, sc2tog) 6 times, slst in beg ch1 [30]
Begin to fill body with toy stuffing.
Rnd 31: ch1, (sc3, sc2tog) 6 times, slst in beg ch1 [24]
Rnd 32: ch1, (sc2, sc2tog) 6 times, slst in beg ch1 [18]
Rnd 33: ch1, (sc1, sc2tog) 6 times, slst in beg ch1 [12]
Add more toy stuffing to body before final rnd.
Rnd 34: ch1, (sc2tog) 6 times, slst in beg ch1 [6]
Fasten off.

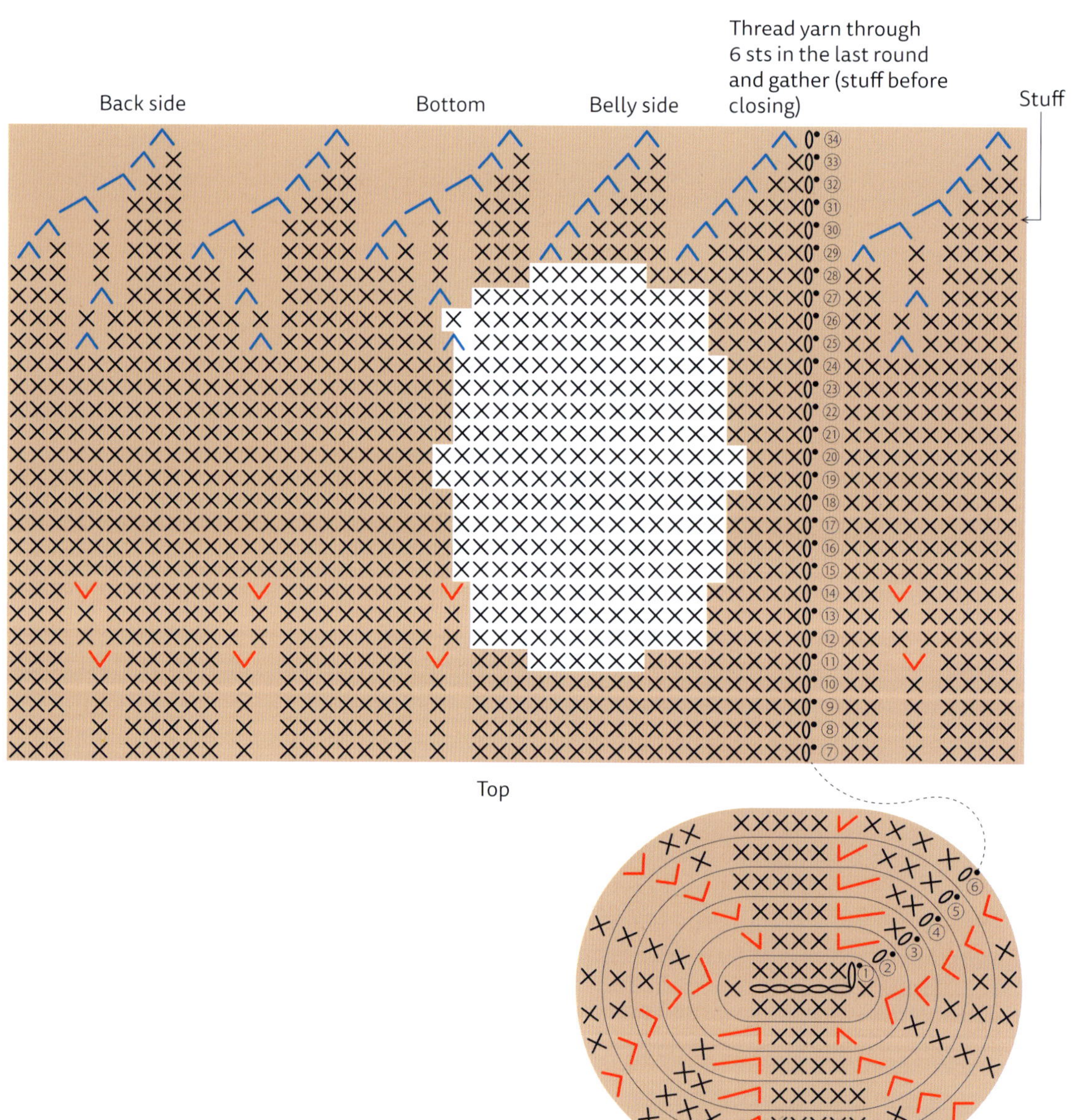

Head & Chest (make 1)

With Yarn A and US 7 hook, ch4.

Rnd 1: skip first ch, sc1 in in next ch, sc1 in next ch, sc3 in last ch, rotate and work along opposite side of chain, sc1 in next ch, sc2 in next ch, slst in skipped ch at beg of round [8]

Place stitch marker in first st of rnd 1 and move it up after each round

Rnd 2: ch1, sc2 in each st to end, slst in beg ch1 [16]

Rnd 3: ch1, sc1, sc2 in next st, sc2, sc2 in next st, sc1, sc2 in next 2 sts, sc1, sc2 in next st, sc2, sc2 in next st, sc1, sc2 in next 2 sts, slst in beg ch1 [24]

Rnd 4: ch1, sc2 in next st, sc6, sc2 in next st, sc4, sc2 in next st, sc6, sc2 in next st, sc4, slst in beg ch1 [28]

Rnd 5: ch1, sc10, sc2 in next st, sc2, sc2 in next st, sc10, sc2 in next st, sc2, sc2 in next st, slst in beg ch1 [32]

Rnd 6: ch1, sc10, sc2 in next st, sc4, sc2 in next st, sc10, sc2 in next st, sc4, sc2 in next st, slst in beg ch1 [36]

Rnds 7-9: in Yarn A sc22, in Yarn B sc2, in Yarn A sc12, slst in beg ch1 (3 rnds)

Rnd 10: in Yarn A sc5, in Yarn B sc2, in Yarn A sc14, in Yarn B sc4, in Yarn A sc11, slst in beg ch1

Rnd 11: in Yarn A sc4, in Yarn B sc4, in Yarn A sc12, in Yarn B sc6, in Yarn A sc10, slst in beg ch1

Continue in Yarn B only.

Rnd 12: ch1, sc18, (sc2tog, sc2) twice, sc2tog, sc8, slst in beg ch1 [33]

Rnd 13: ch1, sc3, sc2 in next st, sc4, sc2 in next st, sc7, (sc2tog, sc1) 3 times, sc2tog, sc6, slst in beg ch1 [31]

Rnds 14-15: ch1, sc1 in each st, slst in beg ch1 (2 rnds)

Rnd 16: ch1, sc18, (sc2 in next st, sc2) twice, sc2 in next st, sc6, slst in beg ch1 [34]

Rnd 17: ch1, sc3, sc2 in next st, sc6, sc2 in next st, sc7, sc2 in next st, sc8, sc2 in next st, sc6, slst in beg ch1 [38]

Rnds 18-19: ch1, sc1 in each st, slst in beg ch1 (2 rnds)

Rnd 20: ch1, sc20, sc2 in next st, sc10, sc2 in next st, sc6, slst in beg ch1 [40]

Rnd 21: ch1, sc20, sc2 in next st, sc12, sc2 in next st, sc6, slst in beg ch1 [42]

Rnds 22-27: ch1, sc1 in each st, slst in beg ch1 (6 rnds)

Rnd 28: ch1, (sc5, sc2tog) 6 times, slst in beg ch1 [36]

Rnd 29: ch1, (sc4, sc2tog) 6 times, slst in beg ch1 [30]

Begin to fill with toy stuffing.

Rnd 30: ch1, (sc3, sc2tog) 6 times, slst in beg ch1 [24]

Rnd 31: ch1, (sc2, sc2tog) 6 times, slst in beg ch1 [18]

Rnd 32: ch1, (sc1, sc2tog) 6 times, slst in beg ch1 [12]

Add more toy stuffing before final rnd.

Rnd 33: ch1, (sc2tog) 6 times, slst in beg ch1 [6]

Fasten off.

TIP

- If the crochet pattern is distorted, adjust the shape by using a steam iron while pulling it straight.

Front Legs

Left (make 1)

With Yarn B and US 7 hook, make a magic ring.
Rnd 1: ch1 (does not count as a st throughout), sc8 in magic ring, slst in beg ch1 [8]
Place stitch marker in first st of rnd 1 and move it up after each round
Rnd 2: ch1, sc2, (hdc-cl in next st) 4 times, sc2, slst in beg ch1
Rnds 3-7: ch1, sc1 in each st, slst in beg ch1 (5 rnds)
Rnd 8: ch1, sc2, sc2 in next st, sc5, slst in beg ch1 [9]
Rnd 9: ch1, sc3, sc2 in next st, sc5, slst in beg ch1 [10]
Rnd 10: ch1, sc4, sc2 in next st, sc5, slst in beg ch1 [11]
Rnd 11: ch1, sc4, sc2 in next st, sc6, slst in beg ch1 [12]
Rnd 12: ch1, sc4, sc2 in next st, sc7, slst in beg ch1 [13]
Rnd 13: ch1, sc4, sc2 in next st, sc8, slst in beg ch1 [14]
Rnd 14: ch1, sc4, sc2 in next st, sc9, slst in beg ch1 [15]
Rnd 15: ch1, sc4, hdc2 in next st, hdc1, sc9, slst in beg ch1 [16]
Rnd 16: ch1, sc4, hdc2 in next st, hdc1, sc10, slst in beg ch1 [17]
Rnd 17: ch1, sc1 in each st, slst in beg ch1.
Fasten off.

Right (make 1)

With Yarn B and US 7 hook, make a magic ring.
Rnd 1: ch1 (does not count as a st throughout), sc8 in magic ring, slst in beg ch1 [8]
Place stitch marker in first st of rnd 1 and move it up after each round
Rnd 2: ch1, sc2, (hdc-cl in next st) 4 times, sc2, slst in beg ch1
Rnds 3-7: ch1, sc1 in each st, slst in beg ch1 (5 rnds)
Rnd 8: ch1, sc5, sc2 in next st, sc2, slst in beg ch1 [9]
Rnd 9: ch1, sc6, sc2 in next st, sc2, slst in beg ch1 [10]
Rnd 10: ch1, sc7, sc2 in next st, sc2, slst in beg ch1 [11]
Rnd 11: ch1, sc8, sc2 in next st, sc2, slst in beg ch1 [12]
Rnd 12: ch1, sc9, sc2 in next st, sc2, slst in beg ch1 [13]
Rnd 13: ch1, sc10, sc2 in next st, sc2, slst in beg ch1 [14]
Rnd 14: ch1, sc11, sc2 in next st, sc2, slst in beg ch1 [15]
Rnd 15: ch1, sc11, hdc1, hdc2 in next st, sc2, slst in beg ch1 [16]
Rnd 16: ch1, sc12, hdc1, hdc2 in next st, sc2, slst in beg ch1 [17]
Rnd 17: ch1, sc1 in each st, slst in beg ch1.
Fasten off.

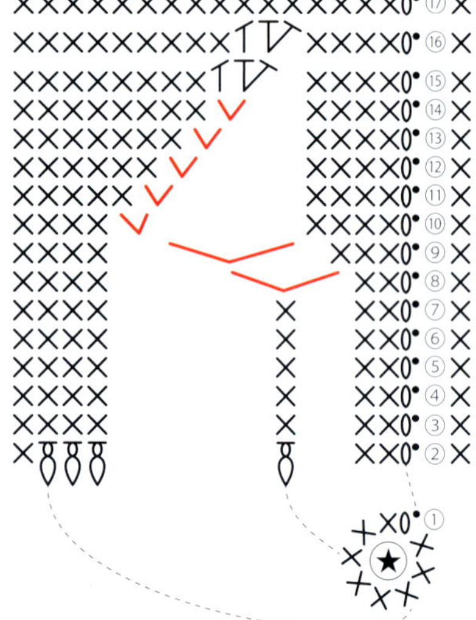

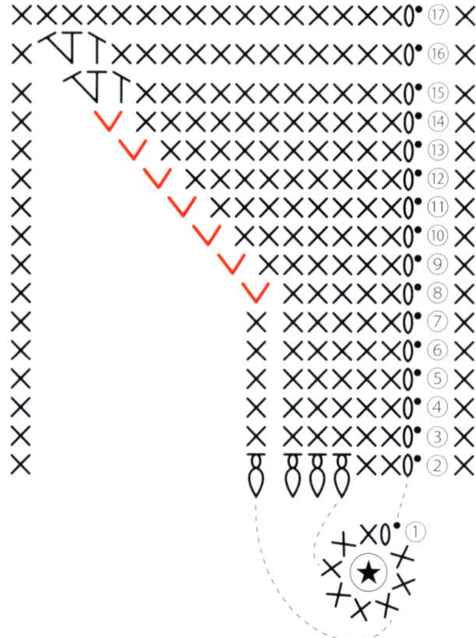

Back Legs (make 2)

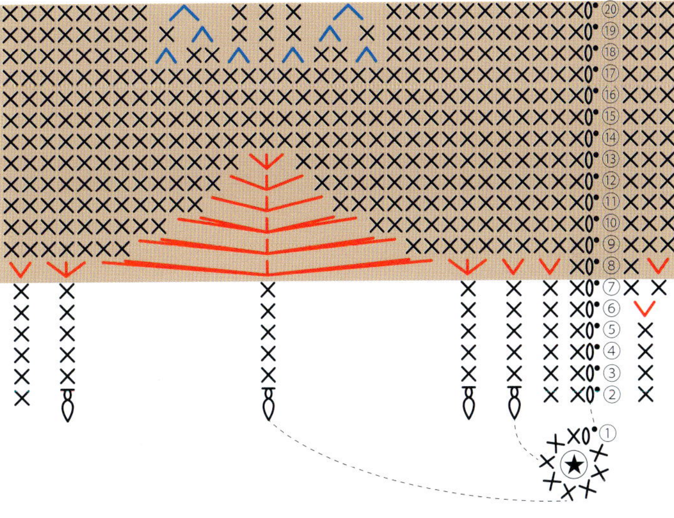

With Yarn B and US 7 hook, make a magic ring.
Rnd 1: ch1 (does not count as a st throughout), sc8 in magic ring, slst in beg ch1 [8]
Place stitch marker in first st of rnd 1 and move it up after each round
Rnd 2: ch1, sc2, hdc-cl in next 4 sts, sc2, slst in beg ch1
Rnds 3-5: ch1, sc1 in each st, slst in beg ch1 (3 rnds)
Rnd 6: ch1, sc7, sc2 in next st, slst in beg ch1 [9]
Rnd 7: ch1, sc1 in each st, slst in beg ch1
Change to Yarn A.
Rnd 8: ch1, sc1, (sc2 in next st) twice, sc3 in next st, sc5 in next st, sc3 in next st, (sc2 in next st) twice, sc1, slst in beg ch1 [21]
Rnd 9: ch1, sc10, sc5 in next st, sc10, slst in beg ch1 [25]
Rnd 10: ch1, sc12, sc5 in next st, sc12, slst in beg ch1 [29]
Rnd 11: ch1, sc14, sc3 in next st, sc14, slst in beg ch1 [31]
Rnd 12: ch1, sc15, sc3 in next st, sc15, slst in beg ch1 [33]
Rnd 13: ch1, sc16, sc3 in next st, sc16, slst in beg ch1 [35]
Rnds 14-17: ch1, sc1 in each st, slst in beg ch1 (4 rnds)
Rnd 18: ch1, sc11, sc2tog, sc2, sc2tog, sc1, sc2tog, sc2, sc2tog, sc11, slst in beg ch1 [31]
Rnd 19: ch1, sc12, sc2tog, sc3, sc2tog, sc12, slst in beg ch1 [29]
Rnd 20: ch1, sc11, sc2tog, sc3, sc2tog, sc11, slst in beg ch1 [27]
Fasten off.

Tail (make 1)

With Yarn A and US 7 hook, make a magic ring.
Rnd 1: ch1 (does not count as a st throughout), sc6 in magic ring, slst in beg ch1 [6]
Place stitch marker in first st of rnd 1 and move it up after each round
Rnd 2: ch1, (sc1, sc2 in next st) 3 times, slst in beg ch1 [9]
Rnds 3-4: ch1, sc1 in each st, slst in beg ch1 (2 rnds)
Rnd 5: ch1, (sc2, sc2 in next st) 3 times, slst in beg ch1 [12]
Rnds 6-23: ch1, sc1 in each st, slst in beg ch1 (18 rnds)
Fasten off.

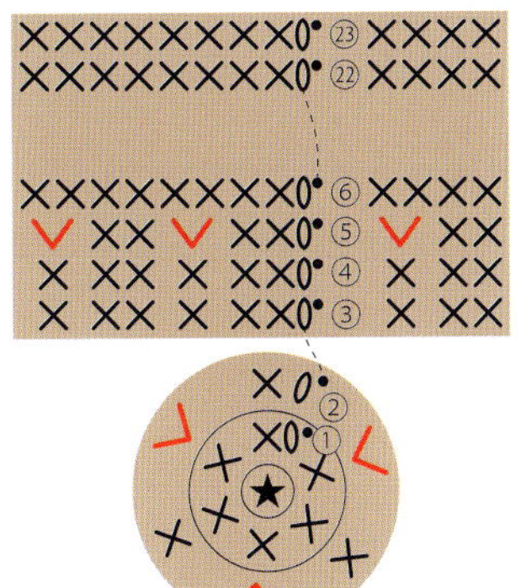

Mouth (make 1)

With Yarn F and US C-2 hook, ch10.
Rnd 1: skip first ch, sc1 in next ch, hdc1, dc2, sc1, dc2, hdc1, sc3 in last ch, rotate and work along opposite side of chain, hdc1, dc2, sc1, dc2, hdc1, sc2 in last ch, slst in skipped ch at beg of rnd [20]
Place stitch marker in first st of rnd 1 and move it up after each round
Rnd 2: ch1, sc4, slst in next st, sc9, slst in next st, sc5, slst in beg ch1
Rnd 3: ch1, sc12, ch2, dc4tog over next 4 sc (and skipping the slst), ch2, sc3, slst in beg ch1 [20]
Fasten off. Use the wrong side as the right side.

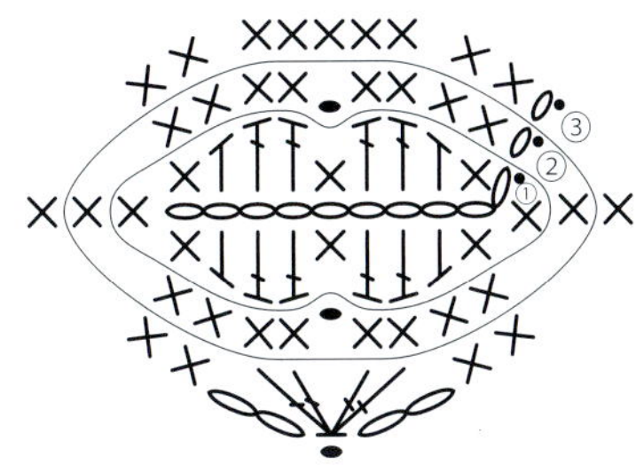

Nose (make 1)

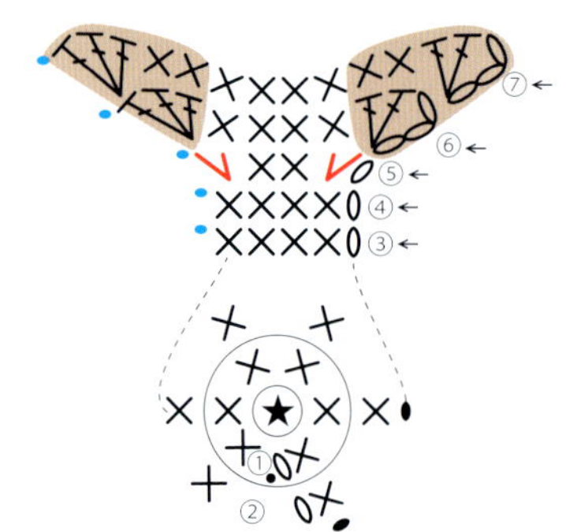

With Yarn F and US C-2 hook, make a magic ring.
Rnd 1: ch1 (does not count as a st throughout), sc6 in magic ring, slst in beg ch1 [6]
Place stitch marker in first st of rnd 1 and move it up after each round
Rnd 2: ch1, sc1 in each st, slst in beg ch1
Slst in next 2 sts, then continue in rows.
Row 3: ch1, sc1 in next 4 sts, lengthen loop from hook and pass yarn through, pull tight to make a knot, do not turn [4]
Row 4: pass yarn across back of work, pull through beg ch1 of prev row, and rep row 3.
Row 5: pass yarn across back of work, pull through beg ch1 of prev row, ch1, sc2 in first st, sc2, sc2 in last st, lengthen loop from hook and pass yarn through, pull tight to make a knot, do not turn [6]
Row 6: pass yarn across back of work, pull through beg ch1 of prev row, change to Yarn E and ch3 (counts as dc), dc2 in first st, change to Yarn F sc4, change to Yarn E dc3 in last st, lengthen loop from hook and pass yarn through, pull tight to make a knot, do not turn [10]
Row 7: pass yarn across back of work, pull through top of beg ch3 of prev row, (ch3, dc2) in same st (beg ch3 counts as dc), sc2, in Yarn F sc4, in Yarn E sc2, dc3 in last st, lengthen loop from hook and pass yarn through, pull tight to make a knot [14]
Fasten off.

Ears

Right Ear (make 1 each of outer and inner ear)

Outer Ear

With Yarn A and US 7 hook, ch9, leaving a 12" (30 cm) tail of yarn.
Work in rows.
Row 1: dc1 in fifth ch from hook (counts as 2dc), dc1, hdc1, sc1, sc3 in last chain, rotate and work along opposite side of chain stitches, hdc2, dc2, 2dc in next ch, turn [14]
Cut a 6" (15 cm) long piece of armature wire, fold in half, position the folded area at the corner of the ear, and crochet next rnd over the wire to trap it into the sts.
Row 2: ch1 (does not count as a st throughout), sc7, sc2 in next st, sc6 [15]
Fasten off.

Inner Ear

Make inner ear in the same way with Yarn E and US C-2 hook, omitting wire.

Left Ear (make 1 each of outer and inner ear)

Outer Ear

With Yarn A and US 7 hook, ch9, leaving a 12" (30 cm) tail of yarn.
Work in rows.
Row 1: dc1 in fourth ch from hook (counts as 2dc), dc2, hdc2, sc3 in last chain, rotate and work along opposite side of chain stitches, sc1, hdc1, dc3, turn [14]
Cut a 6" (15 cm) long piece of armature wire, fold in half, position the folded area at the corner of the ear, and crochet next rnd over the wire to trap it into the sts.
Row 2: ch1 (does not count as a st throughout), sc6, sc2 in next st, sc7 [15]
Fasten off.

Inner Ear

Make inner ear in the same way with Yarn E and US C-2 hook, omitting wire.

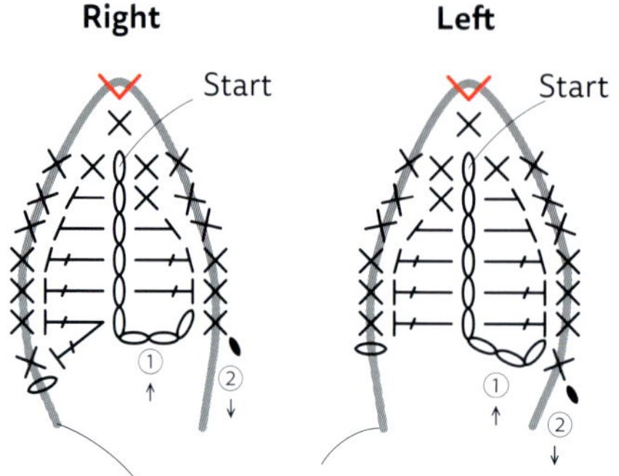

Align a 6" (15 cm) long piece of armature wire with the corner of the ear and crochet around the wire (for outer ear only)

GRAFTING

Placement & Yarn Length Key

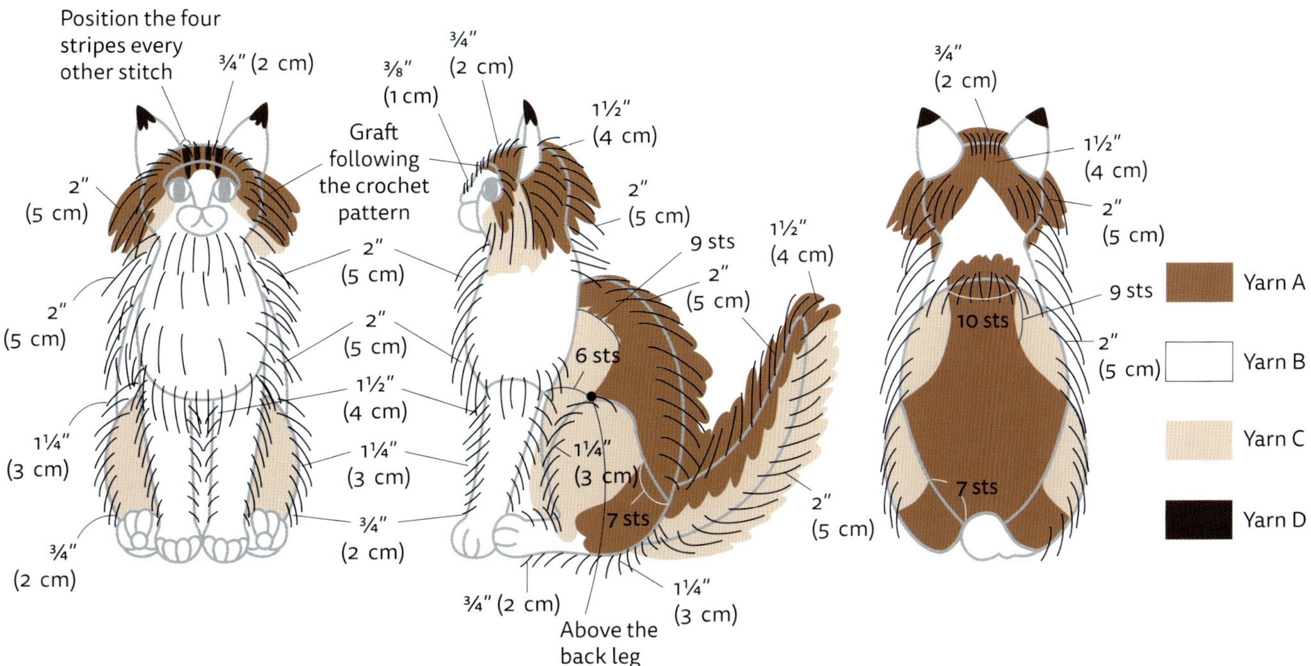

TIPS

- Do not graft ears, toes, or stomach area.
- Graft Yarns C and D to the face in the areas noted in the photo.
- Brush the back of the ears with a slicker brush to make them fuzzy.

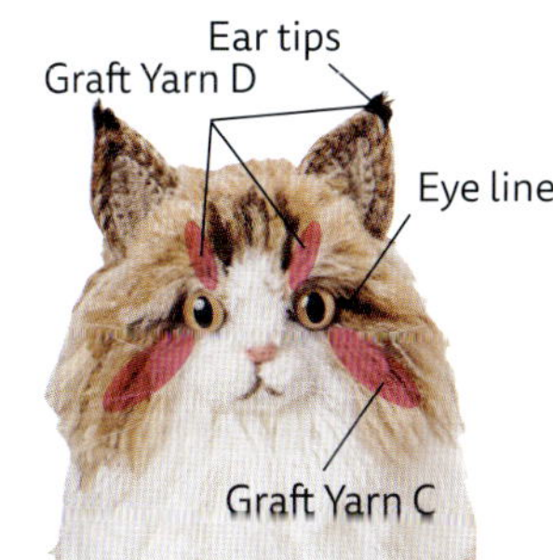

British Shorthair

SHOWN ON PAGE 9

TOOLS & MATERIALS

- US 7 (4.5 mm) crochet hook
- US C-2 (2.5 mm) crochet hook
- Sport weight acrylic yarn
  - 972 yds (888 m) in gray
- Light-fingering weight acrylic/mohair blend yarn
  - 963 yds (880 m) in dark gray
- About 36" (90 cm) of sport weight acrylic yarn in black for embroidering the eyes, nose, and mouth [12" (30 cm) long pieces for each]
- Pair of 18 mm cat eye buttons in yellow
- 2¾" (7 cm) long clear whiskers
- Polyester fiber fill toy stuffing (about 70 g)
- 2 yds (1.9 m) of armature wire
  - Cut two 6" (15 cm) long pieces for the ears
  - Cut two 20" (50 cm) long pieces for the front legs
  - Cut one 24" (60 cm) long piece for the tail
- Stitch marker
- Yarn needle
- Felting needle
- Slicker brush

CONSTRUCTION STEPS

1. Crochet the body, head and chest, front legs, back legs, tail, nose, mouth, and ears following the instructions on page 79 (also see pages 37–49).
2. Stuff as required and assemble the body parts following the instructions on pages 50–56. Make sure to attach the eye buttons to the head before stuffing (refer to page 36).
3. Graft yarn as noted in the diagrams on page 79. Loosen the yarn and trim the fur into shape. Embroider the facial features. Refer to pages 57–61 for general grafting instructions and use these photos as a reference.

FINISHED SIZE

Height: 13" (33 cm)
Length: 8" (20 cm)
Tail: 8" (20 cm)

Front

Back

Side

YARN COMBINATION CHART

	Area	Yarn Used	Yarn Color	Strands	Total Strands	Yarn	Hook Size
Crocheting the Foundation	• Head and chest • Body • Front legs • Back legs • Tail • Outer ears	Sport weight acrylic	Gray	2	4	A	US 7 (4.5 mm)
		Light-fingering weight acrylic/mohair blend	Dark gray	2			
	• Inner ears • Nose • Mouth	Sport weight acrylic	Gray	1	2	B	US C-2 (2.5 mm)
		Light-fingering weight acrylic/mohair blend	Dark gray	1			
Grafting the Fur						A*	

*Graft using the same yarn used to crochet the foundation

CROCHET INSTRUCTIONS

Refer to the following pages to crochet the body parts, but use the yarn colors listed above:

Body ➤ See page 65
Head and chest ➤ See page 63
Front legs ➤ See page 74
Back legs ➤ See page 110
Tail ➤ See page 75
Nose, mouth, and ears ➤ See page 68

TIPS

- Do not graft ears, toes, or stomach area.
- Graft the muzzle to create a rounded shape, resembling a pompom.
- After grafting the whole body, trim to create a rounded silhouette. Trim the grafted fur at the neck to different lengths, referring to the photo on page 9.
- Brush the back of the ears with a slicker brush to make them fuzzy.

GRAFTING

Yarn Length Key

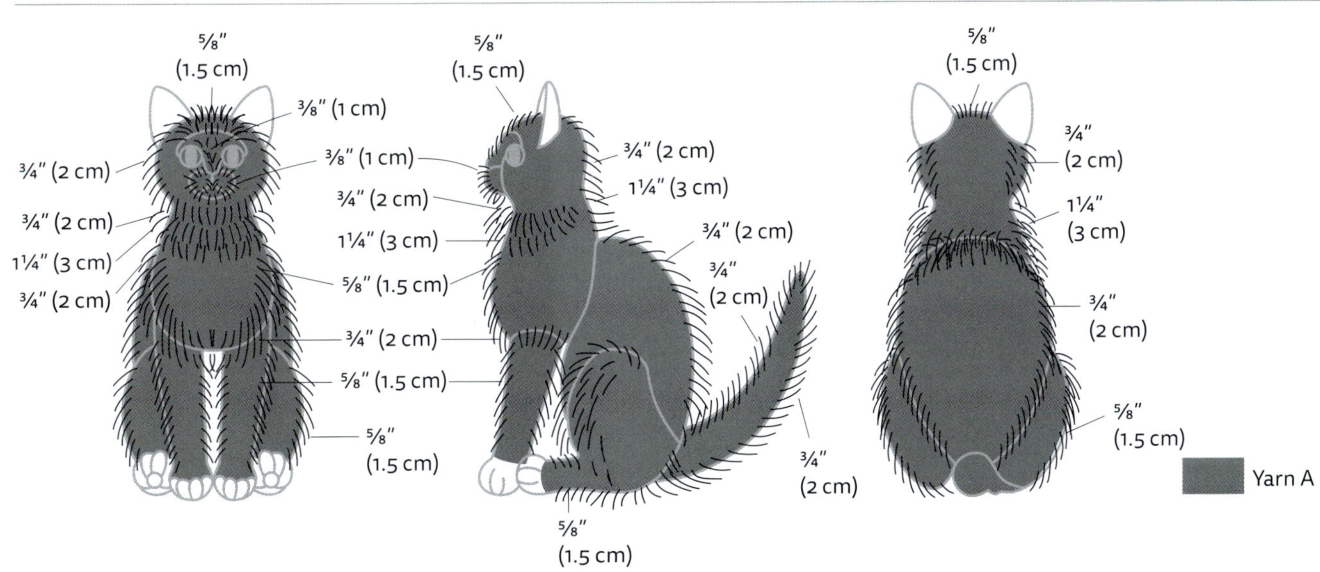

Ragdoll

SHOWN ON PAGE 16

TOOLS & MATERIALS

TOOLS & MATERIALS

- US 7 (4.5 mm) crochet hook
- US C-2 (2.5 mm) crochet hook
- Sport weight acrylic yarn
  - 788 yds (720 m) in white
  - 237 yds (216 m) in light beige
  - 40 yds (36 m) in brown
- Light-fingering weight acrylic/mohair blend yarn
  - 875 yds (800 m) in white
  - 263 yds (240 m) in cream
  - 44 yds (40 m) in brown
- About 12″ (30 cm) of sport weight acrylic yarn in pink for embroidering the nose
- About 24″ (60 cm) of light-fingering weight acrylic/mohair blend yarn in dark brown for embroidering the eyes
- About 12″ (30 cm) of light-fingering weight acrylic/mohair blend yarn in brown for embroidering the mouth
- Pair of 15 mm crystal eye buttons in blue
- 2¾″ (7 cm) long clear whiskers
- Polyester fiber fill toy stuffing (about 70 g)
- 2 yds (1.9 m) of armature wire
  - Cut two 6″ (15 cm) long pieces for the ears
  - Cut two 20″ (50 cm) long pieces for the front legs
  - Cut one 24″ (60 cm) long piece for the tail
- Stitch marker
- Yarn needle
- Felting needle
- Slicker brush

CONSTRUCTION STEPS

1. Crochet the body, head and chest, front legs, back legs, tail, nose, mouth, and ears following the instructions on pages 81–82 (also see pages 37–49).

2. Stuff as required and assemble the body parts following the instructions on pages 50–56. Make sure to attach the eye buttons to the head before stuffing (refer to page 36).

3. Graft yarn as noted in the diagrams on page 82. Loosen the yarn and trim the fur into shape. Embroider the facial features. Refer to pages 57–61 for general grafting instructions and use these photos as a reference.

FINISHED SIZE

Height: 13″ (33 cm)
Length: 8″ (20 cm)
Tail: 8″ (20 cm)

Front

Back

Side

YARN COMBINATION CHART

	Area	Yarn Used	Yarn Color	Strands	Total Strands	Yarn	Hook Size
Crocheting the Foundation	• Head and chest • Tail	Sport weight acrylic	Light beige	2	4	A (Alternate A and B to crochet the head)	US 7 (4.5 mm)
		Light-fingering weight acrylic/mohair blend	Cream	2			
	• Body • Front legs • Back legs	Sport weight acrylic	White	2	4	B	US 7 (4.5 mm)
		Light-fingering weight acrylic/mohair blend	White	2			
	• Outer ears	Sport weight acrylic	Beige	2	4	F	US C-2 (2.5 mm)
		Light-fingering weight acrylic/mohair blend	Brown	2			
	• Inner ears • Nose	Sport weight acrylic	Light beige	1	2	D	
		Light-fingering weight acrylic/mohair blend	Cream	1			
	• Nose • Mouth	Sport weight acrylic	White	1	2	E	
		Light-fingering weight acrylic/mohair blend	White	1			
Grafting the Fur						A, B**	
	Face (around eyes)	Light-fingering weight acrylic/mohair blend	Brown	1*	2	C	

*Use a double strand of the same yarn

**Graft using the same yarn used to crochet the foundation

CROCHET INSTRUCTIONS

Refer to the following pages to crochet the body parts, but use the yarn colors listed above:

Body ➤ See page 65
Head and chest ➤ See page 73
Front legs ➤ See page 74
Back legs ➤ See page 110
Tail ➤ See page 75
Nose ➤ See page 82
Mouth ➤ See page 75

Nose (make 1)

With Yarn E and US C-2 hook, make a magic ring.
Rnd 1: ch1 (does not count as a st throughout), sc6 in magic ring, slst in beg ch1 [6]
Place stitch marker in first st of rnd 1 and move it up after each round
Rnd 2: ch1, sc1 in each st, slst in beg ch1
Slst in next 2 sts, then continue in rows.
Row 3: ch1, sc1 in next 4 sts, lengthen loop from hook and pass yarn through, pull tight to make a knot, do not turn [4]
Row 4: pass yarn across back of work, pull through beg ch1 of prev row, and rep row 3.
Row 5: pass yarn across back of work, pull through beg ch1 of prev row, ch1, sc2 in first st, sc2, sc2 in last st, lengthen loop from hook and pass yarn through, pull tight to make a knot, do not turn [6]
Row 6: pass yarn across back of work, pull through beg ch1 of prev row, change to Yarn D and ch3 (counts as dc), dc2 in first st, change to Yarn E sc4, change to Yarn D dc3 in last st, lengthen loop from hook and pass yarn through, pull tight to make a knot, do not turn [10]
Row 7: pass yarn across back of work, pull through top of beg ch3 of prev row, (ch3, dc2) in same st (beg ch3 counts as dc), sc2, in Yarn E sc4, in Yarn D sc2, dc3 in last st, lengthen loop from hook and pass yarn through, pull tight to make a knot [14]
Fasten off.

Crochet Symbol Key

- ★ = magic ring
- 0 = ch st
- • = slst
- ∧ = ⩓ = sc2tog
- ∨ = ∨ = sc2 in next st
- ∨ = sc3 in next st
- ∨ = sc5 in next st
- • = make a knot (see page 46)

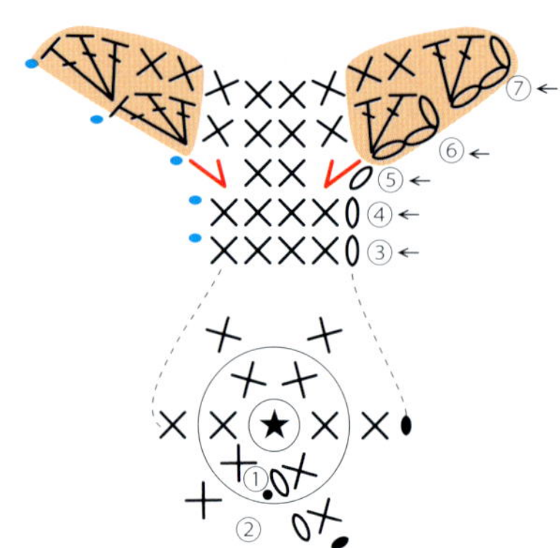

GRAFTING

Placement & Yarn Length Key

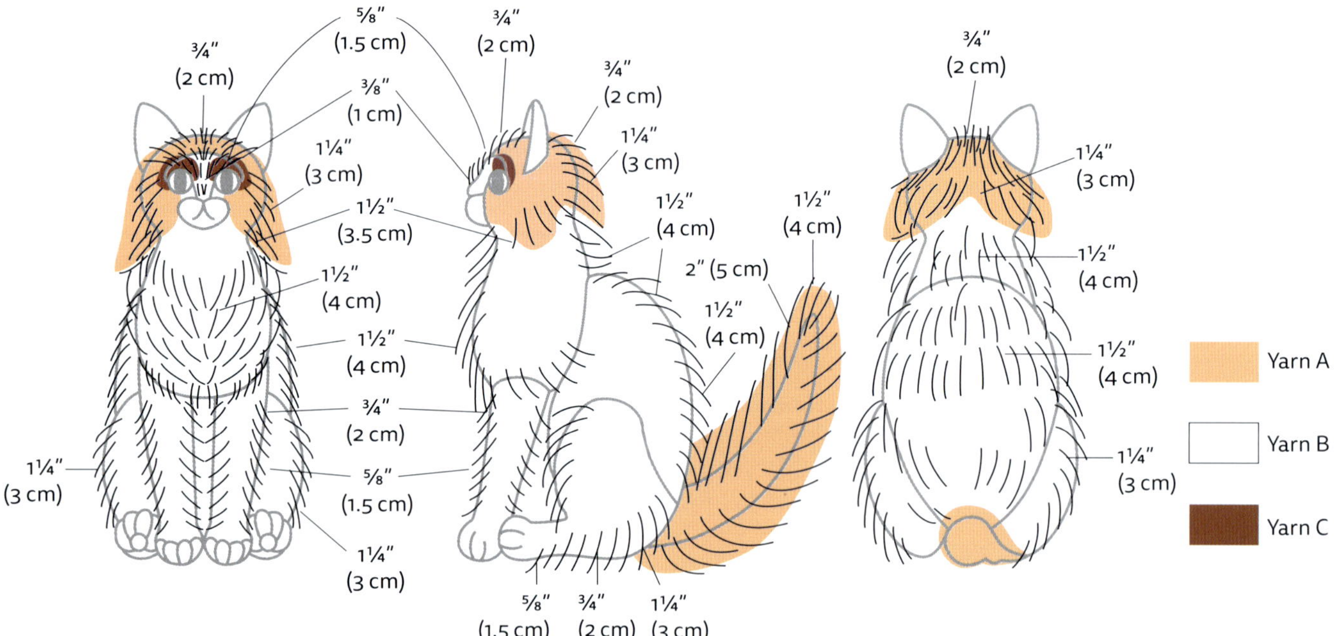

TIPS

- Do not graft ears, toes, or stomach area.
- Graft following the crochet pattern of the body.

Calico (Adult)

SHOWN ON PAGE 19

TOOLS & MATERIALS

- US 7 (4.5 mm) crochet hook
- US C-2 (2.5 mm) crochet hook
- Sport weight acrylic yarn
  - 749 yds (684 m) in white
  - 99 yds (90 m) in golden brown
  - 60 yds (54 m) in black
- Light-fingering weight acrylic/mohair blend yarn
  - 832 yds (760 m) in white
  - 110 yds (100 m) in brown
  - 66 yds (60 m) in black
- About 12" (30 cm) of sport weight acrylic yarn in light pink for embroidering the nose
- About 12" (30 cm) of light-fingering weight acrylic/mohair blend yarn in brown for embroidering the mouth
- Pair of 18 mm cat eye buttons in green
- 2¾" (7 cm) long clear whiskers
- Polyester fiber fill toy stuffing (about 70 g)
- 1.4 yds (1.3 m) of armature wire
  - Cut two 6" (15 cm) long pieces for the ears
  - Cut two 20" (50 cm) long pieces for the front legs
- Stitch marker
- Yarn needle
- Felting needle
- Slicker brush

CONSTRUCTION STEPS

1. Crochet the body, head and chest, front legs, back legs, tail, nose, mouth, and ears following the instructions on page 84 (also see pages 37–49).
2. Stuff as required and assemble the body parts following the instructions on pages 50–56. Make sure to attach the eye buttons to the head before stuffing (refer to page 36).
3. Graft yarn as noted in the diagrams on page 85. Loosen the yarn and trim the fur into shape. Embroider the facial features. Refer to pages 57–61 for general grafting instructions and use these photos as a reference.

FINISHED SIZE

Height: 13" (33 cm)
Length: 8" (20 cm)
Tail: 8" (20 cm)

Front

Back

Side

Side

YARN COMBINATION CHART

	Area	Yarn Used	Yarn Color	Strands	Total Strands	Yarn	Hook Size
Crocheting the Foundation	• Head and chest • Body • Front legs • Back legs	Sport weight acrylic	White	2	4	A	US 7 (4.5 mm)
		Light-fingering weight acrylic/mohair blend	White	2			
	• Tail	Sport weight acrylic	Black	2	4	B	US 7 (4.5 mm)
		Light-fingering weight acrylic/mohair blend	Black	2			
	• Outer ears	Sport weight acrylic	Golden brown	2	4	C	US 7 (4.5 mm)
		Light-fingering weight acrylic/mohair blend	Brown	2			
	•Inner ears	Light-fingering weight acrylic/mohair blend	Brown	1*	2	D	US C-2 (2.5 mm)
	• Nose •Mouth	Sport weight acrylic	White	1	2	E	US C-2 (2.5 mm)
		Light-fingering weight acrylic/mohair blend	White	1			
Grafting the Fur						A, B, C**	

*Use a double strand of the same yarn

**Graft using the same yarn used to crochet the foundation

CROCHET INSTRUCTIONS

Refer to the following pages to crochet the body parts, but use the yarn colors listed above:

Body ➤ See page 65
Head and chest ➤ See page 63
Front legs ➤ See page 74
Back legs ➤ See page 110
Nose ➤ See page 68
Mouth ➤ See page 68
Ears ➤ See page 68

Crochet Symbol Key

★ = magic ring
0 = ch st
• = slst
∧ = ⩓ = sc2tog
∨ = ⩔ = sc2 in next st
sc3 in next st
sc5 in next st
• = make a knot (see page 46)

Tail (make 1)

With Yarn B and US 7 hook, make a magic ring.
Rnd 1: ch1 (does not count as a st throughout), sc6 in magic ring, slst in beg ch1 [6]
Place stitch marker in first st of rnd 1 and move it up after each round
Rnd 2: ch1, (sc2 in next st) 6 times, slst in beg ch1 [12]
Rnds 3-7: ch1, sc1 in each st, slst in beg ch1 (5 rnds)
Fasten off.

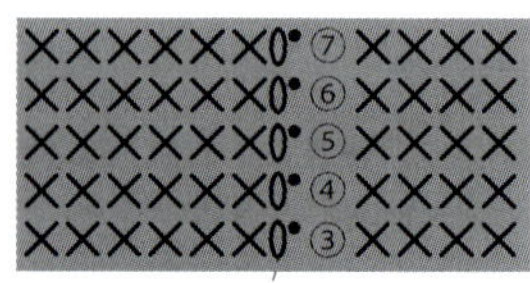

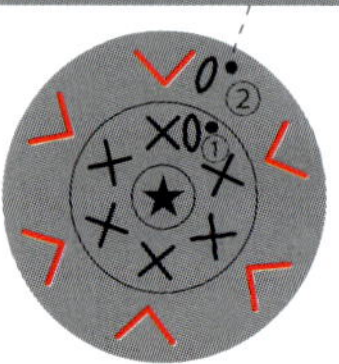

GRAFTING

Placement Key

Note: The appearance of the spotted pattern may differ for your cat depending on how you graft the yarn.

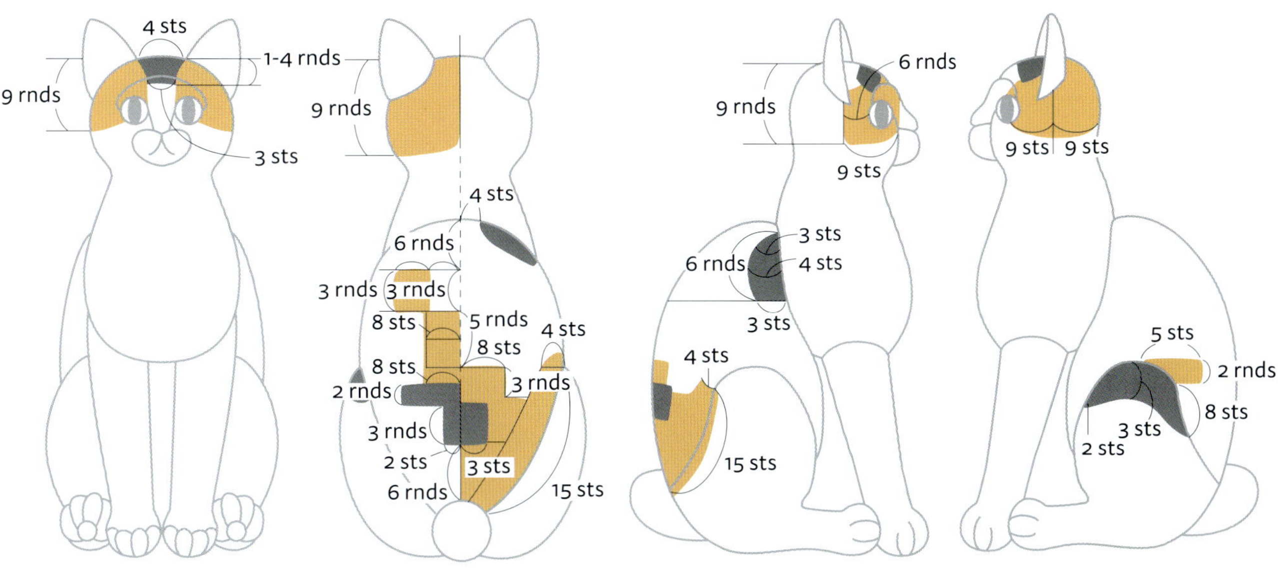

Yarn Length Key

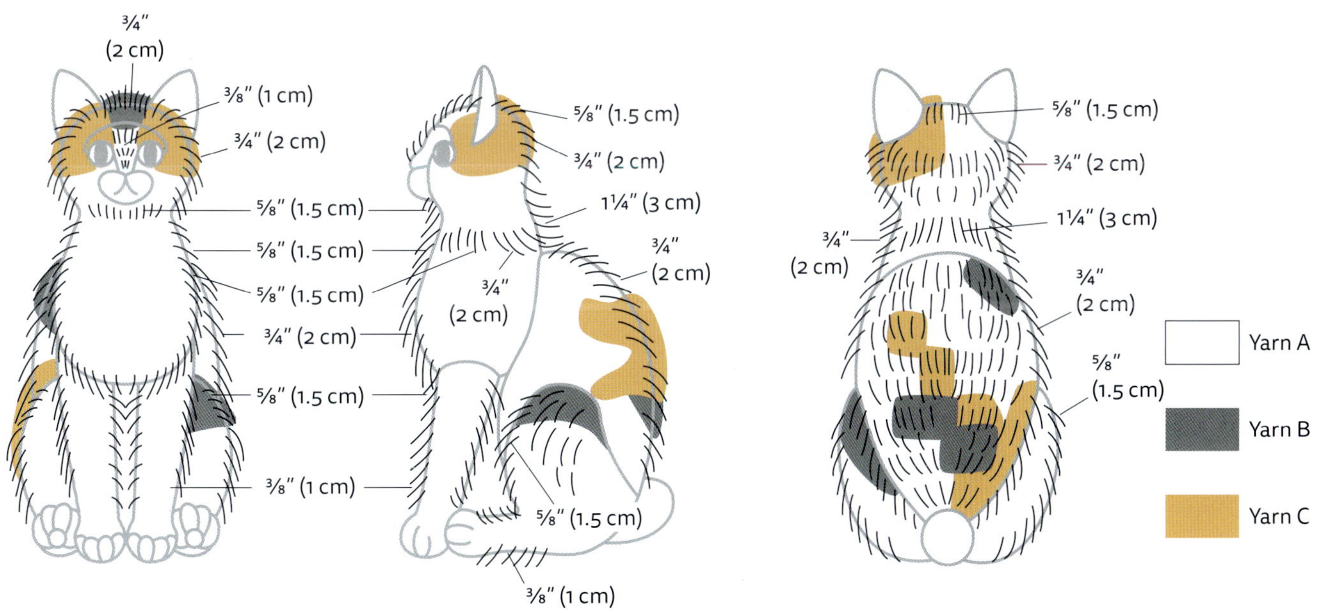

TIPS

- Do not graft ears, toes, or stomach area.
- Graft the patterned areas of the body first, then graft the rest of the body with white yarn.
- Brush the back of the ears with a slicker brush to make them fuzzy.

Calico (Kitten)

SHOWN ON PAGE 18

TOOLS & MATERIALS

- US G-6 (4 mm) crochet hook
- US C-2 (2.5 mm) crochet hook
- US B-1 (2.25 mm) crochet hook
- Sport weight acrylic yarn
  - 315 yds (288 m) in white
  - 60 yds (54 m) in golden brown
  - 40 yds (36 m) in black
- Light-fingering weight acrylic/mohair blend yarn
  - 329 yds (300 m) in white
  - 66 yds (60 m) in brown
  - 44 yds (40 m) in black
- About 12″ (30 cm) of sport weight acrylic yarn in light pink for embroidering the nose
- About 12″ (30 cm) of light-fingering weight acrylic/mohair blend yarn in brown for embroidering the mouth
- Pair of 15 mm cat eye buttons in blue
- 2¾″ (7 cm) long clear whiskers
- Polyester fiber fill toy stuffing (about 30 g)
- 38″ (96 cm) of armature wire
  - Cut two 4¾″ (12 cm) long pieces for the ears
  - Cut two 14½″ (36 cm) long pieces for the front legs
- Stitch marker
- Yarn needle
- Felting needle
- Slicker brush

CONSTRUCTION STEPS

1. Crochet the body, head and chest, front legs, back legs, tail, nose, mouth, and ears following the instructions on pages 87–91 (also see pages 37–49).
2. Stuff as required and assemble the body parts following the instructions on page 91. Make sure to attach the eye buttons to the head before stuffing (refer to page 36).
3. Graft yarn as noted in the diagrams on page 92. Loosen the yarn and trim the fur into shape. Embroider the facial features. Refer to pages 57–61 for general grafting instructions and use these photos as a reference.

FINISHED SIZE

Height: 8¼″ (21 cm)
Length: 7½″ (19 cm)
Tail: 1¼″ (3 cm)

Front

Back

Side

Side

YARN COMBINATION CHART

	Area	Yarn Used	Yarn Color	Strands	Total Strands	Yarn	Hook Size
Crocheting the Foundation	• Head and chest • Body • Front legs • Back legs	Sport weight acrylic	White	2	4	A	US G-6 (4 mm)
		Light-fingering weight acrylic/mohair blend	White	2			
	• Tail	Sport weight acrylic	Golden brown	2	4	B	US G-6 (4 mm)
		Light-fingering weight acrylic/mohair blend	Brown	2			
	• Outer ears	Sport weight acrylic	Golden brown	1	2	E	US C-2 (2.5 mm)
		Light-fingering weight acrylic/mohair blend	Brown	1			
	• Inner ears	Light-fingering weight acrylic/mohair blend	Brown	1	1	D	US B-1 (2.25 mm)
	• Nose • Mouth	Light-fingering weight acrylic/mohair blend	White White	1 1	2	F	US C-2 (2.5 mm)
Grafting the Fur						A, B*	
		Sport weight acrylic	Black	2	4	C	
		Light-fingering weight acrylic/mohair blend	Black	2			

*Graft using the same yarn used to crochet the foundation

CROCHET INSTRUCTIONS

Head & Chest (make 1)

With Yarn A and US G-6 hook, ch4.

Rnd 1: skip first ch, sc1 in in next ch, sc1 in next ch, sc3 in last ch, rotate and work along opposite side of chain, sc1 in next ch, sc2 in next ch, slst in skipped ch at beg of round [8]

Place stitch marker in first st of rnd 1 and move it up after each round

Rnd 2: ch1, sc2 in each st to end, slst in beg ch1 [16]

Rnd 3: ch1, sc1, sc2 in next st, sc2, sc2 in next st, sc1, sc2 in next 2 sts, sc1, sc2 in next st, sc2, sc2 in next st, sc1, sc2 in next 2 sts, slst in beg ch1 [24]

Rnd 4: ch1, sc2 in next st, sc6, sc2 in next st, sc4, sc2 in next st, sc6, sc2 in next st, sc4, slst in beg ch1 [28]

Rnds 5-10: ch1, sc1 in each st, slst in beg ch1 (6 rnds)

Rnd 11: ch1, sc13, sc2tog, sc1, sc2tog, sc2, sc2tog, sc1, sc2tog, sc3, slst in beg ch1 [24]

Rnd 12: ch1, sc4, sc2 in next st, sc3, sc2 in next st, sc4, (sc2tog, sc1) twice, sc2tog, sc3, slst in beg ch1 [23]

Crochet Symbol Key

★ = magic ring
0 = ch st
• = slst
∧ = ∧ = sc2tog
∨ = ∨ = sc2 in next st
= sc3 in next st
= sc5 in next st
• = make a knot (see page 46)

Rnd 13: ch1, sc1 in each st, slst in beg ch1
Rnd 14: ch1, sc4, sc2 in next st, sc5, sc2 in next st, sc12, slst in beg ch1 [25]
Rnd 15: ch1, sc17, sc2 in next st, sc3, sc2 in next st, sc3, slst in beg ch1 [27]
Rnd 16: ch1, sc1 in each st, slst in beg ch1
Rnd 17: ch1, sc17, sc2 in next st, sc5, sc2 in next st, sc3, slst in beg ch1 [29]
Rnd 18: ch1, sc1 in each st, slst in beg ch1
Rnd 19: ch1, sc21, sc2 in next st, sc7, slst in beg ch1 [30]
Rnd 20: ch1, sc1 in each st, slst in beg ch1
Begin to fill with toy stuffing.
Rnd 21: ch1, (sc3, sc2tog) 6 times, slst in beg ch1 [24]
Rnd 22: ch1, (sc2, sc2tog) 6 times, slst in beg ch1 [18]
Rnd 23: ch1, (sc1, sc2tog) 6 times, slst in beg ch1 [12]
Add more toy stuffing before final rnd.
Rnd 24: ch1, (sc2tog) 6 times, slst in beg ch1 [6]
Fasten off.

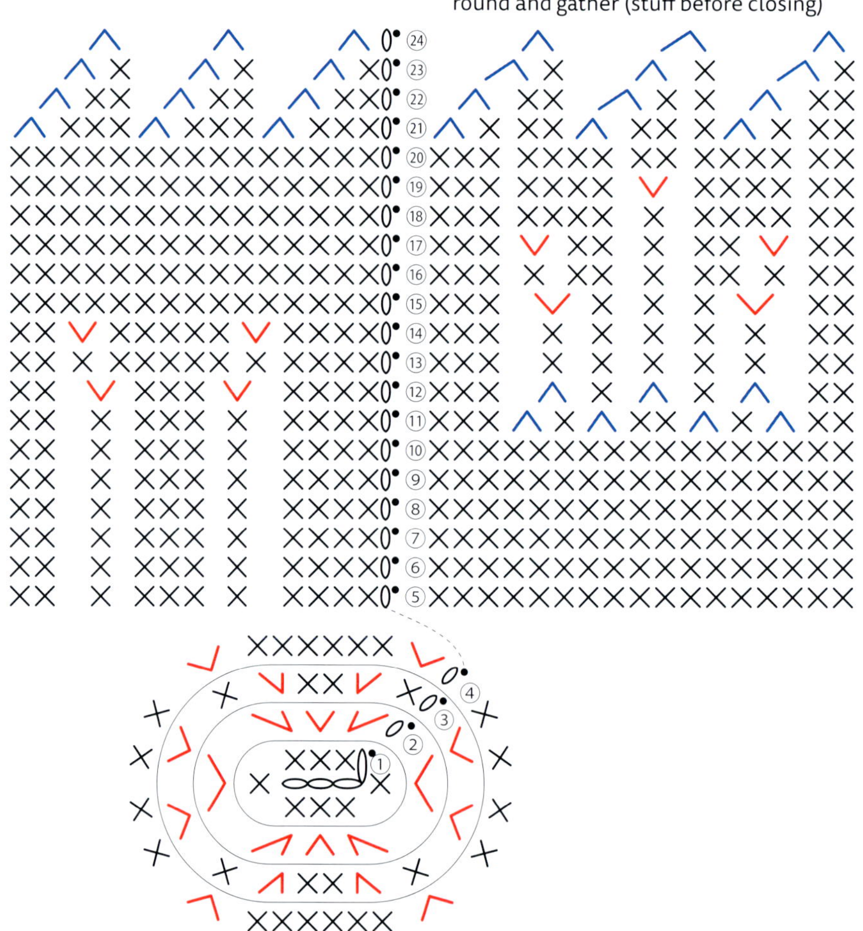

Body (make 1)

With Yarn A and US G-6 hook, make a magic ring.

Rnd 1: ch1 (does not count as a st throughout), sc6 in magic ring, slst in beg ch1 [6]

Place stitch marker in first st of rnd 1 and move it up after each round

Rnd 2: ch1, (sc2 in next st) 6 times, slst in beg ch1 [12]

Rnd 3: ch1, (sc1, sc2 in next st) 6 times, slst in beg ch1 [18]

Rnd 4: ch1, (sc2, sc2 in next st) 6 times, slst in beg ch1 [24]

Rnd 5: ch1, (sc3, sc2 in next st) 6 times, slst in beg ch1 [30]

Rnd 6: ch1, sc1, sc2 in next st, sc26, sc2 in next st, sc1, slst in beg ch1 [32]

Rnds 7-9: ch1, sc1 in each st, slst in beg ch1 (3 rnds)

Rnd 10: ch1, sc12, sc2tog, sc4, sc2tog, sc12, slst in beg ch1 [30]

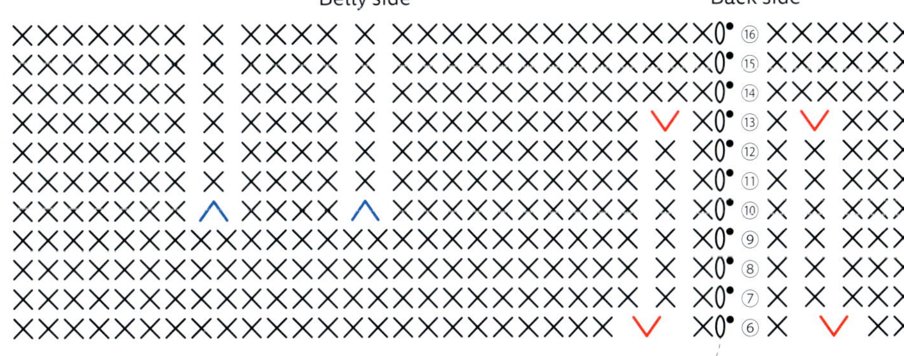

Rnds 11-12: ch1, sc1 in each st, slst in beg ch1 (2 rnds)

Rnd 13: ch1, sc1, sc2 in next st, sc26, sc2 in next st, sc1, slst in beg ch1 [32]

Rnds 14-16: ch1, sc1 in each st, slst in beg ch1 (3 rnds)

Fasten off.

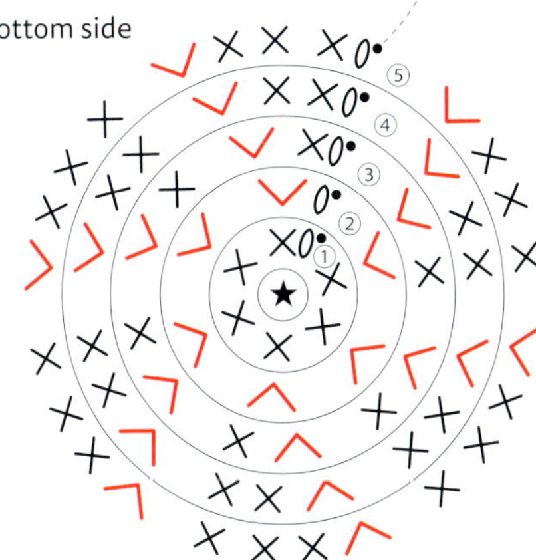

Front Legs

Left (make 1)

With Yarn A and US G-6 hook, make a magic ring.

Rnd 1: ch1 (does not count as a st throughout), sc8 in magic ring, slst in beg ch1 [8]

Place stitch marker in first st of rnd 1 and move it up after each round

Rnd 2: ch1, sc2, (hdc-cl in next st) 4 times, sc2, slst in beg ch1

Rnds 3-5: ch1, sc1 in each st, slst in beg ch1 (3 rnds)

Rnd 6: ch1, sc2, sc2 in next st, sc5, slst in beg ch1 [9]

Rnd 7: ch1, sc3, sc2 in next st, sc5, slst in beg ch1 [10]

Rnd 8: ch1, sc4, sc2 in next st, sc5, slst in beg ch1 [11]

Rnd 9: ch1, sc4, hdc2 in next st, hdc1, sc5, slst in beg ch1 [12]

Rnd 10: ch1, sc4, hdc2 in next st, hdc1, sc6, slst in beg ch1 [13]

Fasten off.

Right (make 1)

With Yarn A and US G-6 hook, make a magic ring.

Rnd 1: ch1 (does not count as a st throughout), sc8 in magic ring, slst in beg ch1 [8]

Place stitch marker in first st of rnd 1 and move it up after each round

Rnd 2: ch1, sc2, (hdc-cl in next st) 4 times, sc2, slst in beg ch1

Rnds 3-5: ch1, sc1 in each st, slst in beg ch1 (3 rnds)

Rnd 6: ch1, sc5, sc2 in next st, sc2, slst in beg ch1 [9]

Rnd 7: ch1, sc6, sc2 in next st, sc2, slst in beg ch1 [10]

Rnd 8: ch1, sc7, sc2 in next st, sc2, slst in beg ch1 [11]

Rnd 9: ch1, sc7, hdc1, hdc2 in next st, sc2, slst in beg ch1 [12]

Rnd 10: ch1, sc8, hdc1, hdc2 in next st, sc2, slst in beg ch1 [13]

Fasten off.

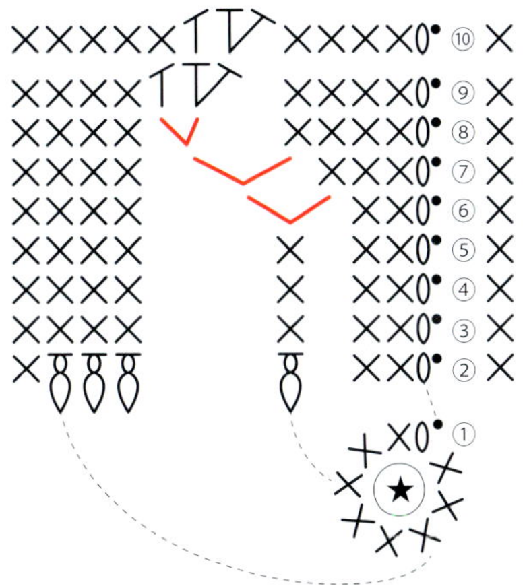

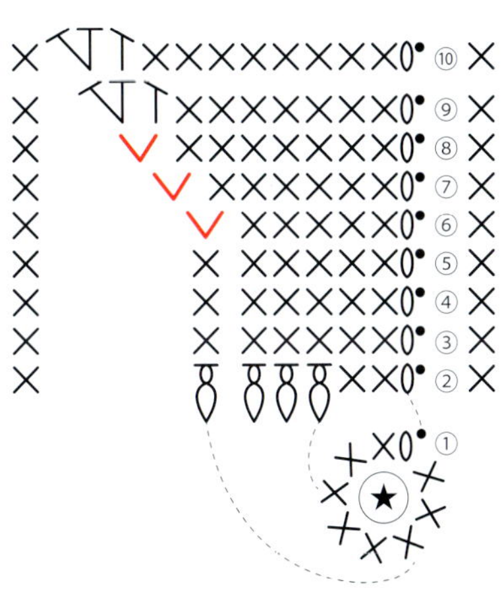

Back Legs (make 2)

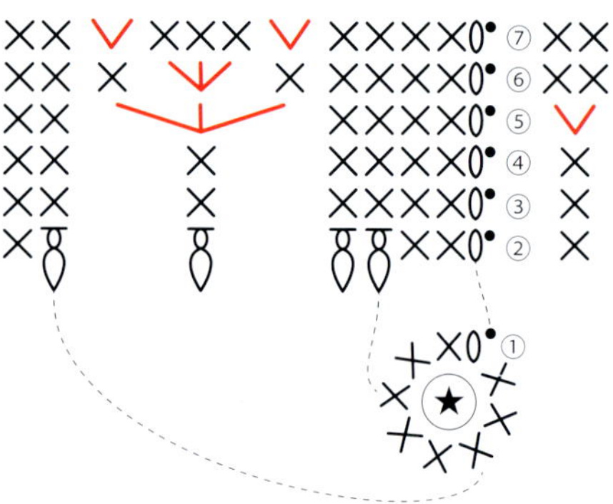

With Yarn A and US G-6 hook, make a magic ring.
Rnd 1: ch1 (does not count as a st throughout), sc8 in magic ring, slst in beg ch1 [8]
Place stitch marker in first st of rnd 1 and move it up after each round
Rnd 2: ch1, sc2, (hdc-cl in next st) 4 times, sc2, slst in beg ch1
Rnds 3-4: ch1, sc1 in each st, slst in beg ch1 (2 rnds)
Rnd 5: ch1, sc4, sc3 in next st, sc2, sc2 in next st, slst in beg ch1 [11]
Rnd 6: ch1, sc5, sc3 in next st, sc5, slst in beg ch1 [13]
Rnd 7: ch1, sc4, sc2 in next st, sc3, sc2 in next st, sc4, slst in beg ch1 [15]
Fasten off.

Tail (make 1)

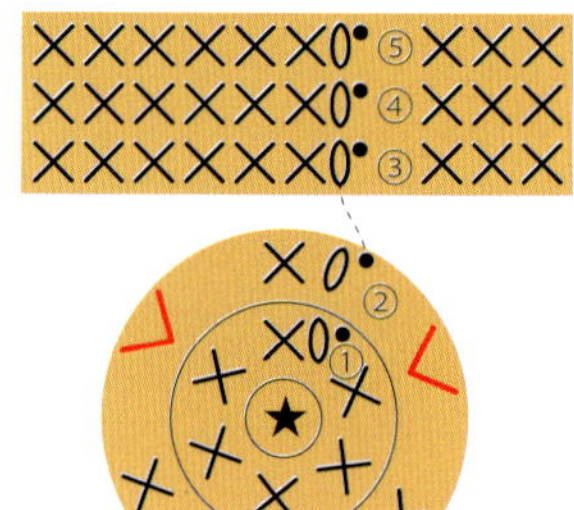

With Yarn B and US G-6 hook, make a magic ring.
Rnd 1: ch1 (does not count as a st throughout), sc6 in magic ring, slst in beg ch1 [6]
Place stitch marker in first st of rnd 1 and move it up after each round
Rnd 2: ch1, (sc1, sc2 in next st) 3 times, slst in beg ch1 [9]
Rnds 3-5: ch1, sc1 in each st, slst in beg ch1 (3 rnds)
Fasten off.

Nose (make 1)

With Yarn F and US C-2 hook, make a magic ring.
Rnd 1: ch1 (does not count as a st throughout), sc5 in magic ring, slst in beg ch1 [5]
Place stitch marker in first st of rnd 1 and move it up after each round
Rnd 2: ch1, sc4, sc2 in next st, slst in beg ch1
Slst in next st, then continue in rows.
Row 3: ch1, sc1 in next 4 sts, lengthen loop from hook and pass yarn through, pull tight to make a knot, do not turn [4]
Rows 4-5: pass yarn across back of work, pull through beg ch1 of prev row, and rep row 3.
Row 6: pass yarn across back of work, pull through beg ch1 of prev row, ch1, sc2 in first st, sc2, sc2 in last st, lengthen loop from hook and pass yarn through, pull tight to make a knot, do not turn [6]
Fasten off.

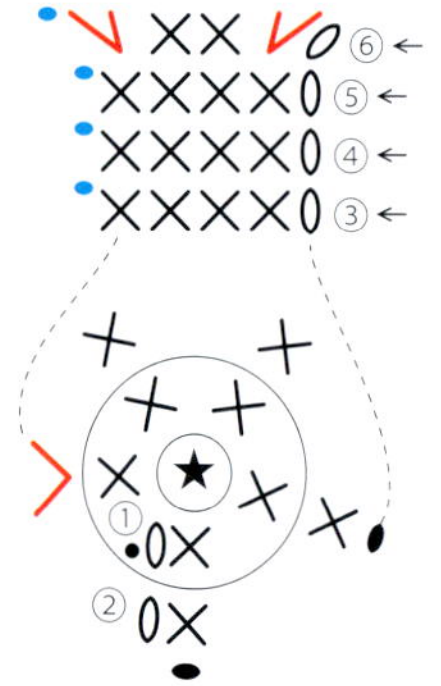

Mouth (make 1)

With Yarn F and US C-2 hook, ch8.
Rnd 1: skip first ch, sc1 in next ch, hdc1, dc1, sc1, dc1, hdc1, sc3 in last ch, rotate and work along opposite side of chain, hdc1, dc1, sc1, dc1, hdc1, sc2 in last ch, slst in skipped ch at beg of rnd [16]
Place stitch marker in first st of rnd 1 and move it up after each round
Rnd 2: ch1, sc3, slst in next st, sc6, ch2, dc3tog over next 3 sts, ch2, sc3, slst in beg ch1 [18]
Fasten off. Use the wrong side as the right side.

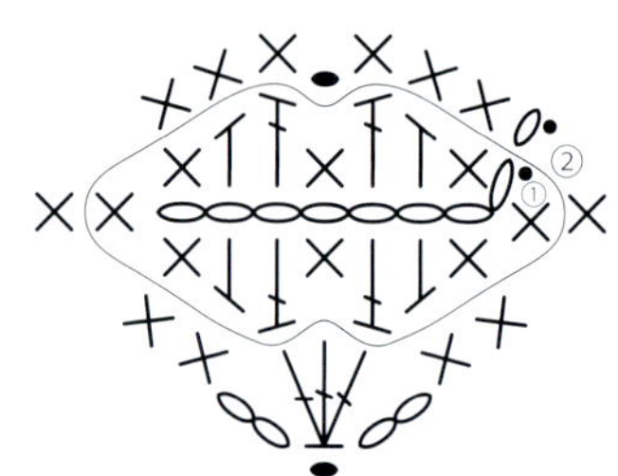

Ears

Right Ear (make 1 each of outer and inner ear)

Outer Ear

With Yarn E and US C-2 hook, ch8, leaving a 12″ (30 cm) tail of yarn.

Work in rows.

Row 1: dc1 in fifth ch from hook (counts as 2dc), hdc2, sc3 in last chain, rotate and work along opposite side of chain stitches, hdc2, dc1, dc2 in next ch, turn [12]

Cut a 4¾″ (12 cm) long piece of armature wire, fold in half, position the folded area at the corner of the ear, and crochet next rnd over the wire to trap it into the sts.

Row 2: ch1 (does not count as a st throughout), sc6, sc2 in next st, sc5 [13]

Fasten off.

Inner Ear

Make inner ear in the same way with Yarn D and US B-1 hook, omitting wire, and working row 1 only.

Left Ear (make 1 each of outer and inner ear)

Outer Ear

With Yarn E and US C-2 hook, ch8, leaving a 12″ (30 cm) tail of yarn.

Work in rows.

Row 1: dc1 in fourth ch from hook (counts as 2dc), dc1, hdc2, sc3 in last chain, rotate and work along opposite side of chain stitches, hdc2, dc2, turn [12]

Cut a 4¾″ (12 cm) long piece of armature wire, fold in half, position the folded area at the corner of the ear, and crochet next rnd over the wire to trap it into the sts.

Row 2: ch1 (does not count as a st throughout), sc5, sc2 in next st, sc6 [13]

Fasten off.

Inner Ear

Make inner ear in the same way with Yarn D and US B-1 hook, omitting wire, and working row 1 only.

Outer Ears

Right Start ① ②

Left Start ① ②

Align a 4¾″ (12 cm) long piece of armature wire with the corner of the ear and crochet around the wire (for outer ear only)

Inner Ears

Right Start ①

Left Start ①

ASSEMBLY DIAGRAM

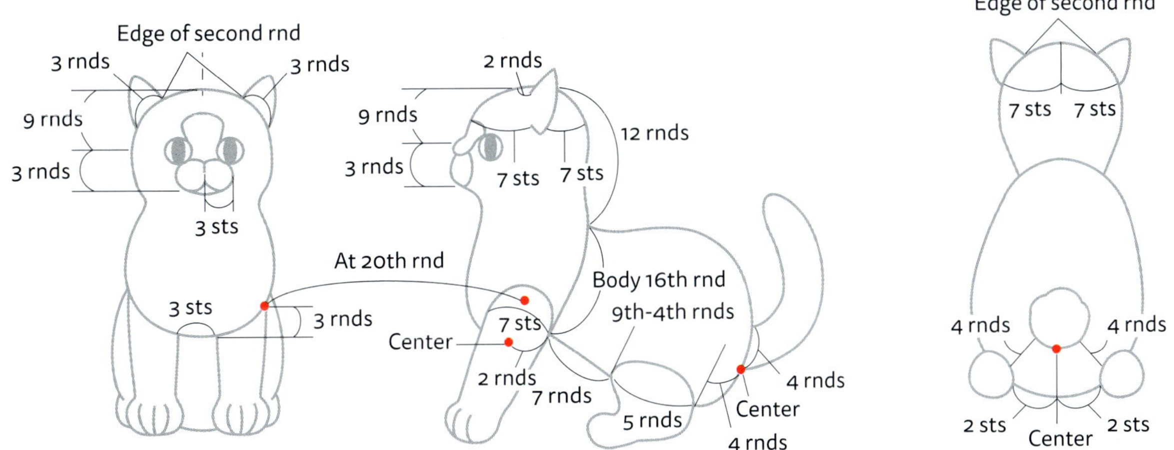

GRAFTING

Placement Key

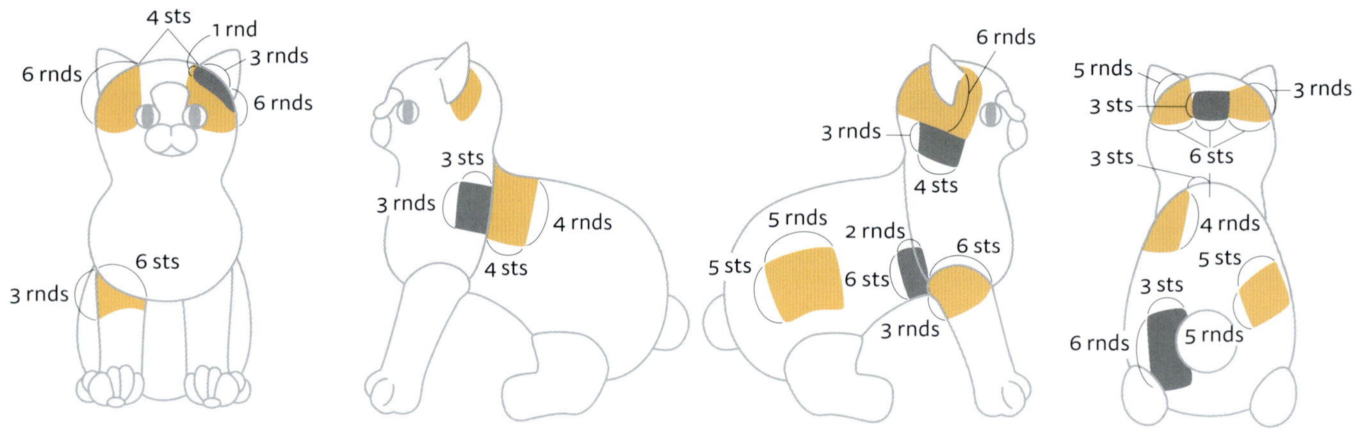

Yarn Length Key

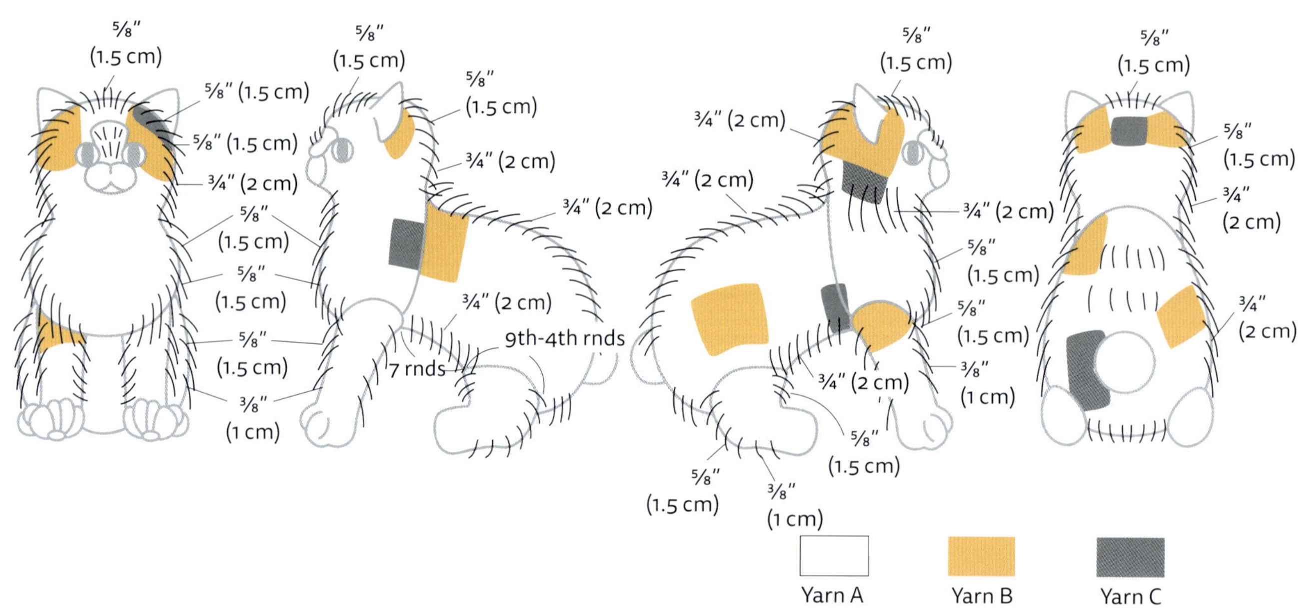

TIPS

- Do not graft ears, toes, or stomach area.
- Graft the patterned areas of the body first, then graft the rest of the body with white yarn.
- Brush the back of the ears with a slicker brush to make them fuzzy.

Mandalay

SHOWN ON PAGE 10

TOOLS & MATERIALS

- US 7 (4.5 mm) crochet hook
- US C-2 (2.5 mm) crochet hook
- 630 yds (576 m) of sport weight acrylic yarn in black
- 613 yds (560 m) of light-fingering weight acrylic/mohair blend yarn in black
- Pair of 18 mm cat eye buttons in beige
- One 15 mm triangular safety nose button in black
- 2¾" (7 cm) long black whiskers
- Polyester fiber fill toy stuffing (about 70 g)
- 3 yds (2.6 m) of armature wire
    - Cut two 20" (50 cm) long pieces for the front legs
    - Cut two 20" (50 cm) long pieces for the back legs
    - Cut one 24" (60 cm) long pieces for the tail
- Stitch marker
- Yarn needle
- Felting needle
- Slicker brush

YARN COMBINATION CHART

	Area	Yarn Used	Yarn Color	Strands	Total Strands	Yarn	Hook Size
Crocheting the Foundation	• Body	Sport weight acrylic	Black	2	4	A	US 7 (4.5 mm)
	• Head and chest • Front legs • Back legs • Tail	Light-fingering weight acrylic/mohair blend	Black	2			
	• Ears	Sport weight acrylic	Black	1	2	B	US C-2 (2.5 mm)
	• Nose • Mouth	Light-fingering weight acrylic/mohair blend	Black	1			

CONSTRUCTION STEPS

1. Crochet the body, head and chest, front legs, back legs, tail, nose, mouth, and ears following the instructions on pages 94–98 (also see pages 37–49).

2. Using the wrong side of the crocheted fabric as the right side for all body parts except the nose, stuff as required, then brush each body part with a slicker brush 5-6 times to make it fuzzy. Assemble the body parts as noted in the diagrams on pages 98–99 (also refer to pages 50–56). Make sure to attach the eye and nose buttons to the head before stuffing (refer to page 36).

3. There is no grafted fur for this cat. Instead, trim and shape the yarn that has been made fuzzy, then brush the entire body with a slicker brush. Use the photos below as a reference.

FINISHED SIZE

Height: 12¼" (31 cm)
Length: 10¾" (27 cm)
Tail: 6¼" (16 cm)

Front Back Side

CROCHET INSTRUCTIONS

Body (make 1)

With Yarn A and US 7 hook, make a magic ring.
Rnd 1: ch1 (does not count as a st throughout), sc6 in magic ring, slst in beg ch1 [6]
Place stitch marker in first st of rnd 1 and move it up after each round
Rnd 2: ch1, (sc2 in next st) 6 times, slst in beg ch1 [12]
Rnd 3: ch1, (sc1, sc2 in next st) 6 times, slst in beg ch1 [18]
Rnd 4: ch1, (sc2, sc2 in next st) 6 times, slst in beg ch1 [24]
Rnd 5: ch1, (sc3, sc2 in next st) 6 times, slst in beg ch1 [30]
Rnd 6: ch1, sc1 in each st, slst in beg ch1
Rnd 7: ch1, sc13, sc2 in next st, sc2, sc2 in next st, sc13, slst in beg ch1 [32]
Rnd 8: ch1, sc1 in each st, slst in beg ch1
Rnd 9: ch1, sc13, sc2 in next st, sc4, sc2 in next st, sc13, slst in beg ch1 [34]
Rnds 10-11: ch1, sc1 in each st, slst in beg ch1 (2 rnds)
Rnd 12: ch1, sc14, sc2 in next st, sc4, sc2 in next st, sc14, slst in beg ch1 [36]
Rnds 13-17: ch1, sc1 in each st, slst in beg ch1 (5 rnds)
Rnd 18: ch1, sc1, sc2 in next st, sc32, sc2 in next st, sc1, slst in beg ch1 [38]
Rnds 19-20: ch1, sc1 in each st, slst in beg ch1 (2 rnds)
Rnd 21: ch1, sc15, sc2tog, sc4, sc2tog, sc15, slst in beg ch1 [36]
Rnds 22-25: ch1, sc1 in each st, slst in beg ch1 (4 rnds)
Fasten off. Use the wrong side as the right side.

Crochet Symbol Key

★ = magic ring
0 = ch st
• = slst
∧ = ⩓ = sc2tog
∨ = ⩔ = sc2 in next st
⩛ = sc3 in next st
⩛ = sc5 in next st
• = make a knot (see page 46)

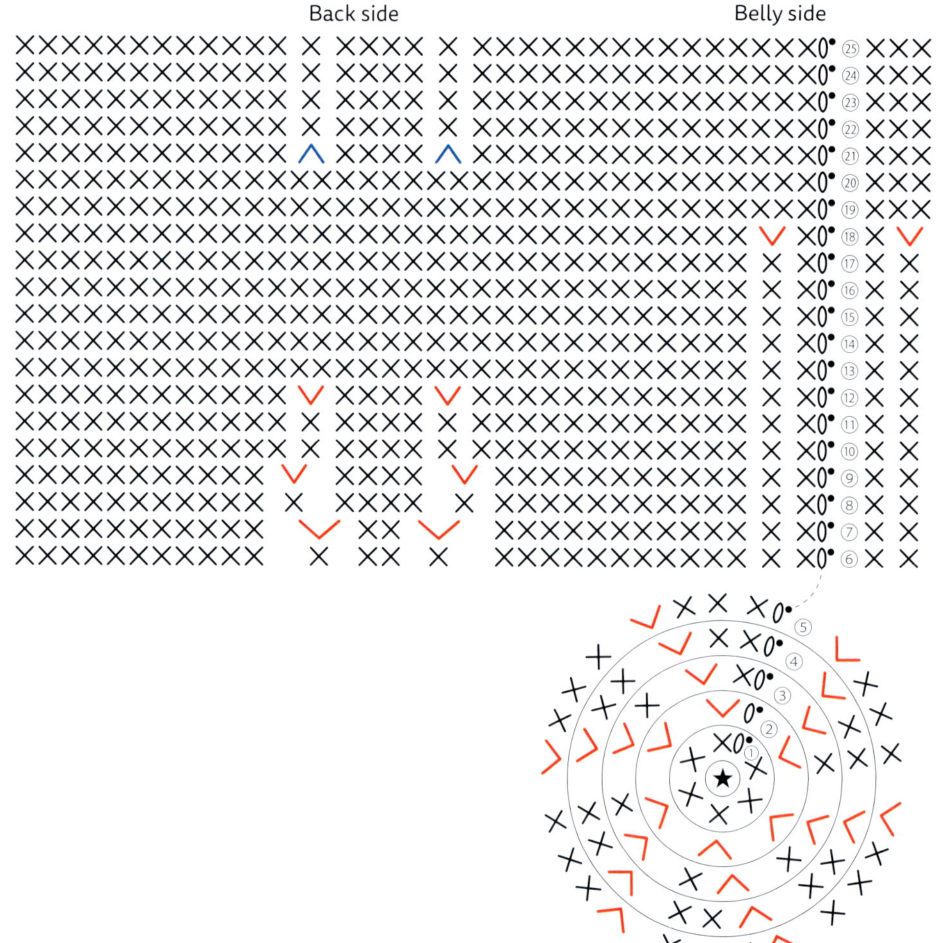

Head & Chest (make 1)

With Yarn A and US 7 hook, ch4.

Rnd 1: skip first ch, sc1 in in next ch, sc1 in next ch, sc3 in last ch, rotate and work along opposite side of chain, sc1 in next ch, sc2 in next ch, slst in skipped ch at beg of round [8]

Place stitch marker in first st of rnd 1 and move it up after each round

Rnd 2: ch1, (sc2 in next st) 8 times, slst in beg ch1 [16]

Rnd 3: ch1, sc1, sc2 in next st, sc2, sc2 in next st, sc1, (sc2 in next st) twice, sc1 in next st, sc2 in next st, sc2, sc2 in next st, sc1, (sc2 in next st) twice, slst in beg ch1 [24]

Rnd 4: ch1, sc2 in next st, sc6, sc2 in next st, sc4, sc2 in next st, sc6, sc2 in next st, sc4, slst in beg ch1 [28]

Rnd 5: ch1, sc10, sc2 in next st, sc2, sc2 in next st, sc10, sc2 in next st, sc2, sc2 in next st, slst in beg ch1 [32]

Rnds 6-10: ch1, sc1 in each st, slst in beg ch1 (5 rnds)

Rnd 11: ch1, sc17, sc2tog, (sc2, sc2tog) twice, sc5, slst in beg ch1 [29]

Rnd 12: ch1, sc3, sc2 in next st, sc6, sc2 in next st, sc4, sc2tog, (sc1, sc2tog) 3 times, sc3, slst in beg ch1 [27]

Rnds 13-14: ch1, sc1 in each st, slst in beg ch1 (2 rnds)

Rnd 15: ch1, sc17, (sc2 in next st, sc2) twice, sc2 in next st, sc3, slst in beg ch1 [30]

Rnd 16: ch1, sc3, sc2 in next st, sc9, sc2 in next st, sc3, sc2 in next st, sc8, sc2 in next st, sc3, slst in beg ch1 [34]

Rnds 17-18: ch1, sc1 in each st, slst in beg ch1 (2 rnds)

Rnd 19: ch1, sc19, sc2 in next st, sc10, sc2 in next st, sc3, slst in beg ch1 [36]

Rnd 20: ch1, sc19, sc2 in next st, sc12, sc2 in next st, sc3, slst in beg ch1 [38]

Rnds 21-24: ch1, sc1 in each st, slst in beg ch1 (4 rnds)

Rnd 25: ch1, sc18, sc2tog, sc13, sc2tog, sc3, slst in beg ch1 [36]

Begin to fill with toy stuffing.

Rnd 26: ch1, (sc4, sc2tog) 6 times, slst in beg ch1 [30]

Rnd 27: ch1, (sc3, sc2tog) 6 times, slst in beg ch1 [24]

Rnd 28: ch1, (sc2, sc2tog) 6 times, slst in beg ch1 [18]

Rnd 29: ch1, (sc1, sc2tog) 6 times, slst in beg ch1 [12]

Add more toy stuffing before final rnd.

Rnd 30: ch1, (sc2tog) 6 times, slst in beg ch1 [6]

Fasten off. Use the wrong side as the right side.

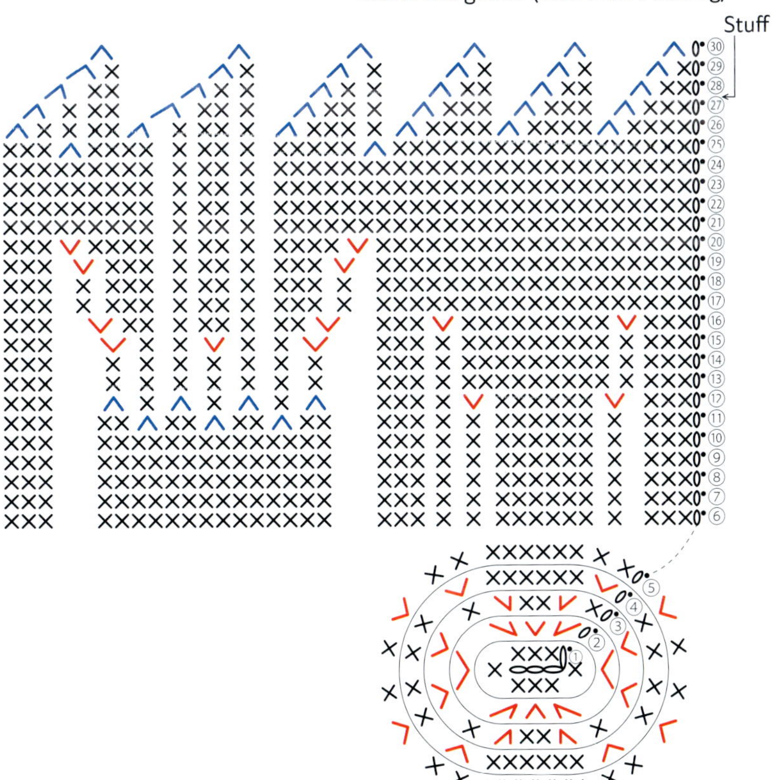

Front Legs

Note: Since the wrong side is used as the right side, the crochet diagrams are the same as other designs in this book, but the left and right sides are different.

Left (make 1)

With Yarn A and US 7 hook, make a magic ring.
Rnd 1: ch1 (does not count as a st throughout), sc7 in magic ring, slst in beg ch1 [7]
Place stitch marker in first st of rnd 1 and move it up after each round
Rnd 2: ch1, sc1, (hdc-cl in next st) 4 times, sc2, slst in beg ch1
Rnds 3-7: ch1, sc1 in each st, slst in beg ch1 (5 rnds)
Rnd 8: ch1, sc4, sc2 in next st, sc2 [8]
Rnd 9: ch1, sc5, sc2 in next st, sc2 [9]
Rnd 10: ch1, sc6, sc2 in next st, sc2 [10]
Rnd 11: ch1, sc7, sc2 in next st, sc2 [11]
Rnd 12: ch1, sc8, sc2 in next st, sc2 [12]
Rnd 13: ch1, sc9, sc2 in next st, sc2 [13]
Rnd 14: ch1, sc10, sc2 in next st, sc2 [14]
Rnd 15: ch1, sc10, hdc1, hdc2 in next st, sc2, slst in beg ch1 [15]
Rnd 16: ch1, sc11, hdc1, hdc2 in next st, sc2, slst in beg ch1 [16]
Rnd 17: ch1, sc1 in each st, slst in beg ch1
Fasten off. Use the wrong side as the right side.

Right (make 1)

Work as given for left front leg to the end of rnd 7
Rnd 8: ch1, sc1, sc2 in next st, sc5 [8]
Rnd 9: ch1, sc2, sc2 in next st, sc5 [9]
Rnd 10: ch1, sc3, sc2 in next st, sc5 [10]
Rnd 11: ch1, sc3, sc2 in next st, sc6 [11]
Rnd 12: ch1, sc3, sc2 in next st, sc7 [12]
Rnd 13: ch1, sc3, sc2 in next st, sc8 [13]
Rnd 14: ch1, sc3, sc2 in next st, sc9 [14]
Rnd 15: ch1, sc3, hdc2 in next st, hdc1, sc9, slst in beg ch1 [15]
Rnd 16: ch1, sc3, hdc2 in next st, hdc1, sc10, slst in beg ch1 [16]
Rnd 17: ch1, sc1 in each st, slst in beg ch1
Fasten off. Use the wrong side as the right side.

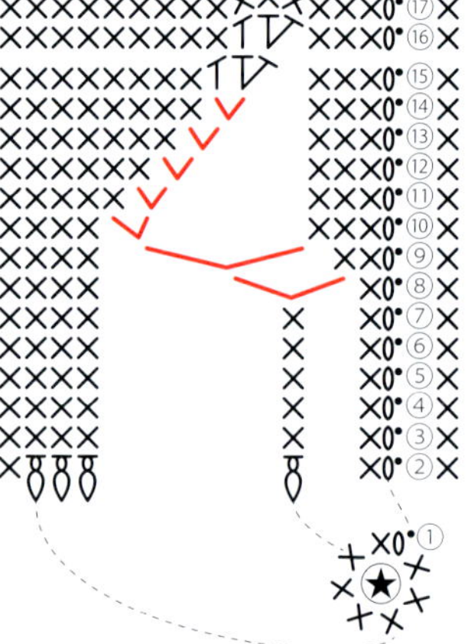

Back Legs (make 2)

Work as given for left front leg to the end of rnd 7
Rnd 8: ch1, sc2 in next st, sc5, sc2 in next st, slst in beg ch1 [9]
Rnds 9-10: ch1, sc1 in each st, slst in beg ch1 (2 rnds)
Rnd 11: ch1, sc4, sc5 in next st, sc4, slst in beg ch1 [13]
Rnd 12: ch1, sc6, sc5 in next st, sc6, slst in beg ch1 [17]
Rnd 13: ch1, sc8, sc5 in next st, sc8, slst in beg ch1 [21]
Rnd 14: ch1, sc10, sc3 in next st, sc10, slst in beg ch1 [23]
Rnd 15: ch1, sc11, sc3 in next st, sc11, slst in beg ch1 [25]
Rnd 16: ch1, sc12, sc3 in next st, sc12, slst in beg ch1 [27]
Rnd 17: ch1, sc1 in each st, slst in beg ch1
Rnd 18: ch1, sc10, sc2tog, sc3, sc2tog, sc10, slst in beg ch1 [25]
Rnd 19: ch1, sc9, sc2tog, sc3, sc2tog, sc9, slst in beg ch1 [23]
Fasten off. Use the wrong side as the right side.

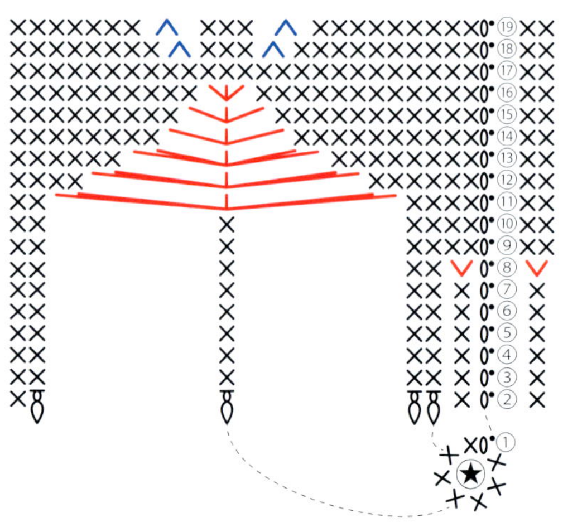

Tail (make 1)

With Yarn A and US 7 hook, make a magic ring.
Rnd 1: ch1 (does not count as a st throughout), sc5 in magic ring, slst in beg ch1 [5]
Place stitch marker in first st of rnd 1 and move it up after each round
Rnd 2: ch1, sc4, sc2 in next st, slst in beg ch1 [6]
Rnd 3: ch1, sc5, sc2 in next st, slst in beg ch1 [7]
Rnd 4: ch1, sc6, sc2 in next st, slst in beg ch1 [8]
Rnds 5-7: ch1, sc1 in each st, slst in beg ch1 (3 rnds)
Rnd 8: ch1, sc7, sc2 in next st, slst in beg ch1 [9]
Rnds 9-11: ch1, sc1 in each st, slst in beg ch1 (3 rnds)
Rnd 12: ch1, sc8, sc2 in next st, slst in beg ch1 [10]
Rnds 13-20: ch1, sc1 in each st, slst in beg ch1 (8 rnds)
Rnd 21: ch1, sc9, sc2 in next st, slst in beg ch1 [11]
Rnds 22-23: ch1, sc1 in each st, slst in beg ch1 (2 rnds)
Fasten off. Use the wrong side as the right side.

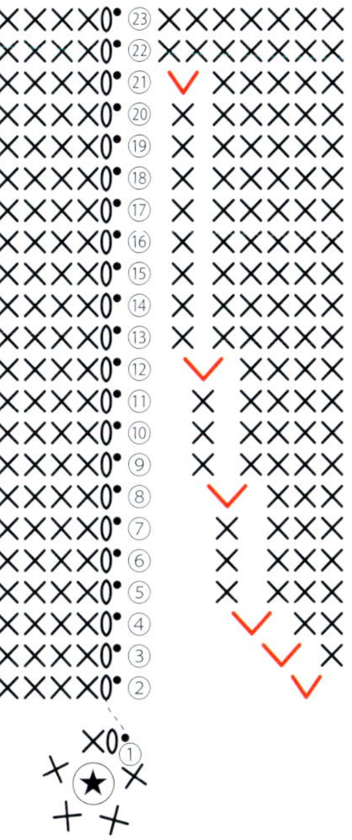

Nose (make 1)

With Yarn B and US C-2 hook, make a magic ring.
Rnd 1: ch1 (does not count as a st throughout), sc6 in magic ring, slst in beg ch1 [6]
Place stitch marker in first st of rnd 1 and move it up after each round
Rnd 2: ch1, sc1 in each st, slst in beg ch1
Slst in next st, then continue in rows.
Row 3: ch1, sc1 in next 4 sts, lengthen loop from hook and pass yarn through, pull tight to make a knot, do not turn [4]
Row 4: pass yarn across back of work, pull through beg ch1 of prev row, and rep row 3.
Row 5: pass yarn across back of work, pull through beg ch1 of prev row, ch1, sc2 in first st, sc2, sc2 in last st, lengthen loop from hook and pass yarn through, pull tight to make a knot, do not turn [6]
Row 6: pass yarn across back of work, pull through beg ch1 of prev row, ch3, dc2 in same st at base of ch3, sc4, dc3 in last st, lengthen loop from hook and pass yarn through, pull tight to make a knot [10]
Fasten off.

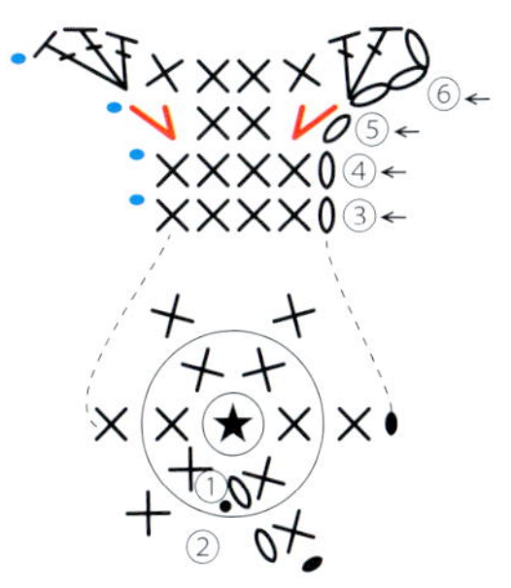

Mouth (make 1)

With Yarn B and US C-2 hook, ch10.
Rnd 1: skip first ch, sc1 in next ch, hdc1, dc2, sc1, dc2, hdc1, sc3 in last ch, rotate and work along opposite side of chain, hdc1, dc2, sc1, dc2, hdc1, sc2 in last ch, slst in skipped ch at beg of rnd [20]
Place stitch marker in first st of rnd 1 and move it up after each round
Rnd 2: ch1, sc4, slst in next st, sc9, slst in next st, sc5, slst in beg ch1
Rnd 3: ch1, sc12, ch2, dc4tog over next 4 sc (and skipping the slst), ch2, sc3, slst in beg ch1 [20]
Fasten off. Use the wrong side as the right side.

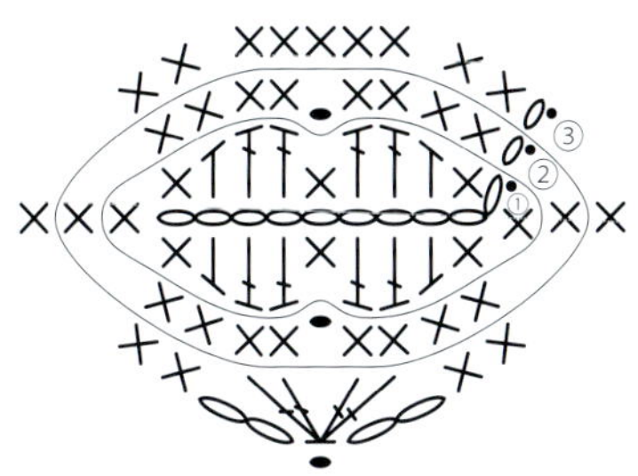

Ears (make 2)

With Yarn B and US C-2 hook, make a magic ring.

Rnd 1: ch1 (does not count as a st throughout), sc6 in magic ring, slst in beg ch1 [6]

Place stitch marker in first st of rnd 1 and move it up after each round

Rnd 2: ch1, sc2 in first st, sc in each st to last st, sc2 in last st, slst in beg ch1 [8]

Rnds 3-8: rep rnd 2 (6 rnds) [20]

Rnd 9: ch2 (does not count as a st), hdc2 in first st, sc1 in each st to last st, hdc2 in last st, slst in beg ch1 [22]

Rnds 10-11: rep rnd 9 (2 rnds) [26]

Fasten off. Use the wrong side as the right side.

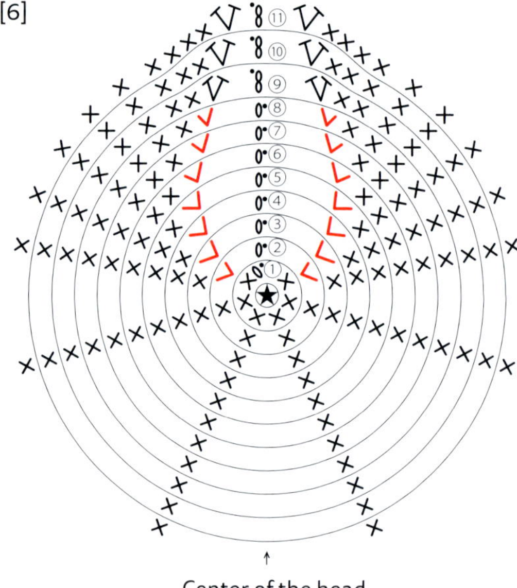

ASSEMBLY DIAGRAM

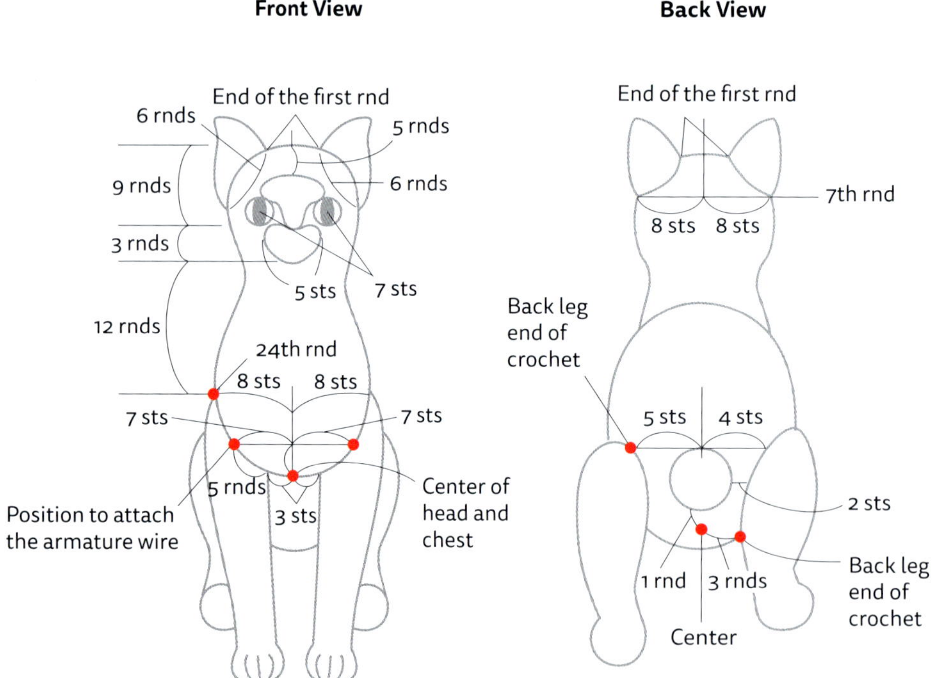

Side View

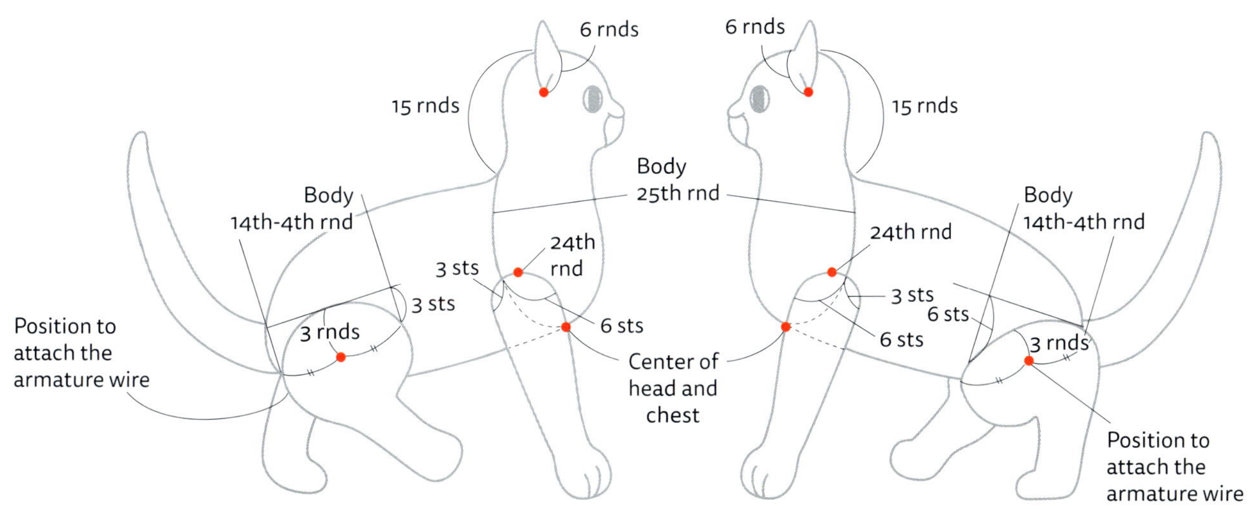

How to Attach the Back Legs

Wrap stuffing and yarn around the armature wire to shape the back leg. Add extra stuffing at the base of the leg. **Note:** Gray yarn is used for visual clarity.

Make a few stitches to attach the back leg to the body. Next, sew the top three rows of the leg (above the red line) to the inside of the body (purple line). Push the top of the leg in so that it is hidden underneath the stitching. This will create a naturally rounded haunch.

TIPS

- Use the wrong side of the crocheted fabric as the right side for all body parts, except the nose.
- Use a safety nose button for the nose. Insert it where the crocheted nose meets the mouth.
- Brush each body part with a slicker brush 5-6 times to make them fuzzy before assembling.
- There is no grafted fur for this cat. Instead, trim and shape the yarn that has been made fuzzy, then brush the entire body with a slicker brush.

American Shorthair

SHOWN ON PAGE 25

TOOLS & MATERIALS

- US 7 (4.5 mm) crochet hook
- US C-2 (2.5 mm) crochet hook
- Sport weight acrylic yarn
  - 630 yds (576 m) in gray
  - 79 yds (72 m) in black
  - 40 yds (36 m) in light pink
- Light-fingering weight acrylic/mohair blend yarn
  - 744 yds (680 m) in dark gray
  - 88 yds (80 m) in black
- About 12″ (30 cm) of sport weight acrylic yarn in pink for embroidering the nose
- About 48″ (120 cm) of sport weight acrylic yarn in black for embroidering the eyes, nose, and mouth [36″ (90 cm) for eyes and nose and 12″ (30 cm) for mouth]
- Pair of 18 mm cat eye buttons in yellow green
- 2¾″ (7 cm) long clear whiskers
- Polyester fiber fill toy stuffing (about 60 g)
- 2 yds (1.8 m) of armature wire
  - Cut two 6″ (15 cm) long pieces for the ears
  - Cut two 20″ (50 cm) long pieces for the front legs
  - Cut one 20″ (50 cm) long piece for the tail
- Stitch marker
- Yarn needle
- Felting needle
- Slicker brush

CONSTRUCTION STEPS

1. Crochet the body, head and chest, front legs, back legs, tail, nose, mouth, and ears following the instructions on pages 101–105 (also see pages 37–49).
2. Stuff as required and assemble the body parts as noted in the diagram on page 105 (also refer to pages 50–56). Make sure to attach the eye buttons to the head before stuffing (refer to page 36).
3. Graft yarn as noted in the diagrams on page 106. Loosen the yarn and trim the fur into shape. Embroider the facial features. Refer to pages 57–61 for general grafting instructions and use these photos as a reference.

FINISHED SIZE

Height: 10¾″ (27 cm)
Length: 8″ (20 cm)
Tail: 6¾″ (17 cm)

Front

Back

Side

YARN COMBINATION CHART

	Area	Yarn Used	Yarn Color	Strands	Total Strands	Yarn	Hook Size
Crocheting the Foundation	• Body • Head and chest • Outer ears	Sport weight acrylic	Gray	2	4	A	US 7 (4.5 mm)
		Light-fingering weight acrylic/mohair blend	Dark gray	2			
	• Front legs • Back legs • Tail	Sport weight acrylic	Black	2	4	B (Alternate A and B as shown in the diagrams)	US 7 (4.5 mm)
		Light-fingering weight acrylic/mohair blend	Black	2			
	• Nose • Mouth	Sport weight acrylic	Gray	1	2	C	US C-2 (2.5 mm)
		Light-fingering weight acrylic/mohair blend	Dark gray	1			
	• Inner ears	Sport weight acrylic	Light Pink	1	2	D	US C-2 (2.5 mm)
		Light-fingering weight acrylic/mohair blend	Dark gray	1			
Grafting the Fur						A, B*	

*Graft using the same yarn used to crochet the foundation

CROCHET INSTRUCTIONS

Body (make 1)

With Yarn A and US 7 hook, ch6.

Rnd 1: skip first ch, sc1 in in next ch, sc1 in next 3 ch, sc3 in last ch, rotate and work along opposite side of chain, sc1 in next 3 ch, sc2 in next ch, slst in skipped ch at beg of round [12]

Place stitch marker in first st of rnd 1 and move it up after each round

Rnd 2: ch1, sc2 in next st, sc3, (sc2 in next st) 3 times, sc3, (sc2 in next st) twice, slst in beg ch1 [18]

Rnd 3: ch1, sc1, sc2 in next st, sc4, (sc2 in next st, sc1) twice, sc2 in next st, sc4, sc2 in next st, sc1, sc2 in next st, slst in beg ch1 [24]

Rnd 4: ch1, sc2, sc2 in next st, sc5, (sc2 in next st, sc2) twice, sc2 in next st, sc5, sc2 in next st, sc2, sc2 in next st, slst in beg ch1 [30]

Rnd 5: ch1, sc3, sc2 in next st, sc6, (sc2 in next st, sc3) twice, sc2 in next st, sc6, sc2 in next st, sc3, sc2 in next st, slst in beg ch1 [36]

Crochet Symbol Key

- ★ = magic ring
- 0 = ch st
- • = slst
- ∧ = ⩓ = sc2tog
- ∨ = ⩔ = sc2 in next st
- sc3 in next st
- sc5 in next st
- • = make a knot (see page 46)

Thread yarn through 6 sts in the last round and gather (stuff before closing)

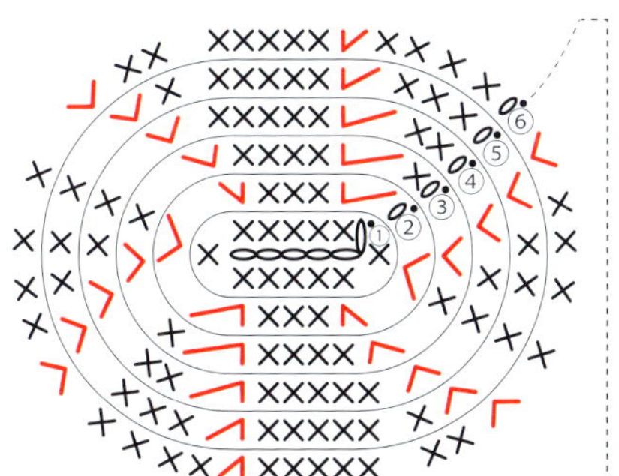

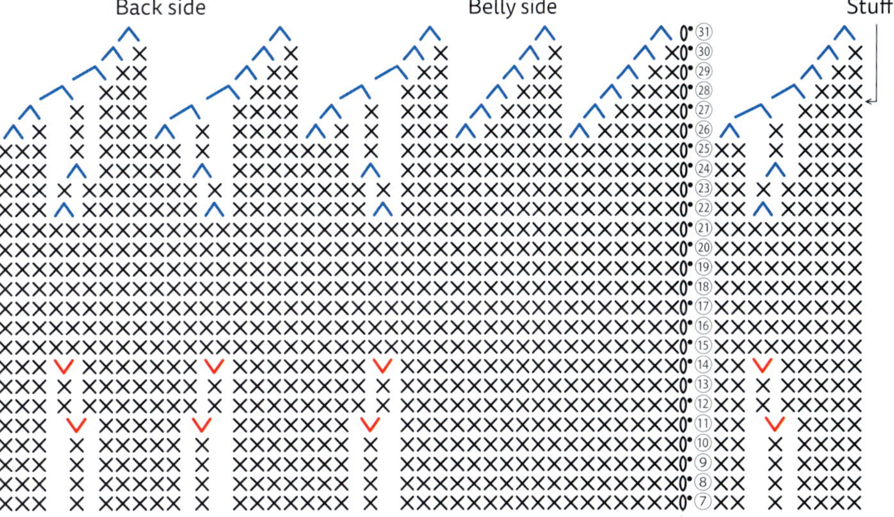

Rnd 6: ch1, sc4, sc2 in next st, sc7, (sc2 in next st, sc4) twice, sc2 in next st, sc7, sc2 in next st, sc4, sc2 in next st, slst in beg ch1 [42]
Rnds 7-10: ch1, sc1 in each st, slst in beg ch1 (4 rnds)
Rnd 11: ch1, sc17, sc2 in next st, sc7, sc2 in next st, sc5, sc2 in next st, sc7, sc2 in next st, sc2, slst in beg ch1 [46]
Rnds 12-13: ch1, sc1 in each st, slst in beg ch1 (2 rnds)
Rnd 14: ch1, sc17, sc2 in next st, sc8, sc2 in next st, sc7, sc2 in next st, sc8, sc2 in next st, sc2, slst in beg ch1 [50]
Rnds 15-21: ch1, sc1 in each st, slst in beg ch1 (7 rnds)
Rnd 22: ch1, sc17, sc2tog, sc8, sc2tog, sc7, sc2tog, sc8, sc2tog, sc2, slst in beginning ch1 [46]
Rnd 23: ch1, sc1 in each st, slst in beg ch1
Rnd 24: ch1, sc17, sc2tog, sc7, sc2tog, sc5, sc2tog, sc7, sc2tog, sc2, slst in beginning ch1 [42]
Rnd 25: ch1, sc1 in each st, slst in beg ch1
Rnd 26: ch1, (sc5, sc2tog) 6 times, slst in beg ch1 [36]
Rnd 27: ch1, (sc4, sc2tog) 6 times, slst in beg ch1 [30]
Begin to fill Body with toy stuffing.
Rnd 28: ch1, (sc3, sc2tog) 6 times, slst in beg ch1 [24]
Rnd 29: ch1, (sc2, sc2tog) 6 times, slst in beg ch1 [18]
Rnd 30: ch1, (sc1, sc2tog) 6 times, slst in beg ch1 [12]
Add more toy stuffing to Body before final rnd.
Rnd 31: ch1, (sc2tog) 6 times, slst in beg ch1 [6]
Fasten off.

Head & Chest (make 1)

With Yarn A and US 7 hook, ch4.
Rnd 1: skip first ch, sc1 in in next ch, sc1 in next ch, sc3 in last ch, rotate and work along opposite side of chain, sc1 in next ch, sc2 in next ch, slst in skipped ch at beg of round [8]
Place stitch marker in first st of rnd 1 and move it up after each round
Rnd 2: ch1, (sc2 in next st) 8 times, slst in beg ch1 [16]
Rnd 3: ch1, sc1, sc2 in next st, sc2, sc2 in next st, sc1, (sc2 in next st) twice, sc1, sc2 in next st, sc2, sc2 in next st, sc1, (sc2 in next st) twice, slst in beg ch1 [24]
Rnd 4: ch1, sc2 in next st, sc6, sc2 in next st, sc4, sc2 in next st, sc6, sc2 in next st, sc4, slst in beg ch1 [28]
Rnd 5: ch1, sc10, sc2 in next st, sc2, sc2 in next st, sc10, sc2 in next st, sc2, sc2 in next st, slst in beg ch1 [32]
Rnd 6: ch1, sc10, sc2 in next st, sc4, sc2 in next st, sc10, sc2 in next st, sc4, sc2 in next st, slst in beg ch1 [36]
Rnds 7-11: ch1, sc1 in each st, slst in beg ch1 (5 rnds)
Rnd 12: ch1, sc18, (sc2tog, sc2) twice, sc2tog, sc8, slst in beg ch1 [33]
Rnd 13: ch1, sc3, sc2 in next st, sc4, sc2 in next st, sc7, (sc2tog, sc1) 3 times, sc2tog, sc6, slst in beg ch1 [31]
Rnds 14-15: ch1, sc1 in each st, slst in beg ch1 (2 rnds)
Rnd 16: ch1, sc18, (sc2 in next st, sc2) twice, sc2 in next st, sc6, slst in beg ch1 [34]
Rnd 17: ch1, sc3, sc2 in next st, sc6, sc2 in next st, sc7, sc2 in next st, sc8, sc2 in next st, sc6, slst in beg ch1 [38]
Rnds 18-19: ch1, sc1 in each st, slst in beg ch1 (2 rnds)
Rnd 20: ch1, sc20, sc2 in next st, sc10, sc2 in next st, sc6, slst in beg ch1 [40]
Rnd 21: ch1, sc20, sc2 in next st, sc12, sc2 in next st, sc6, slst in beg ch1 [42]
Rnds 22-24: ch1, sc1 in each st, slst in beg ch1 (3 rnds)
Rnd 25: ch1, (sc5, sc2tog) 6 times, slst in beg ch1 [36]
Rnd 26: ch1, (sc4, sc2tog) 6 times, slst in beg ch1 [30]
Begin to fill with toy stuffing.
Rnd 27: ch1, (sc3, sc2tog) 6 times, slst in beg ch1 [24]
Rnd 28: ch1, (sc2, sc2tog) 6 times, slst in beg ch1 [18]
Rnd 29: ch1, (sc1, sc2tog) 6 times, slst in beg ch1 [12]
Add more toy stuffing before final rnd.
Rnd 30: ch1, (sc2tog) 6 times, slst in beg ch1 [6]
Fasten off.

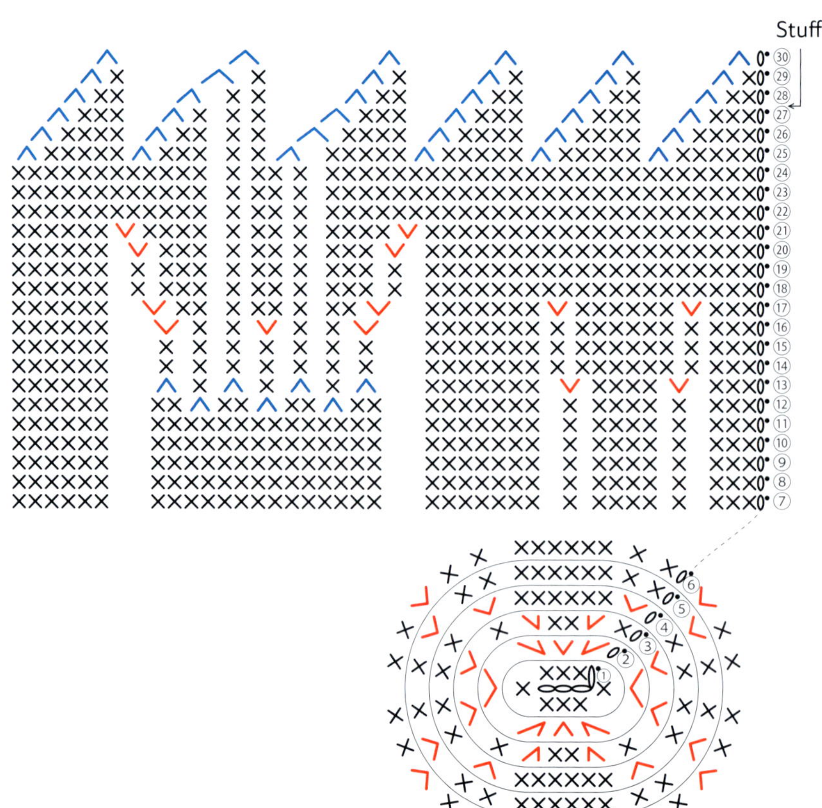

Front Legs

Left (make 1)

With Yarn A and US 7 hook, make a magic ring.
Rnd 1: ch1 (does not count as a st throughout), sc8 in magic ring, slst in beg ch1 [8]
Place stitch marker in first st of rnd 1 and move it up after each round
Rnd 2: ch1, sc2, (hdc-cl in next st) 4 times, sc2, slst in beg ch1
Rnds 3-7: ch1, sc1 in each st, slst in beg ch1 (5 rnds)
Rnd 8: ch1, sc2, sc2 in next st, sc5, slst in beg ch1 [9]
Change to Yarn B
Rnd 9: ch1, sc3, sc2 in next st, sc5, slst in beg ch1 [10]
Change to Yarn A
Rnd 10: ch1, sc4, sc2 in next st, sc5, slst in beg ch1 [11]
Change to Yarn B
Rnd 11: ch1, sc4, hdc2 in next st, hdc1, sc5, slst in beg ch1 [12]
Change to Yarn A
Rnd 12: ch1, sc4, hdc2 in next st, hdc1, sc6, slst in beg ch1 [13]
Fasten off.

Right (make 1)

Work as given for left front leg to the end of rnd 7.
Rnd 8: ch1, sc5, sc2 in next st, sc2, slst in beg ch1 [9]
Change to Yarn B
Rnd 9: ch1, sc6, sc2 in next st, sc2, slst in beg ch1 [10]
Change to Yarn A
Rnd 10: ch1, sc7, sc2 in next st, sc2, slst in beg ch1 [11]
Change to Yarn B
Rnd 11: ch1, sc7, hdc1, hdc2 in next st, sc2, slst in beg ch1 [12]
Change to Yarn A
Rnd 12: ch1, sc8, hdc1, hdc2 in next st, sc2, slst in beg ch1 [13]
Fasten off.

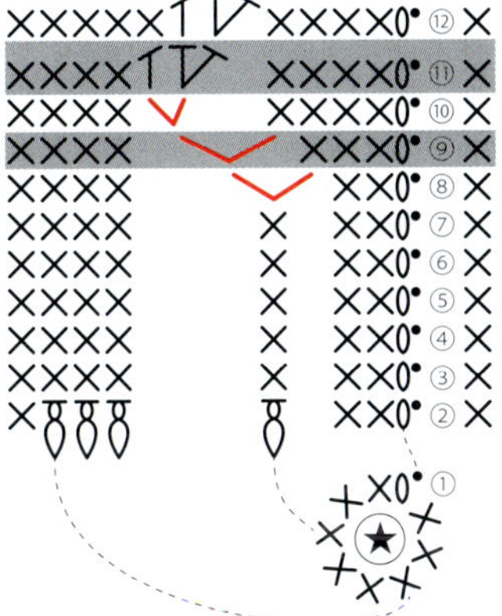

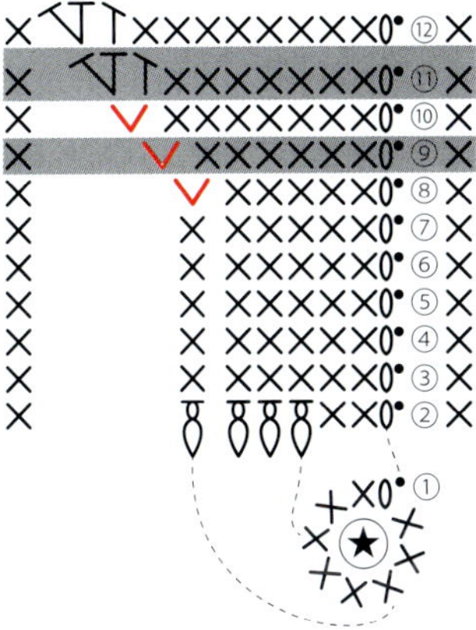

Back Legs (make 2)

With Yarn A and US 7 hook, make a magic ring.
Rnd 1: ch1 (does not count as a st throughout), sc8 in magic ring, slst in beg ch1 [8]
Place stitch marker in first st of rnd 1 and move it up after each round
Rnd 2: ch1, sc2, (hdc-cl in next st) 4 times, sc2, slst in beg ch1
Rnds 3-4: ch1, sc1 in each st, slst in beg ch1 (2 rnds)
Change to Yarn B
Rnd 5: ch1, sc4, sc3 in next st, sc2, sc2 in next st, slst in beg ch1 [11]
Rnd 6: ch1, sc5, sc3 in next st, sc5, slst in beg ch1 [13]
Change to Yarn A
Rnd 7: ch1, sc4, sc2 in next st, sc3, sc2 in next st, sc4 [15]
Fasten off.

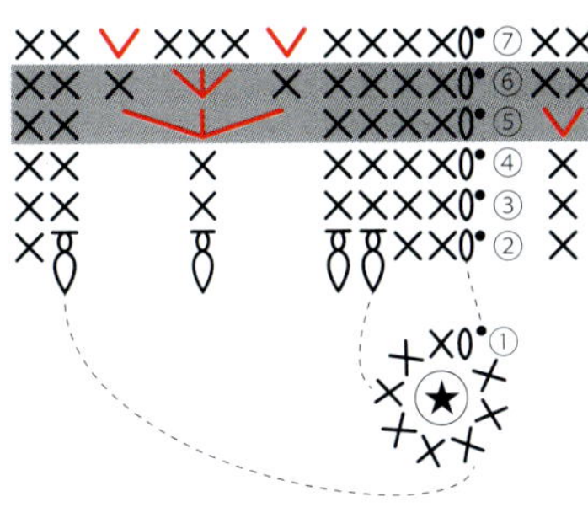

Tail (make 1)

With Yarn B and US 7 hook, make a magic ring.
Rnd 1: ch1 (does not count as a st throughout), sc5 in magic ring, slst in beg ch1 [5]
Place stitch marker in first st of rnd 1 and move it up after each round
Rnd 2: ch1, sc1 in each st to last st, sc2 in last st, slst in beg ch1 [6]
Rnds 3-4: as rnd 2 [8]
Rnd 5: ch1, sc1 in each st, slst in beg ch1
Change to Yarn A
Rnds 6-7: ch1, sc1 in each st, slst in beg ch1 (2 rnds)
Change to Yarn B
Rnd 8: as rnd 2 [9]
Rnd 9: as rnd 5
Rnd 10: as rnd 2 [10]
Change to Yarn A
Rnd 11: as rnd 5
Rnd 12: as rnd 2 [11]
*Change to Yarn B
Rnd 13: ch1, sc1 in each st, slst in beg ch1
Change to Yarn A
Rnd 14: ch1, sc1 in each st, slst in beg ch1*
Rnds 15-16: rep from * to * once more
Change to Yarn B
Rnd 17: as rnd 5
Change to Yarn A
Rnd 18: As rnd 2 [12]
Change to Yarn B
Rnds 19-20: as rnds 6-7
Fasten off.

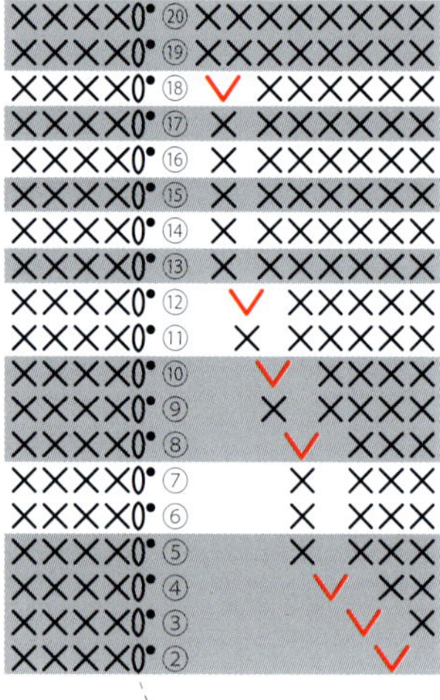

Nose (make 1)

With Yarn C and US C-2 hook, make a magic ring.
Rnd 1: ch1 (does not count as a st throughout), sc6 in magic ring, slst in beg ch1 [6]
Place stitch marker in first st of rnd 1 and move it up after each round
Rnd 2: ch1, sc1 in each st, slst in beg ch1
Slst in next 2 sts, then continue in rows.
Row 3: ch1, sc1 in next 4 sts, lengthen loop from hook and pass yarn through, pull tight to make a knot, do not turn [4]
Row 4: pass yarn across back of work, pull through beg ch1 of prev row, and rep row 3.
Row 5: pass yarn across back of work, pull through beg ch1 of prev row, ch1, sc2 in first st, sc2, sc2 in last st, lengthen loop from hook and pass yarn through, pull tight to make a knot, do not turn [6]
Row 6: pass yarn across back of work, pull through beg ch1 of prev row, ch3 (counts as dc), dc2 in first st, sc4, dc3 in last st, lengthen loop from hook and pass yarn through, pull tight to make a knot, do not turn [10]

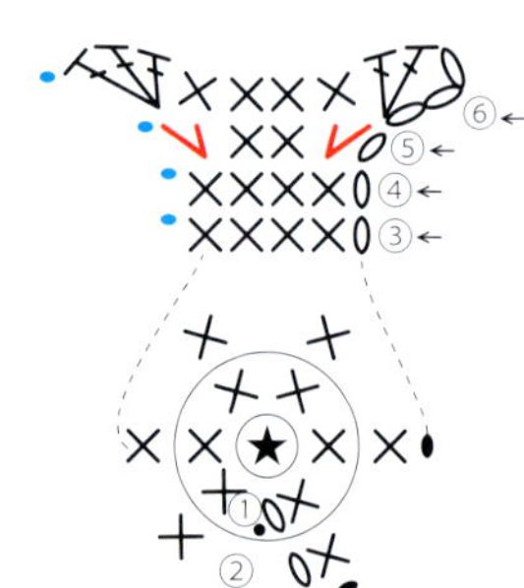

Mouth (make 1)

With Yarn C and US C-2 hook, ch10.
Rnd 1: skip first ch, sc1 in next ch, hdc1, dc2, sc1, dc2, hdc1, sc3 in last ch, rotate and work along opposite side of chain, hdc1, dc2, sc1, dc2, hdc1, sc2 in last ch, slst in skipped ch at beg of rnd [20]
Place stitch marker in first st of rnd 1 and move it up after each round
Rnd 2: ch1, sc4, slst in next st, sc9, slst in next st, sc5, slst in beg ch1
Rnd 3: ch1, sc12, ch2, dc4tog over next 4 sc (and skipping the slst), ch2, sc3, slst in beg ch1 [20]
Fasten off. Use the wrong side as the right side.
Fasten off.

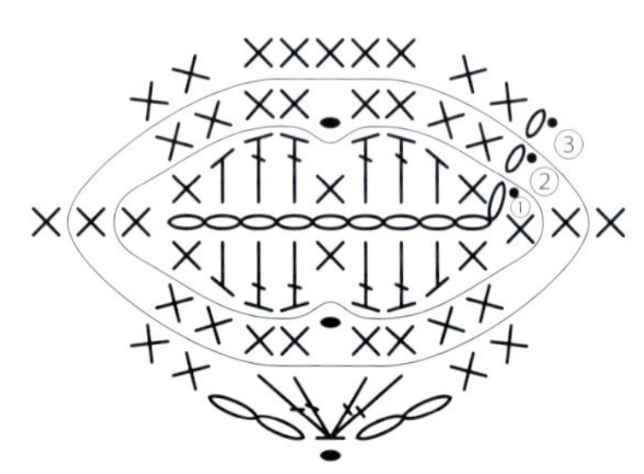

Ears

Right Ear (make 1 each of outer and inner ear)

Outer Ear

With Yarn A and US 7 hook, ch9, leaving a 12" (30 cm) tail of yarn.

Work in rows.

Row 1: dc1 in fifth ch from hook (counts as 2dc), dc1, hdc1, sc1, sc3 in last chain, rotate and work along opposite side of chain stitches, hdc2, dc2, dc2 in next ch, turn [14]

Cut a 6" (15 cm) long piece of armature wire, fold in half, position the folded area at the corner of the ear, and crochet next rnd over the wire to trap it into the sts.

Row 2: ch1 (does not count as a st throughout), sc7, sc2 in next st, sc6 [15]

Fasten off.

Inner Ear

Make inner ear in the same way with Yarn D and US C-2 hook, omitting wire.

Left Ear (make 1 each of outer and inner ear)

Outer Ear

With Yarn A and US 7 hook, ch9, leaving a 12" (30 cm) tail of yarn.

Work in rows.

Row 1: dc1 in fourth ch from hook (counts as 2dc), dc2, hdc2, sc3 in last chain, rotate and work along opposite side of chain stitches, sc1, hdc1, dc3, turn [14]

Cut a 6" (15 cm) long piece of armature wire, fold in half, position the folded area at the corner of the ear, and crochet next rnd over the wire to trap it into the sts.

Row 2: Ch1 (does not count as a st throughout), sc6, sc2 in next st, sc7 [15]

Fasten off.

Inner Ear

Make inner ear in the same way with Yarn D and US C-2 hook, omitting wire.

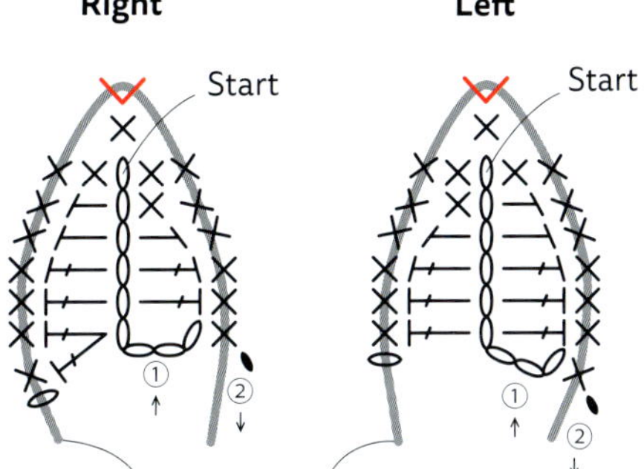

ASSEMBLY DIAGRAM

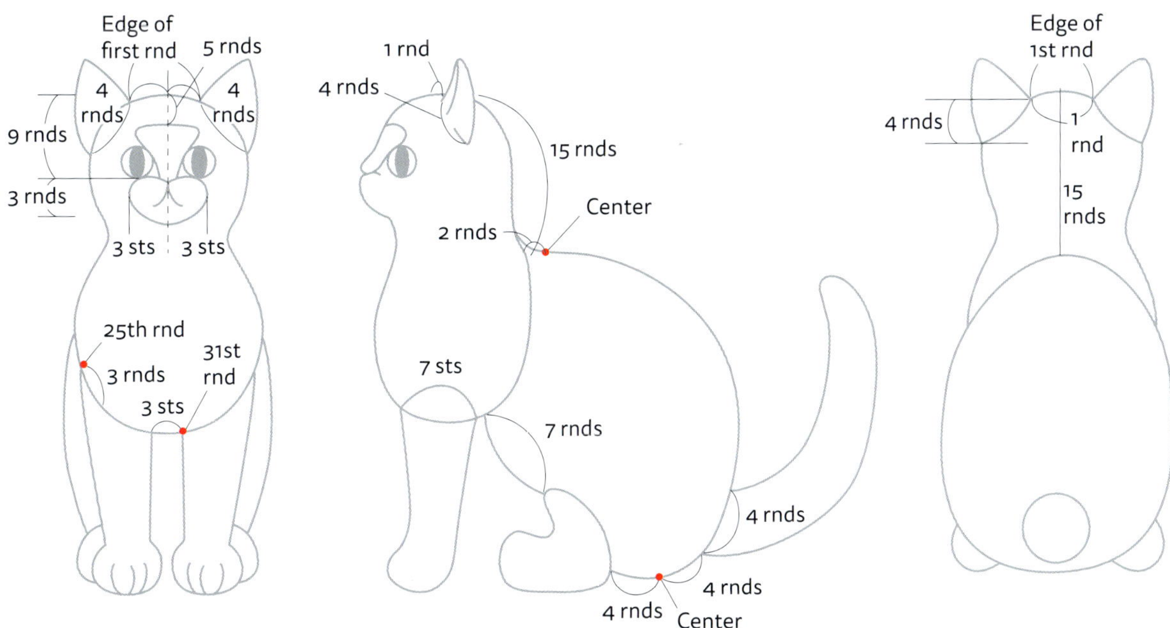

GRAFTING

Placement Key

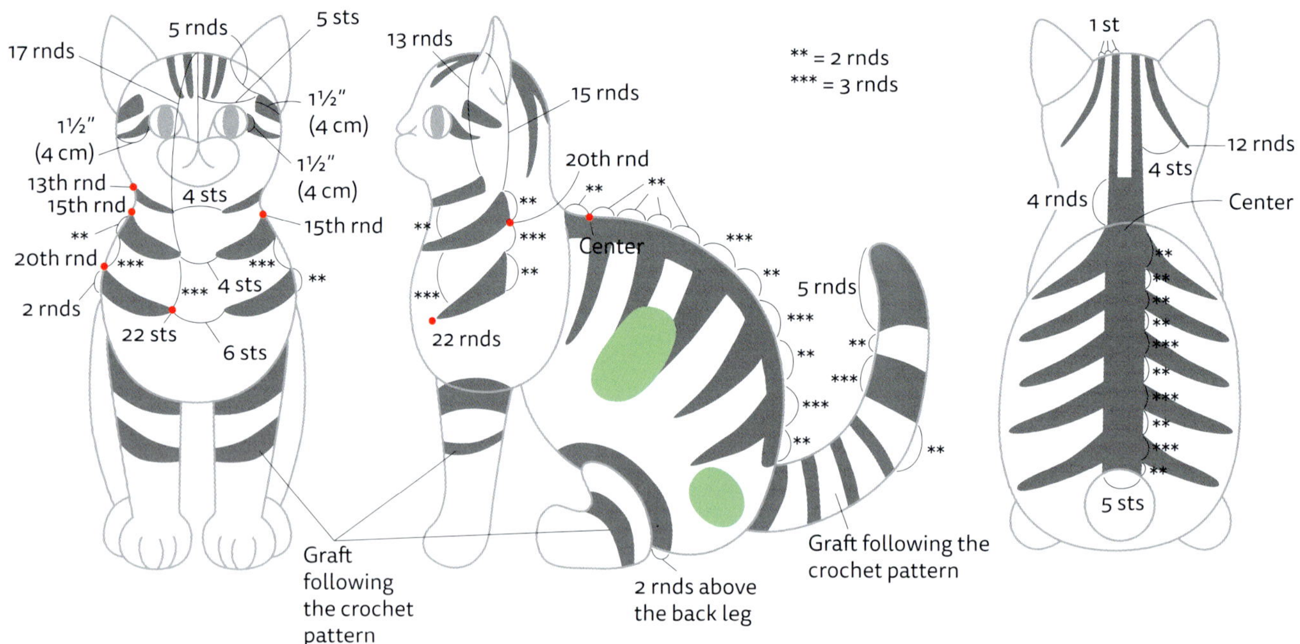

Note: The diagrams above illustrate how to graft a striped pattern. To create a marbled pattern, also graft small and large circular areas using Yarn B, as noted by the green areas in the diagrams above.

Yarn Length Key

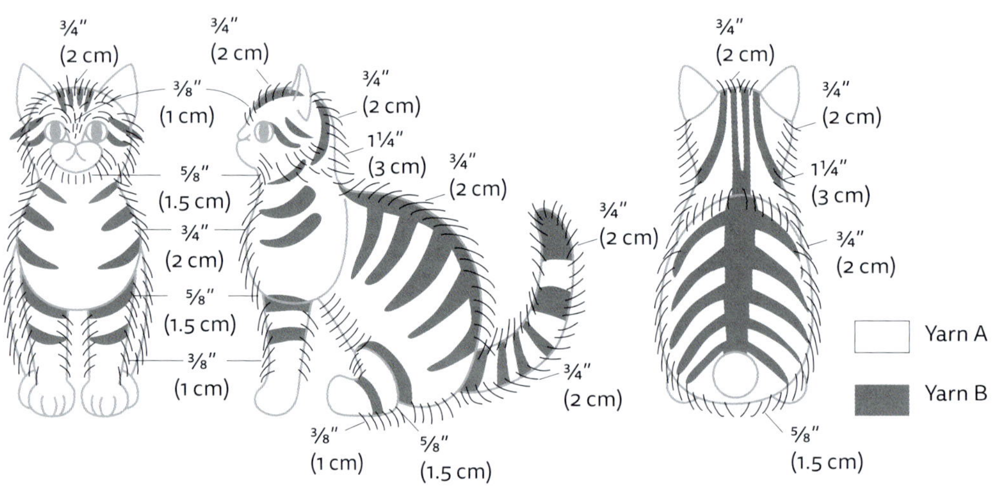

TIPS

- Do not graft ears, toes or stomach area.
- Brush the back of the ears with a slicker brush to make them fuzzy.
- To create a marbled fur pattern, connect the stripes with large splotches of color.
- Refer to page 61 for instructions on embroidering the nose.

Persian (Adult)

SHOWN ON PAGE 27

TOOLS & MATERIALS

- US 7 (4.5 mm) crochet hook
- US C-2 (2.5 mm) crochet hook
- Sport weight acrylic yarn
  - 867 yds (792 m) in white
  - 20 yds (18 m) in light pink
- Light-fingering weight acrylic/mohair blend yarn
  - 919 yds (840 m) in white
- About 12" (30 cm) of sport weight acrylic yarn in light pink for embroidering the nose
- About 12" (30 cm) of light-fingering weight acrylic/mohair blend yarn in dark gray for embroidering the mouth
- Pair of 18 mm crystal eye buttons in blue
- Polyester fiber fill toy stuffing (about 70 g)
- 2.1 yds (1.9 m) of armature wire
  - Cut two 6" (15 cm) long pieces for the ears
  - Cut two 20" (50 cm) long pieces for the front legs
  - Cut one 24" (60 cm) long piece for the tail
- Stitch marker
- Yarn needle
- Felting needle
- Slicker brush

CONSTRUCTION STEPS

1. Crochet the body, head and chest, front legs, back legs, tail, mouth, and ears following the instructions on pages 108–111 (also see pages 37–49).
2. Stuff as required and assemble the body parts as noted in the diagram on page 112 (also refer to pages 50–56). Make sure to attach the eye buttons to the head before stuffing (refer to page 36).
3. Graft yarn as noted in the diagram on page 112. Loosen the yarn and trim the fur into shape. Embroider the facial features as noted in the diagram on page 112. Refer to pages 57–61 for general grafting instructions and use the photos on the next page as a reference.

FINISHED SIZE

Height: 9" (23 cm)
Length: 12" (30 cm)
Tail: 8" (20 cm)

YARN COMBINATION CHART

	Area	Yarn Used	Yarn Color	Strands	Total Strands	Yarn	Hook Size
Crocheting the Foundation	• Body • Head and chest • Front legs • Back legs • Tail • Outer ears	Sport weight acrylic	White	2	4	A	US 7 (4.5 mm)
		Light-fingering weight acrylic/mohair blend	White	2			
	• Mouth	Sport weight acrylic	White	1	2	B	US C-2 (2.5 mm)
		Light-fingering weight acrylic/mohair blend	White	1			
	• Inner ears	Sport weight acrylic	Light pink	1*	2	C	US C-2 (2.5 mm)
Grafting the Fur						A**	

*Use a double strand of the same yarn

**Graft using the same yarn used to crochet the foundation

Front

Back

Side

CROCHET INSTRUCTIONS

Body (make 1)

With Yarn A and US 7 hook, make a magic ring.
Rnd 1: ch1 (does not count as a st throughout), sc6 in magic ring, slst in beg ch1 [6]
Place stitch marker in first st of rnd 1 and move it up after each round
Rnd 2: ch1, (sc2 in next st) 6 times, slst in beg ch1 [12]
Rnd 3: ch1, (sc1, sc2 in next st) 6 times, slst in beg ch1 [18]
Rnd 4: ch1, (sc2, sc2 in next st) 6 times, slst in beg ch1 [24]
Rnd 5: ch1, (sc3, sc2 in next st) 6 times, slst in beg ch1 [30]
Rnd 6: ch1, (sc4, sc2 in next st) 6 times, slst in beg ch1 [36]
Rnd 7: ch1, (sc5, sc2 in next st) 6 times, slst in beg ch1 [42]
Rnd 8: ch1, sc1 in each st, slst in beg ch1
Rnd 9: ch1, sc21, sc2 in next st, sc5, sc2 in next st, sc6, sc2 in next st, sc5, sc2 in next st, sc1, slst in beg ch1 [46]
Rnds 10-12: ch1, sc1 in each st, slst in beg ch1 (3 rnds)
Rnd 13: ch1, sc22, sc2 in next st, (sc6, sc2 in next st) 3 times, sc2, slst in beg ch1 [50]
Rnds 14-21: ch1, sc1 in each st, slst in beg ch1 (8 rnds)
Rnd 22: ch1, sc1, sc2tog, sc14, sc2tog, sc10, sc2tog, sc8, sc2tog, sc9, slst in beg ch1 [46]
Rnd 23: ch1, sc1 in each st, slst in beg ch1
Rnd 24: ch1, sc1, sc2tog, sc12, sc2tog, sc9, sc2tog, sc8, sc2tog, sc8, slst in beg ch1 [42]
Rnds 25-26: ch1, sc1 in each st, slst in beg ch1 (2 rnds)
Rnd 27: ch1, sc1, sc2tog, sc10, sc2tog, sc27, slst in beg ch1 [40]
Rnds 28-30: ch1, sc1 in each st, slst in beg ch1 (3 rnds)
Fasten off.

Crochet Symbol Key

- ★ = magic ring
- 0 = ch st
- • = slst
- ^ = sc2tog
- V = sc2 in next st
- sc3 in next st
- sc5 in next st
- • = make a knot (see page 46)

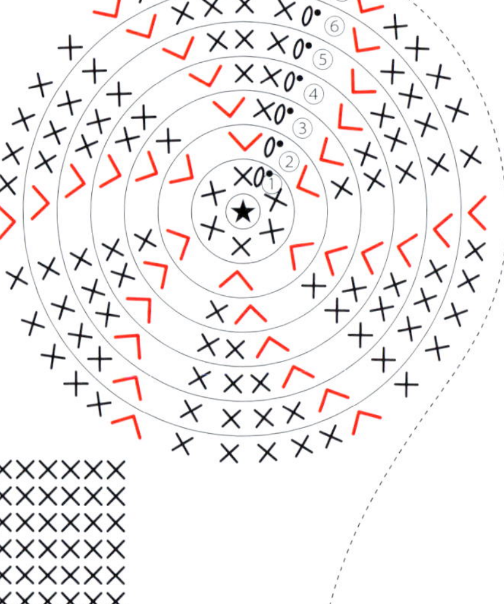

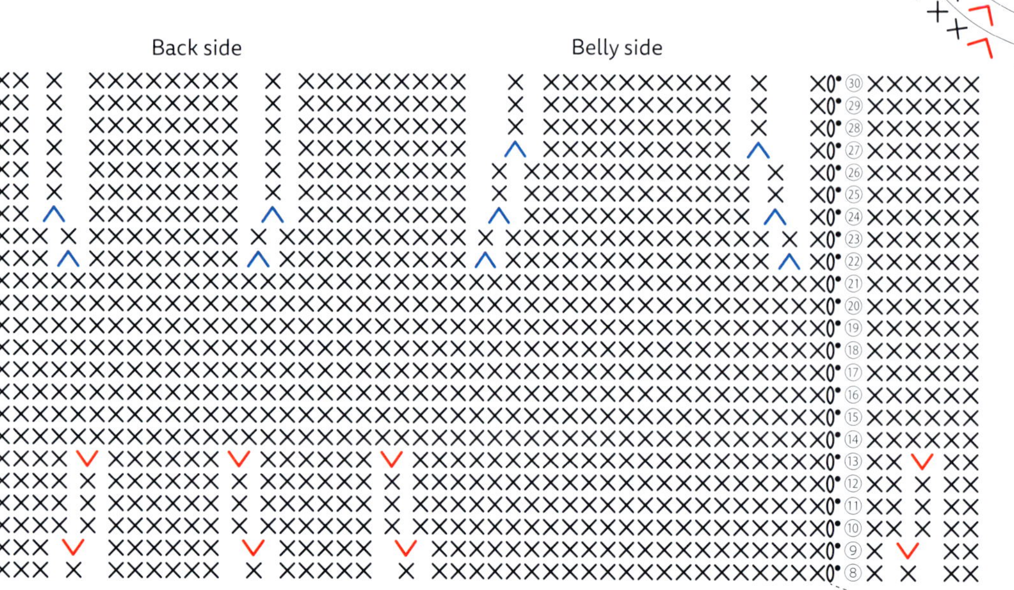

Head & Chest (make 1)

With Yarn A and US 7 hook, ch4.

Rnd 1: skip first ch, sc1 in next ch, sc1 in next ch, sc3 in last ch, rotate and work along opposite side of chain, sc1 in next ch, sc2 in next ch, slst in skipped ch at beg of round [8]

Place stitch marker in first st of rnd 1 and move it up after each round

Rnd 2: ch1, (sc2 in next st) 8 times, slst in beg ch1 [16]

Rnd 3: ch1, sc1, sc2 in next st, sc2, sc2 in next st, sc1, (sc2 in next st) twice, sc1, sc2 in next st, sc2, sc2 in next st, sc1, (sc2 in next st) twice, slst in beg ch1 [24]

Rnd 4: ch1, sc2 in next st, sc6, sc2 in next st, sc4, sc2 in next st, sc6, sc2 in next st, sc4, slst in beg ch1 [28]

Rnd 5: ch1, sc10, sc2 in next st, sc2, sc2 in next st, sc10, sc2 in next st, sc2, sc2 in next st, slst in beg ch1 [32]

Rnd 6: ch1, sc10, sc2 in next st, sc4, sc2 in next st, sc10, sc2 in next st, sc4, sc2 in next st, slst in beg ch1 [36]

Rnds 7-11: ch1, sc1 in each st, slst in beg ch1 (5 rnds)

Rnd 12: ch1, sc18, (sc2tog, sc2) twice, sc2tog, sc8, slst in beg ch1 [33]

Rnd 13: ch1, sc3, sc2 in next st, sc4, sc2 in next st, sc7, (sc2tog, sc1) 3 times, sc2tog, sc6, slst in beg ch1 [31]

Rnds 14-15: ch1, sc1 in each st, slst in beg ch1 (2 rnds)

Rnd 16: ch1, sc18, (sc2 in next st, sc2) twice, sc2 in next st, sc6, slst in beg ch1 [34]

Rnd 17: ch1, sc3, sc2 in next st, sc6, sc2 in next st, sc7, sc2 in next st, sc8, sc2 in next st, sc6, slst in beg ch1 [38]

Rnds 18-19: ch1, sc1 in each st, slst in beg ch1 (2 rnds)

Rnd 20: ch1, sc20, sc2 in next st, sc10, sc2 in next st, sc6, slst in beg ch1 [40]

Rnd 21: ch1, sc20, sc2 in next st, sc12, sc2 in next st, sc6, slst in beg ch1 [42]

Rnds 22-24: ch1, sc1 in each st, slst in beg ch1 (3 rnds)

Begin to fill with toy stuffing.

Rnd 25: ch1, (sc5, sc2tog) 6 times, slst in beg ch1 [36]

Rnd 26: ch1, (sc4, sc2tog) 6 times, slst in beg ch1 [30]

Rnd 27: ch1, (sc3, sc2tog) 6 times, slst in beg ch1 [24]

Rnd 28: ch1, (sc2, sc2tog) 6 times, slst in beg ch1 [18]

Rnd 29: ch1, (sc1, sc2tog) 6 times, slst in beg ch1 [12]

Add more toy stuffing before final rnd.

Rnd 30: ch1, (sc2tog) 6 times, slst in beg ch1 [6]

Fasten off.

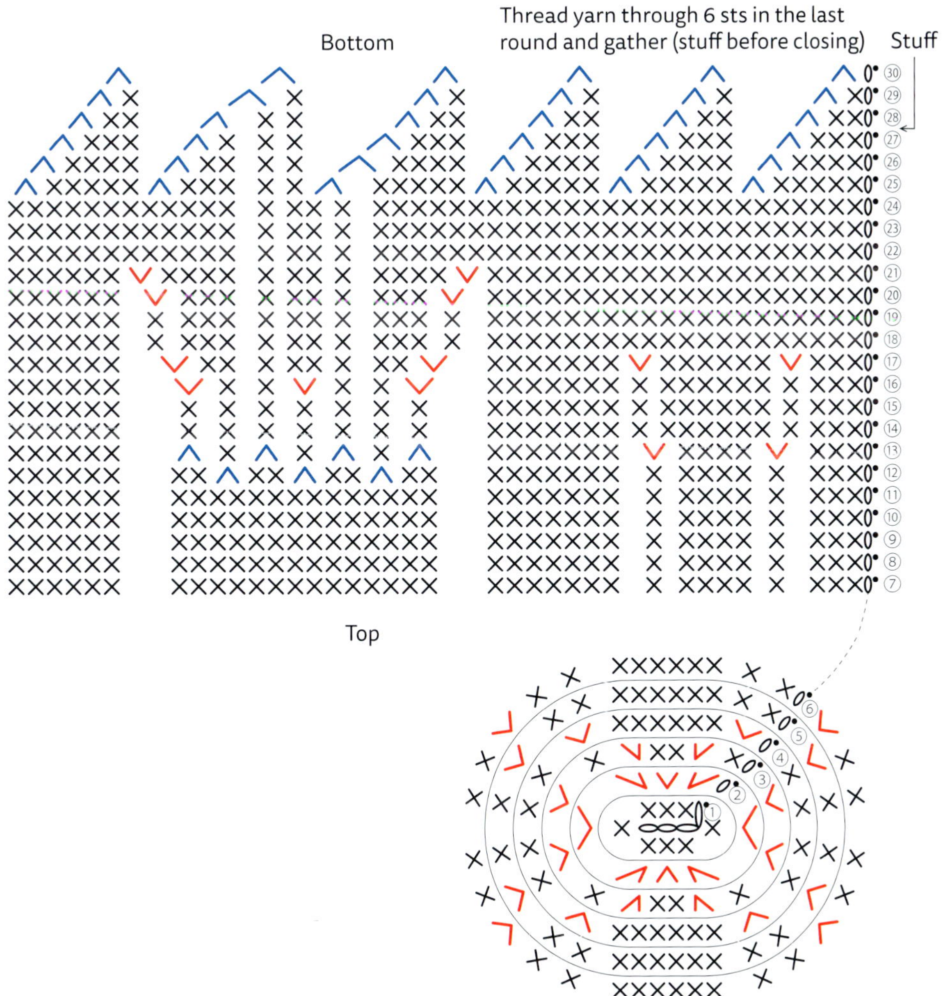

Front Legs (make 2)

With Yarn A and US 7 hook, make a magic ring.
Rnd 1: ch1 (does not count as a st throughout), sc8 in magic ring, slst in beg ch1 [8]
Place stitch marker in first st of rnd 1 and move it up after each round
Rnd 2: ch1, sc2, (hdc-cl in next st) 4 times, sc2, slst in beg ch1
Rnds 3-7: ch1, sc1 in each st, slst in beg ch1 (5 rnds)
Rnd 8: ch1, sc7, sc2 in next st, slst in beg ch1 [9]
Rnd 9: ch1, sc8, sc2 in next st, slst in beg ch1 [10]
Rnd 10: ch1, sc9, sc2 in next st, slst in beg ch1 [11]
Rnd 11: ch1, sc10, sc2 in next st, slst in beg ch1 [12]
Rnd 12: ch1, sc6, sc3 in next st, sc4, sc2 in next st, slst in beg ch1 [15]
Rnd 13: ch1, sc7, sc3 in next st, sc6, sc2 in next st, slst in beg ch1 [18]
Rnd 14: ch1, sc8, sc3 in next st, sc9, slst in beg ch1 [20]
Rnd 15: ch1, sc1 in each st, slst in beg ch1
Rnd 16: ch1, sc9, sc3 in next st, sc10, slst in beg ch1 [22]
Rnd 17: ch1, sc1 in each st, slst in beg ch1
Fasten off.

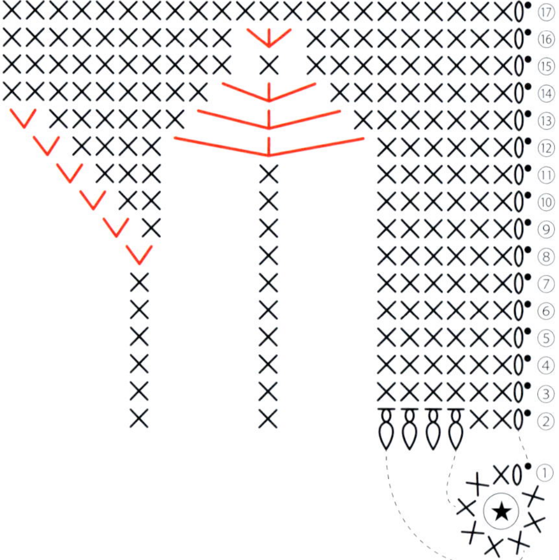

Back Legs (make 2)

With Yarn A and US 7 hook, make a magic ring.
Work as given for Front Legs to end of rnd 5 [8]
Rnd 6: ch1, sc7, sc2 in next st, slst in beg ch1 [9]
Rnd 7: ch1, sc1 in each st, slst in beg ch1
Rnd 8: ch1, sc1, (sc2 in next st) twice, sc3 in next st, sc5 in next st, sc3 in next st, (sc2 in next st) twice, sc1, slst in beg ch1 [21]
Rnd 9: ch1, sc10, sc5 in next st, sc10, slst in beg ch1 [25]
Rnd 10: ch1, sc12, sc5 in next st, sc12, slst in beg ch1 [29]
Rnd 11: ch1, sc14, sc3 in next st, sc14, slst in beg ch1 [31]
Rnd 12: ch1, sc15, sc3 in next st, sc15, slst in beg ch1 [33]
Rnd 13: ch1, sc16, sc3 in next st, sc16, slst in beg ch1 [35]
Rnds 14-17: ch1, sc1 in each st, slst in beg ch1 (4 rnds)
Rnd 18: ch1, sc11, sc2tog, sc2, sc2tog, sc1, sc2tog, sc2, sc2tog, sc11, slst in beg ch1 [31]
Rnd 19: ch1, sc12, sc2tog, sc3, sc2tog, sc12, slst in beg ch1 [29]
Rnd 20: ch1, sc11, sc2tog, sc3, sc2tog, sc11, slst in beg ch1 [27]
Fasten off.

Tail (make 1)

With Yarn A and US 7 hook, make a magic ring.
Rnd 1: ch1 (does not count as a st throughout), sc6 in magic ring, slst in beg ch1 [6]
Place stitch marker in first st of rnd 1 and move it up after each round
Rnd 2: ch1, (sc1, sc2 in next st) 3 times, slst in beg ch1 [9]
Rnds 3-4: ch1, sc1 in each st, slst in beg ch1 (2 rnds)
Rnd 5: ch1, (sc2, sc2 in next st) 3 times, slst in beg ch1 [12]
Rnds 6-23: ch1, sc1 in each st, slst in beg ch1 (18 rnds)
Fasten off.

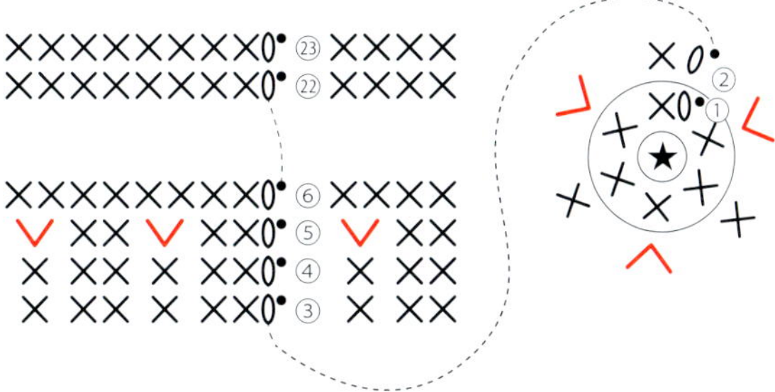

Mouth (make 1)

With Yarn B and US C-2 hook, ch12.
Rnd 1: skip first ch, sc5, sc3 in next ch, sc4, sc3 in last ch, rotate and work along opposite side of chain, sc3, sc3tog, sc3, sc2 in last ch, slst in skipped ch at beg of rnd [24]
Rnd 2: ch1, sc1 in each st, slst in beg ch1
Fasten off. Use the wrong side as the right side.

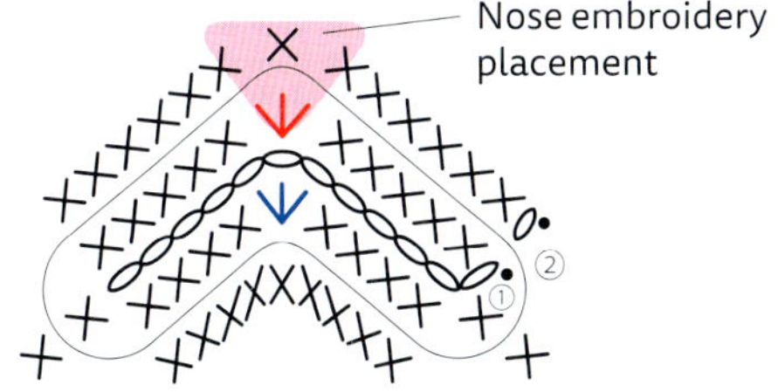

Ears

Right Ear (make 1 each of outer and inner ear)

Outer Ear

With Yarn A and US 7 hook, ch9, leaving a 12" (30 cm) tail of yarn.
Work in rows.
Row 1: dc1 in fifth ch from hook (counts as 2dc), dc1, hdc1, sc1, sc3 in last chain, rotate and work along opposite side of chain stitches, hdc2, dc2, 2dc in next ch, turn [14]
Cut a 6" (15 cm) long piece of armature wire, fold in half, position the folded area at the corner of the ear, and crochet next rnd over the wire to trap it into the sts.
Row 2: ch1 (does not count as a st throughout), sc7, sc2 in next st, sc6 [15]
Fasten off.

Inner Ear

Make inner ear in the same way with Yarn C and US C-2 hook, omitting wire.

Left Ear (make 1 each of outer and inner ear)

Outer Ear

With Yarn A and US 7 hook, ch9, leaving a 12" (30 cm) tail of yarn.
Work in rows.
Row 1: dc1 in fourth ch from hook (counts as 2dc), dc2, hdc2, sc3 in last chain, rotate and work along opposite side of chain stitches, sc1, hdc1, dc3, turn [14]
Cut a 6" (15 cm) long piece of armature wire, fold in half, position the folded area at the corner of the ear, and crochet next rnd over the wire to trap it into the sts.
Row 2: Ch1 (does not count as a st throughout), sc6, sc2 in next st, sc7 [15]
Fasten off.

Inner Ear

Make inner ear in the same way with Yarn C and US C-2 hook, omitting wire.

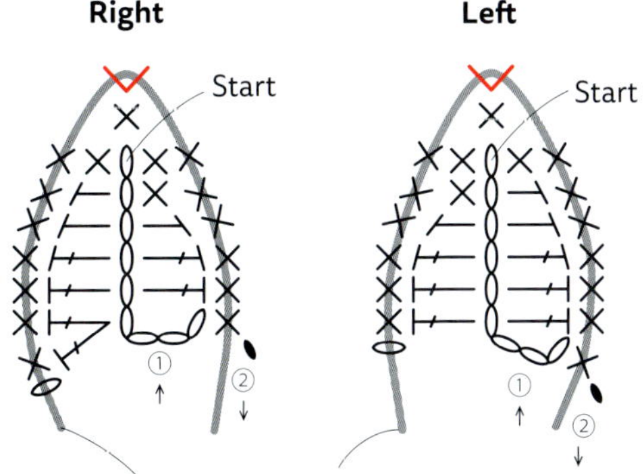

ASSEMBLY DIAGRAM

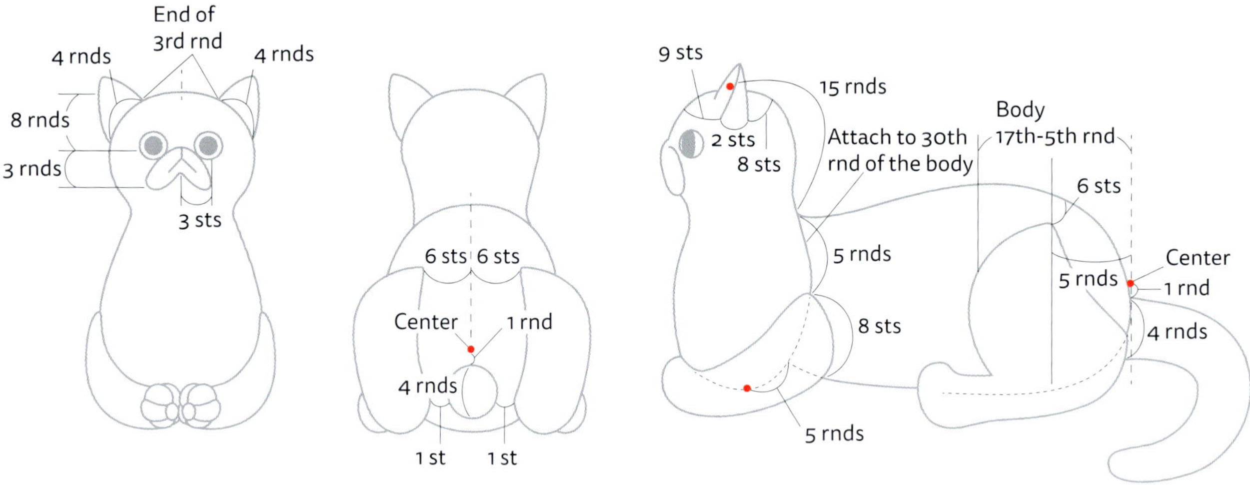

GRAFTING

Yarn Length Key

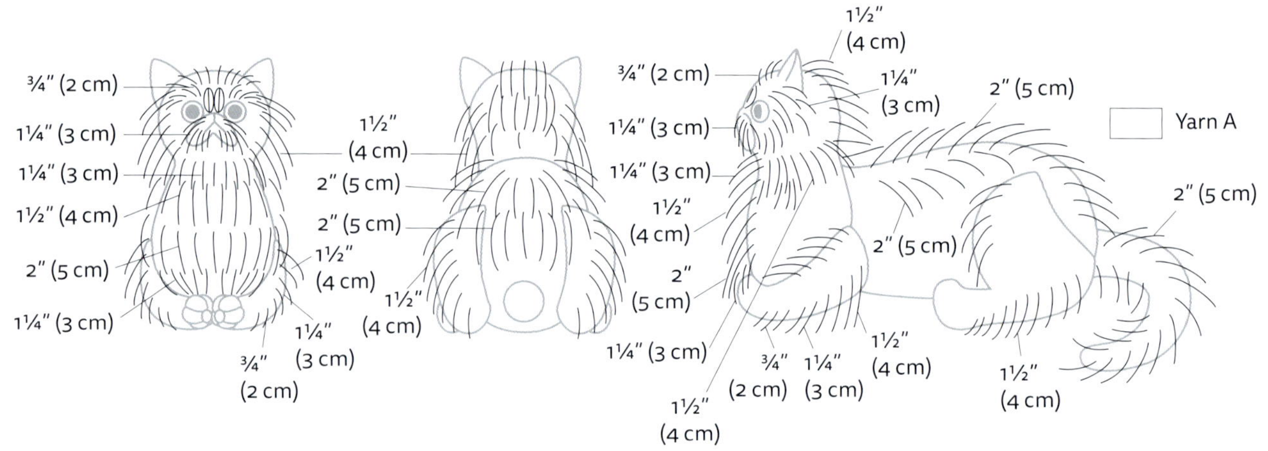

Face Embroidery

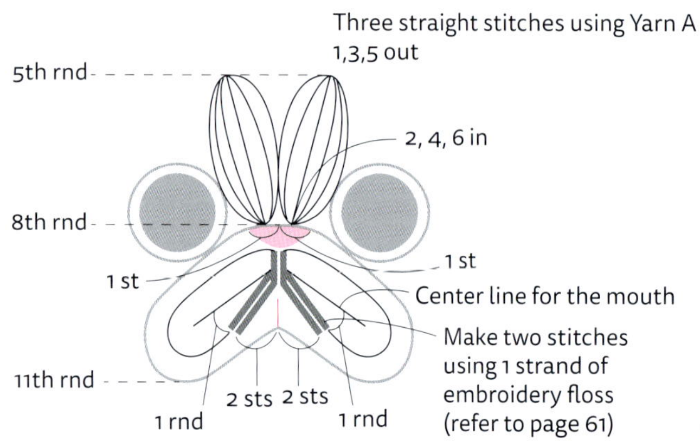

TIPS

- Do not graft ears, toes or stomach area.
- Brush the back of the ears with a slicker brush to make them fuzzy.
- There is no crocheted nose for this cat. Embroider a nose onto the crocheted mouth, as shown in the diagram at left (also refer to page 61).
- This cat does not have whiskers.

Persian (Kitten)

SHOWN ON PAGE 27

TOOLS & MATERIALS

- US G-6 (4 mm) crochet hook
- US C-2 (2.5 mm) crochet hook
- US B-1 (2.25 mm) crochet hook
- Sport weight acrylic yarn
  - 433 yds (396 m) in white
  - 20 yds (18 m) in light pink
- Light-fingering weight acrylic/mohair blend yarn
  - 438 yds (400 m) in white
- About 12" (30 cm) of sport weight acrylic yarn in light pink for embroidering the nose
- About 12" (30 cm) of light-fingering weight acrylic/mohair blend yarn in dark gray for embroidering the mouth
- Pair of 15 mm cat eye buttons in blue
- Polyester fiber fill toy stuffing (about 30 g)
- 1.5 yds (1.3 m) of armature wire
  - Cut two 4¾" (12 cm) long pieces for the ears
  - Cut two 14" (36 cm) long pieces for the front legs
  - Cut one 12" (30 cm) long piece for the tail
- Stitch marker
- Yarn needle
- Felting needle
- Slicker brush

CONSTRUCTION STEPS

1. Crochet the body, head and chest, front legs, back legs, tail, mouth and ears following the instructions on pages 114–117 (also see pages 37–49).
2. Stuff as required and assemble the body parts as noted in the diagram on page 118 (also refer to pages 50–56). Make sure to attach the eye buttons to the head before stuffing (refer to page 36).
3. Graft yarn as noted in the diagram on page 118. Loosen the yarn and trim the fur into shape. Embroider the facial features as noted in the diagram on page 112. Refer to pages 57–61 for general grafting instructions and use the photos on the next page as a reference.

FINISHED SIZE

Height: 8¾" (22 cm)
Length: 7½" (19 cm)
Tail: 4¾" (12 cm)

YARN COMBINATION CHART

	Area	Yarn Used	Yarn Color	Strands	Total Strands	Yarn	Hook Size
Crocheting the Foundation	• Body • Head and chest	Sport weight acrylic	White	2	4	A	US 7 (4.5 mm)
	• Front legs • Back legs • Tail	Light-fingering weight acrylic/mohair blend	White	2			US C-2 (2.5 mm)
	• Outer ears • Mouth	Sport weight acrylic	White	1	2	B	US C-2 (2.5 mm)
		Light-fingering weight acrylic/mohair blend	White	1			
	• Inner ears	Sport weight acrylic	Light pink	1	1	C	US B-1 (2.25 mm)
Grafting the Fur						A*	

*Graft using the same yarn used to crochet the foundation

Front

Back

Side

CROCHET INSTRUCTIONS

Crochet Symbol Key

★ = magic ring
0 = ch st
• = slst
∧ = sc2tog
∨ = sc2 in next st
= sc3 in next st
= sc5 in next st
• = make a knot (see page 46)

Body (make 1)

With Yarn A and US G-6 hook, make a magic ring.
Rnd 1: ch1 (does not count as a st throughout), sc6 in magic ring, slst in beg ch1 [6]
Place stitch marker in first st of rnd 1 and move it up after each round
Rnd 2: ch1, (sc2 in next st) 6 times, slst in beg ch1 [12]
Rnd 3: ch1, (sc1, sc2 in next st) 6 times, slst in beg ch1 [18]
Rnd 4: ch1, (sc2, sc2 in next st) 6 times, slst in beg ch1 [24]
Rnd 5: ch1, (sc3, sc2 in next st) 6 times, slst in beg ch1 [30]
Rnd 6: ch1, sc1, sc2 in next st, sc26, sc2 in next st, sc1, slst in beg ch1 [32]
Rnds 7-9: ch1, sc1 in each st, slst in beg ch1 (3 rnds)
Rnd 10: ch1, sc12, sc2tog, sc4, sc2tog, sc12, slst in beg ch1 [30]
Rnds 11-12: ch1, sc1 in each st, slst in beg ch1 (2 rnds)
Rnd 13: ch1, sc1, sc2 in next st, sc26, sc2 in next st, sc1, slst in beg ch1 [32]
Rnds 14-16: ch1, sc1 in each st, slst in beg ch1 (3 rnds)
Fasten off.

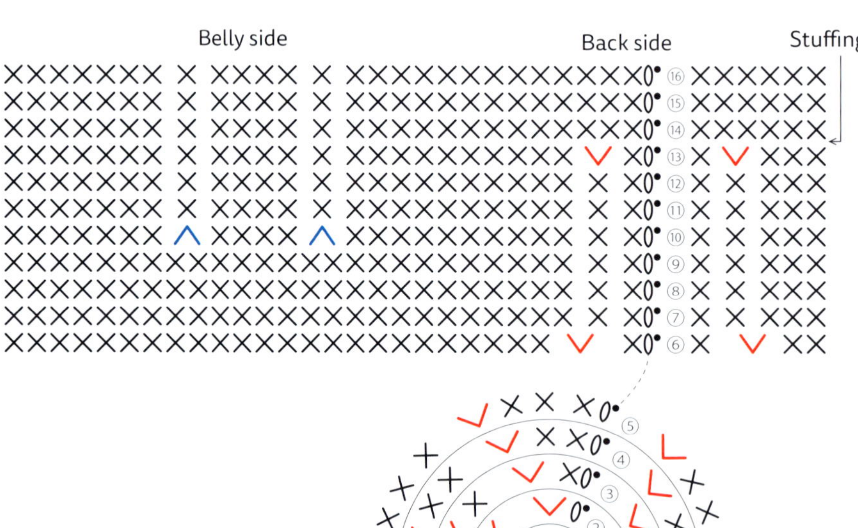

Head & Chest (make 1)

With Yarn A and US G-6 hook, ch4.

Rnd 1: skip first ch, sc1 in in next ch, sc1 in next ch, sc3 in last ch, rotate and work along opposite side of chain, sc1 in next ch, sc2 in next ch, slst in skipped ch at beg of round [8]

Place stitch marker in first st of rnd 1 and move it up after each round

Rnd 2: ch1, (sc2 in next st) 8 times, slst in beg ch1 [16]

Rnd 3: ch1, sc1, sc2 in next st, sc2, sc2 in next st, sc1, (sc2 in next st) twice, sc1, sc2 in next st, sc2, sc2 in next st, sc1, (sc2 in next st) twice, slst in beg ch1 [24]

Rnd 4: ch1, sc2 in next st, sc6, sc2 in next st, sc4, sc2 in next st, sc6, sc2 in next st, sc4, slst in beg ch1 [28]

Rnds 5-10: ch1, sc1 in each st, slst in beg ch1 (6 rnds)

Rnd 11: ch1, sc13, sc2tog, sc1, sc2tog, sc2, sc2tog, sc1, sc2tog, sc3, slst in beg ch1 [24]

Rnd 12: ch1, sc4, sc2 in next st, sc3, sc2 in next st, sc4, (sc2tog, sc1) twice, sc2tog, sc3, slst in beg ch1 [23]

Rnd 13: ch1, sc1 in each st, slst in beg ch1

Rnd 14: ch1, sc4, sc2 in next st, sc5, sc2 in next st, sc12, slst in beg ch1 [25]

Rnd 15: ch1, sc17, (sc2 in next st, sc3) twice, slst in beg ch1 [27]

Rnd 16: ch1, sc1 in each st, slst in beg ch1

Rnd 17: ch1, sc17, sc2 in next st, sc5, sc2 in next st, sc3, slst in beg ch1 [29]

Rnd 18: ch1, sc1 in each st, slst in beg ch1

Rnd 19: ch1, sc21, sc2 in next st, sc7, slst in beg ch1 [30]

Rnd 20: ch1, sc1 in each st, slst in beg ch1

Begin to fill with toy stuffing.

Rnd 21: ch1, (sc3, sc2tog) 6 times, slst in beg ch1 [24]

Rnd 22: ch1, (sc2, sc2tog) 6 times, slst in beg ch1 [18]

Rnd 23: ch1, (sc1, sc2tog) 6 times, slst in beg ch1 [12]

Add more toy stuffing before final rnd.

Rnd 24: ch1, (sc2tog) 6 times, slst in beg ch1 [6]

Fasten off.

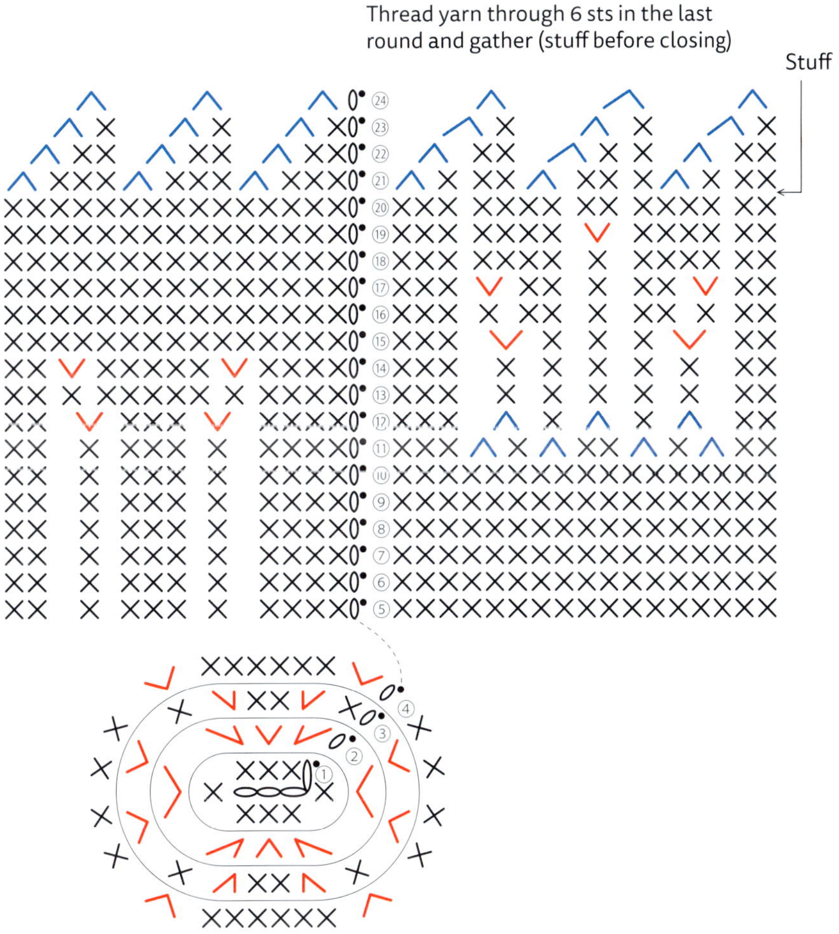

Thread yarn through 6 sts in the last round and gather (stuff before closing)

Stuff

Front Legs

Left (make 1)

With Yarn A and US G-6 hook, make a magic ring.
Rnd 1: ch1 (does not count as a st throughout), sc8 in magic ring, slst in beg ch1 [8]
Place stitch marker in first st of rnd 1 and move it up after each round
Rnd 2: ch1, sc2, (hdc-cl in next st) 4 times, sc2, slst in beg ch1
Rnds 3-5: ch1, sc1 in each st, slst in beg ch1 (3 rnds)
Rnd 6: ch1, sc2, sc2 in next st, sc5, slst in beg ch1 [9]
Rnd 7: ch1, sc3, sc2 in next st, sc5, slst in beg ch1 [10]
Rnd 8: ch1, sc4, sc2 in next st, sc5, slst in beg ch1 [11]
Rnd 9: ch1, sc4, hdc2 in next st, hdc1, sc5, slst in beg ch1 [12]
Rnd 10: ch1, sc4, hdc2 in next st, hdc1, sc6, slst in beg ch1 [13]
Fasten off.

Right (make 1)

Work as given for left front leg to the end of rnd 5.
Rnd 6: ch1, sc5, sc2 in next st, sc2, slst in beg ch1 [9]
Rnd 7: ch1, sc6, sc2 in next st, sc2, slst in beg ch1 [10]
Rnd 8: ch1, sc7, sc2 in next st, sc2, slst in beg ch1 [11]
Rnd 9: ch1, sc7, hdc1, hdc2 in next st, sc2, slst in beg ch1 [12]
Rnd 10: ch1, sc8, hdc1, hdc2 in next st, sc2, slst in beg ch1 [13]
Fasten off.

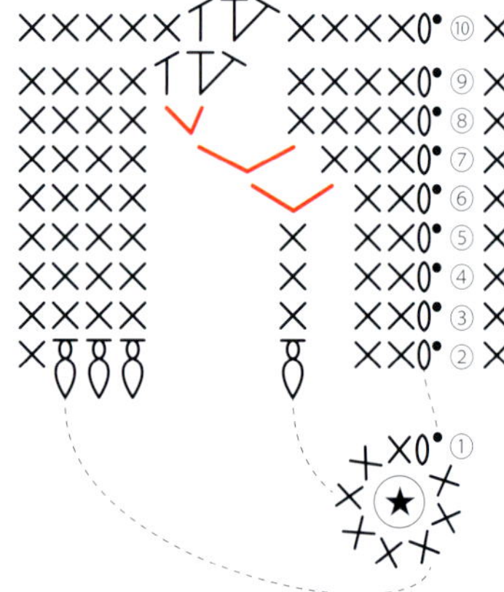

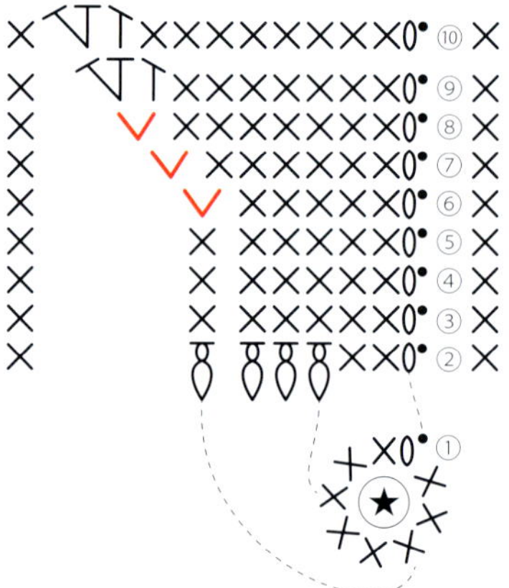

Back Legs (make 2)

With Yarn A and US G-6 hook, make a magic ring.
Rnd 1: ch1 (does not count as a st throughout), sc8 in magic ring, slst in beg ch1 [8]
Place stitch marker in first st of rnd 1 and move it up after each round
Rnd 2: ch1, sc2, (hdc-cl in next st) 4 times, sc2, slst in beg ch1
Rnds 3-4: ch1, sc1 in each st, slst in beg ch1 (2 rnds)
Rnd 5: ch1, sc4, sc3 in next st, sc2, sc2 in next st, slst in beg ch1 [11]
Rnd 6: ch1, sc5, sc3 in next st, sc5, slst in beg ch1 [13]
Rnd 7: ch1, sc4, sc2 in next st, sc3, sc2 in next st, sc4, slst in beg ch1 [15]
Fasten off.

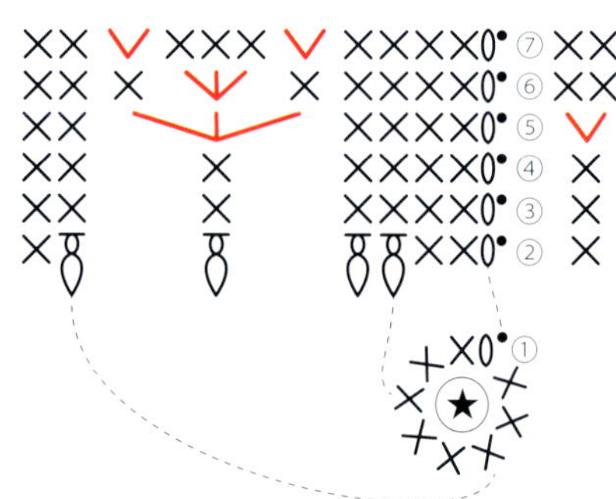

Tail (make 1)

With Yarn A and US G-6 hook, make a magic ring.
Rnd 1: ch1 (does not count as a st throughout), sc6 in magic ring, slst in beg ch1 [6]
Place stitch marker in first st of rnd 1 and move it up after each round
Rnd 2: ch1, (sc1, sc2 in next st) 3 times, slst in beg ch1 [9]
Rnds 3-12: ch1, sc1 in each st, slst in beg ch1 (10 rnds)
Fasten off.

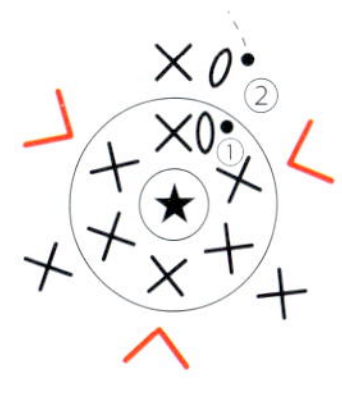

Mouth (make 1)

With Yarn B and US C-2 hook, ch10.
Rnd 1: skip first ch, sc4, sc3 in next ch, sc3, sc3 in last ch, rotate and work along opposite side of chain, sc2, sc3tog, sc2, sc2 in last ch, slst in skipped ch at beg of rnd [20]
Fasten off. Use the wrong side as the right side.

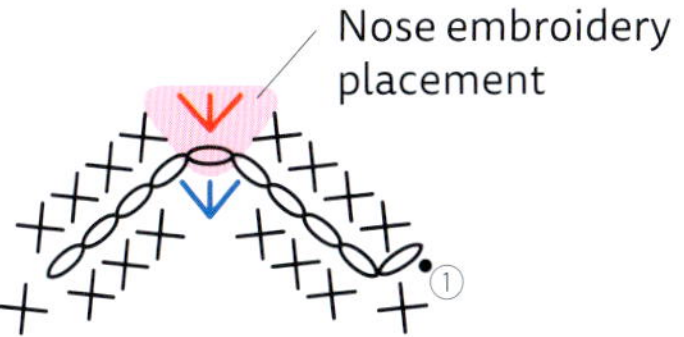

Ears

Right Ear (make 1 each of outer and inner ear)

Outer Ear

With Yarn B and US C-2 hook, ch8, leaving a 12" (30 cm) tail of yarn.
Work in rows.
Row 1: dc1 in fifth ch from hook (counts as 2dc), hdc2, sc3 in last chain, rotate and work along opposite side of chain stitches, hdc2, dc1, 2dc in next ch, turn [12]
Cut a 4.7" (12 cm) long piece of armature wire, fold in half, position the folded area at the corner of the ear, and crochet next rnd over the wire to trap it into the sts.
Row 2: Ch1 (does not count as a st throughout), sc6, sc2 in next st, sc5 [13]
Fasten off.

Inner Ear

Make inner ear in the same way with Yarn C and US B-1 hook, omitting wire, and working 1 row only.

Left Ear (make 1 each of outer and inner ear)

Outer Ear

With Yarn B and US C-2 hook, ch8, leaving a 12" (30 cm) tail of yarn.
Work in rows.
Row 1: dc1 in fourth ch from hook (counts as 2dc), dc1, hdc2, sc3 in last chain, rotate and work along opposite side of chain stitches, hdc2, dc2, turn [12]
Cut a 4.7" (12 cm) long piece of armature wire, fold in half, position the folded area at the corner of the ear, and crochet next rnd over the wire to trap it into the sts.
Row 2: Ch1 (does not count as a st throughout), sc5, sc2 in next st, sc6 [13]
Fasten off.

Inner Ear

Make inner ear in the same way with Yarn C and US B-1 hook, omitting wire, and working 1 row only.

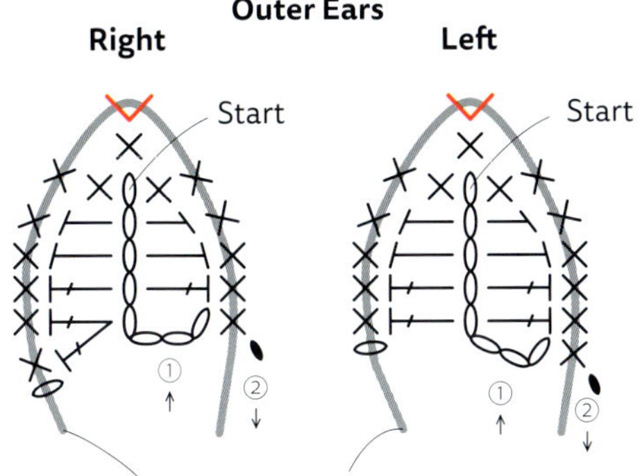

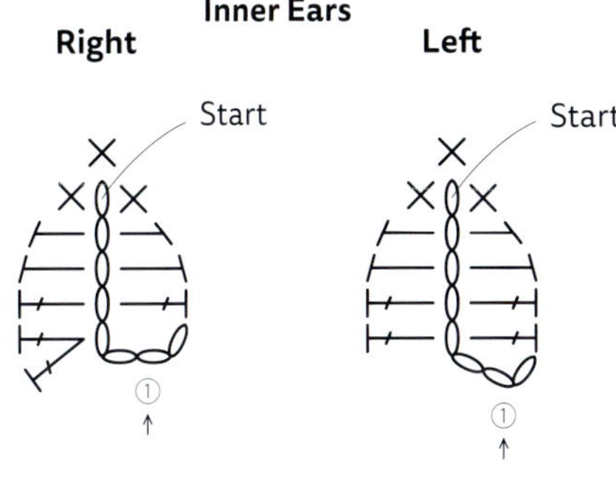

ASSEMBLY DIAGRAM

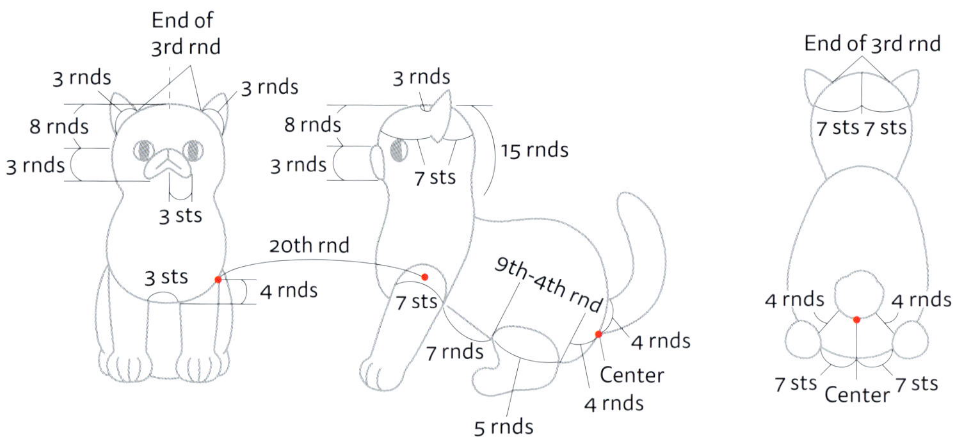

GRAFTING

Yarn Length Key

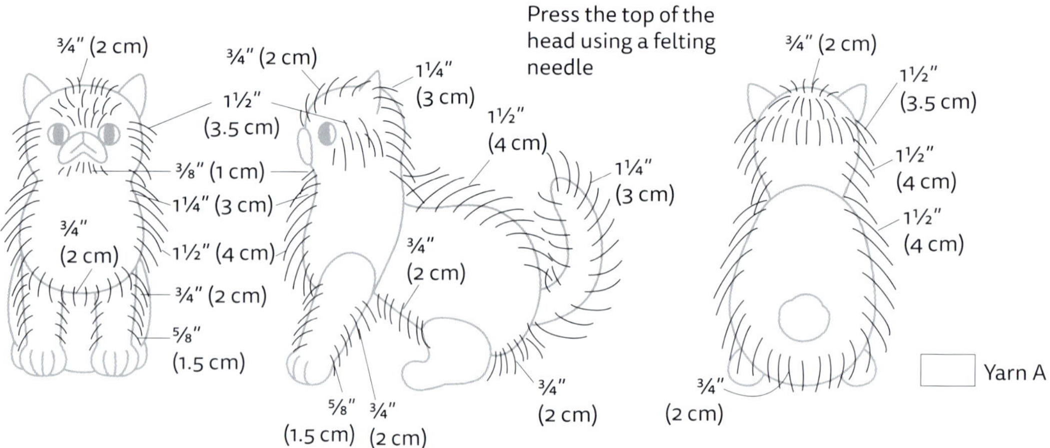

TIPS

- Do not graft ears, toes or stomach area.
- Brush the back of the ears with a slicker brush to make them fuzzy.
- There is no crocheted nose for this cat. Embroider a nose onto the crocheted mouth, as shown in the diagram on page 112 (also refer to page 61).
- This cat does not have whiskers.

Tuxedo

SHOWN ON PAGE 28

TOOLS & MATERIALS

- US 7 (4.5 mm) crochet hook
- US C-2 (2.5 mm) crochet hook
- Sport weight acrylic yarn
    - 197 yds (180 m) in white
    - 630 yds (576 m) in black
    - 40 yds (36 m) in light pink
- Light-fingering weight acrylic/mohair blend yarn
    - 219 yds (200 m) in white
    - 700 yds (640 m) in black
    - 44 yds (40 m) in dark gray
- About 12" (30 cm) of sport weight acrylic yarn in light pink for embroidering the nose
- About 12" (30 cm) of light-fingering weight acrylic/mohair blend yarn in dark gray for embroidering the mouth
- Pair of 18 mm cat eye buttons in green
- 2¾" (7 cm) long clear whiskers
- Polyester fiber fill toy stuffing (about 70 g)
- 2.1 yds (1.9 m) of armature wire
    - Cut two 6" (15 cm) long pieces for the ears
    - Cut two 20" (50 cm) long pieces for the front legs
    - Cut one 24" (60 cm) long piece for the tail
- Stitch marker
- Yarn needle
- Felting needle
- Slicker brush

CONSTRUCTION STEPS

1. Crochet the body, head and chest, front legs, back legs, tail, nose, mouth, and ears following the instructions on pages 120–124 (also see pages 37–49).
2. Stuff as required and assemble the body parts as noted in the diagram on page 125 (also refer to pages 50–56). Make sure to attach the eye buttons to the head before stuffing (refer to page 36).
3. Graft yarn as noted in the diagram on page 125. Loosen the yarn and trim the fur into shape. Embroider the facial features. Refer to pages 57–61 for general grafting instructions and use these photos as a reference.

FINISHED SIZE

Height: 9½" (24 cm)
Length: 14¼" (36 cm)
Tail: 8" (20 cm)

Front

Back

Side

YARN COMBINATION CHART

	Area	Yarn Used	Yarn Color	Strands	Total Strands	Yarn	Hook Size
Crocheting the Foundation	• Body • Tail • Outer ears	Sport weight acrylic	Black	2	4	A	US 7 (4.5 mm)
		Light-fingering weight acrylic/mohair blend	Black	2			
	• Head and chest • Front legs • Back legs	Sport weight acrylic	White	2	4	B*	US 7 (4.5 mm)
		Light-fingering weight acrylic/mohair blend	White	2			
	• Mouth • Nose	Sport weight acrylic	White	1	2	C	US C-2 (2.5 mm)
		Sport weight acrylic	White	1			
	• Nose	Sport weight acrylic	Black	1	2	D**	US C-2 (2.5 mm)
		Sport weight acrylic	Black	1			
	• Inner ears	Sport weight acrylic	Light pink	1	2	E	US C-2 (2.5 mm)
		Light-fingering weight acrylic/mohair blend	Dark gray	1			
Grafting the Fur						A, B***	

*Yarn B will alternate with Yarn A to create the tuxedo pattern

**Yarn D will alternate with Yarn C to create the tuxedo pattern

***Graft using the same yarn used to crochet the foundation

CROCHET INSTRUCTIONS

Body (make 1)

With Yarn A and US 7 hook, make a magic ring.
Rnd 1: ch1 (does not count as a st throughout), sc6 in magic ring, slst in beg ch1 [6]
Place stitch marker in first st of rnd 1 and move it up after each round
Rnd 2: ch1, (sc2 in next st) 6 times, slst in beg ch1 [12]
Rnd 3: ch1, (sc1, sc2 in next st) 6 times, slst in beg ch1 [18]
Rnd 4: ch1, (sc2, sc2 in next st) 6 times, slst in beg ch1 [24]
Rnd 5: ch1, (sc3, sc2 in next st) 6 times, slst in beg ch1 [30]
Rnd 6: ch1, (sc4, sc2 in next st) 6 times, slst in beg ch1 [36]
Rnd 7: ch1, (sc5, sc2 in next st) 6 times, slst in beg ch1 [42]
Rnd 8: ch1, sc1 in each st, slst in beg ch1
Rnd 9: ch1, sc21, sc2 in next st, sc5, sc2 in next st, sc6, sc2 in next st, sc5, sc2 in next st, sc1, slst in beg ch1 [46]
Rnds 10-12: ch1, sc1 in each st, slst in beg ch1 (3 rnds)
Rnd 13: ch1, sc22, sc2 in next st, (sc6, sc2 in next st) 3 times, sc2, slst in beg ch1 [50]
Rnds 14-21: ch1, sc1 in each st, slst in beg ch1 (8 rnds)
Rnd 22: ch1, sc1, sc2tog, sc14, sc2tog, sc10, sc2tog, sc8, sc2tog, sc9, slst in beg ch1 [46]
Rnd 23: ch1, sc1 in each st, slst in beg ch1
Rnd 24: ch1, sc1, sc2tog, sc12, sc2tog, sc9, (sc2tog, sc8) twice, slst in beg ch1 [42]
Rnds 25-26: ch1, sc1 in each st, slst in beg ch1 (2 rnds)
Rnd 27: ch1, sc1, sc2tog, sc10, sc2tog, sc27, slst in beg ch1 [40]
Rnds 28-30: ch1, sc1 in each st, slst in beg ch1 (3 rnds)
Fasten off.

Crochet Symbol Key

★ = magic ring
0 = ch st
• = slst
∧ = ⩓ = sc2tog
∨ = ⩔ = sc2 in next st
sc3 in next st symbol = sc3 in next st
sc5 in next st symbol = sc5 in next st
• = make a knot (see page 46)

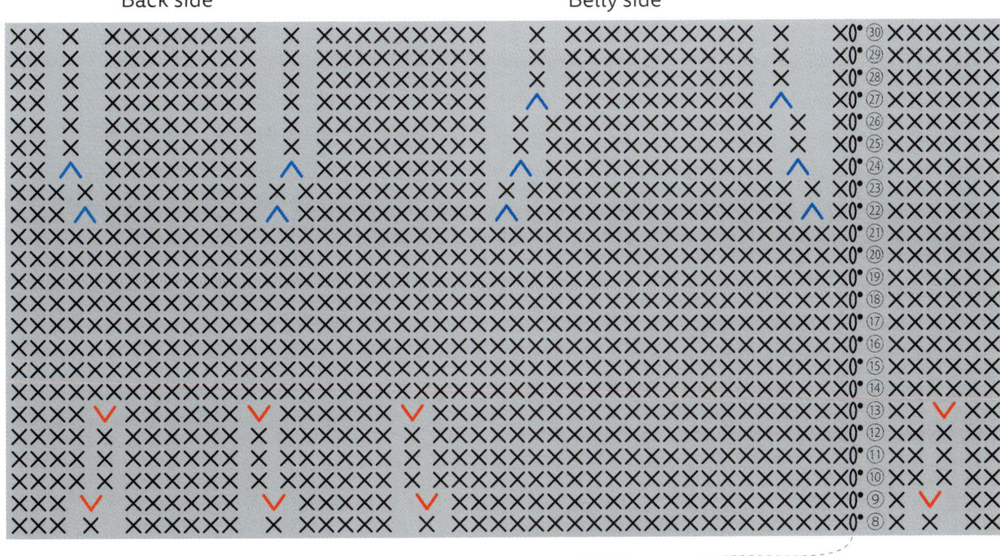

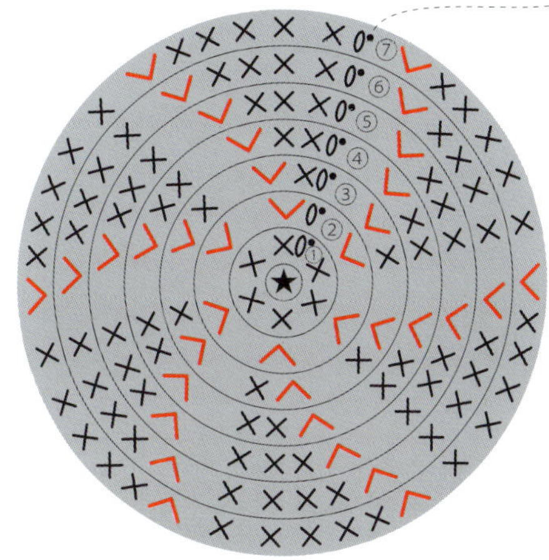

Head & Chest (make 1)

With Yarn A and US 7 hook, ch4.

Rnd 1: skip first ch, sc1 in next ch, sc1 in next ch, sc3 in last ch, rotate and work along opposite side of chain, sc1 in next ch, sc2 in next ch, slst in skipped ch at beg of round [8]

Place stitch marker in first st of rnd 1 and move it up after each round

Rnd 2: ch1, (sc2 in next st) 8 times, slst in beg ch1 [16]

Rnd 3: ch1, sc1, sc2 in next st, sc2, sc2 in next st, sc1, (sc2 in next st) twice, sc1, sc2 in next st, sc2, sc2 in next st, sc1, (sc2 in next st) twice, slst in beg ch1 [24]

Rnd 4: ch1, sc2 in next st, sc6, sc2 in next st, sc4, sc2 in next st, sc6, sc2 in next st, sc4, slst in beg ch1 [28]

Rnd 5: ch1, sc10, sc2 in next st, sc2, sc2 in next st, sc10, sc2 in next st, sc2, sc2 in next st, slst in beg ch1 [32]

Rnd 6: ch1, sc10, sc2 in next st, sc4, sc2 in next st, sc10, sc2 in next st, sc4, sc2 in next st, slst in beg ch1 [36]

Join in Yarn B.

Rnds 7-8: in Yarn A ch1, sc21, in Yarn B sc4, in Yarn A sc11, slst in beg ch1 (2 rnds)

Rnds 9-10: in Yarn A ch1, sc20, in Yarn B sc6, in Yarn A sc10, slst in beg ch1 (2 rnds)

Rnd 11: in Yarn A ch1, sc19, in Yarn B sc8, in Yarn A sc9, slst in beg ch1

Rnd 12: in Yarn A ch1, sc16, in Yarn B (sc2, sc2tog) 3 times, sc2, in Yarn A sc6, slst in beg ch1 [33]

Rnd 13: in Yarn A ch1, sc3, sc2 in next st, sc4, sc2 in next st, sc7, in Yarn B (sc2tog, sc1) 3 times, sc2tog, in Yarn A sc6, slst in beg ch1 [31]

Rnds 14-15: in Yarn A ch1, sc18, in Yarn B sc7, in Yarn A sc6, slst in beg ch1 (2 rnds)

Rnd 16: in Yarn A ch1, sc18, in Yarn B (sc2 in next st, sc2) twice, sc2 in next st, in Yarn A sc6, slst in beg ch1 [34]

Rnd 17: in Yarn A ch1, sc3, sc2 in next st, sc6, sc2 in next st, sc7, in Yarn B sc2 in next st, sc8, sc2 in next st, in Yarn A sc6, slst in beg ch1 [38]

Rnds 18-19: in Yarn A ch1, sc20, in Yarn B sc12, in Yarn A sc6, slst in beg ch1 (2 rnds)

Rnd 20: in Yarn A ch1, sc20, in Yarn B sc2 in next st, sc10, sc2 in next st, in Yarn A sc6, slst in beg ch1 [40]

Rnd 21: in Yarn A ch1, sc20, in Yarn B sc2 in next st, sc12, sc2 in next st, in Yarn A sc6, slst in beg ch1 [42]

Rnds 22-24: in Yarn A ch1, sc20, in Yarn B sc16, in Yarn A sc6, slst in beg ch1 (3 rnds)

Rnd 25: in Yarn A ch1, (sc5, sc2tog) 3 times, sc3, in Yarn B sc2, sc2tog, sc4, in Yarn A sc1, sc2tog, sc5, sc2tog, slst in beg ch1 [36]
Continue in Yarn A only.
Rnd 26: ch1, (sc4, sc2tog) 6 times, slst in beg ch1 [30]
Rnd 27: ch1, (sc3, sc2tog) 6 times, slst in beg ch1 [24]
Begin to fill with toy stuffing.
Rnd 28: ch1, (sc2, sc2tog) 6 times, slst in beg ch1 [18]
Rnd 29: ch1, (sc1, sc2tog) 6 times, slst in beg ch1 [12]
Add more toy stuffing before final rnd.
Rnd 30: ch1, (sc2tog) 6 times, slst in beg ch1 [6]
Fasten off.

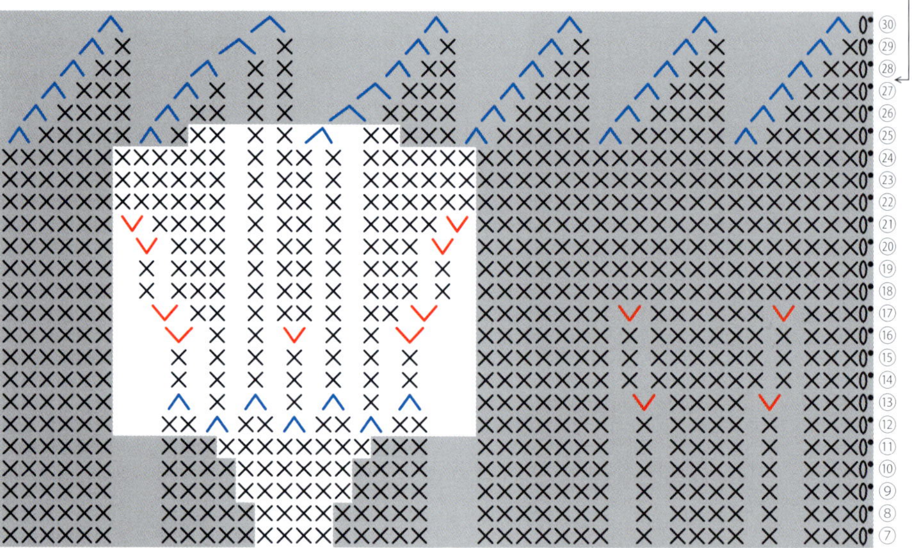

TIP
If the crochet pattern is distorted, adjust the shape by using a steam iron while pulling it straight.

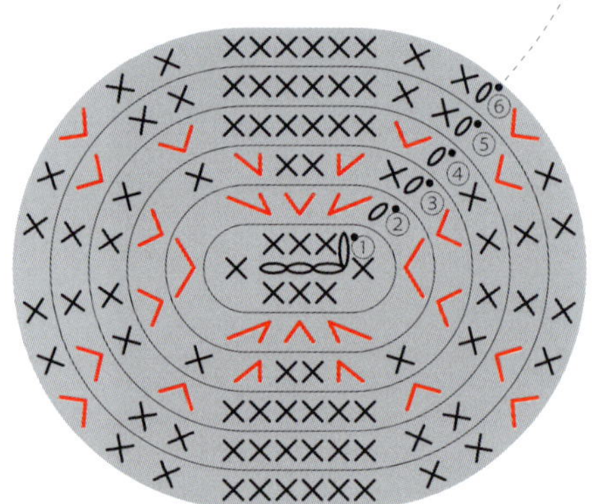

Front Legs (make 2)

With Yarn B and US 7 hook, make a magic ring.
Rnd 1: ch1 (does not count as a st throughout), sc8 in magic ring, slst in beg ch1 [8]
Place stitch marker in first st of rnd 1 and move it up after each round
Rnd 2: ch1, sc2, (hdc-cl in next st) 4 times, sc2, slst in beg ch1
Rnds 3-4: ch1, sc1 in each st, slst in beg ch1 (2 rnds)
Change to Yarn A.
Rnds 5-7: ch1, sc1 in each st, slst in beg ch1 (3 rnds)
Rnd 8: ch1, sc7, sc2 in next st, slst in beg ch1 [9]
Rnd 9: ch1, sc8, sc2 in next st, slst in beg ch1 [10]
Rnd 10: ch1, sc9, sc2 in next st, slst in beg ch1 [11]
Rnd 11: ch1, sc10, sc2 in next st, slst in beg ch1 [12]
Rnd 12: ch1, sc6, sc3 in next st, sc4, sc2 in next st, slst in beg ch1 [15]
Rnd 13: ch1, sc7, sc3 in next st, sc6, sc2 in next st, slst in beg ch1 [18]
Rnd 14: ch1, sc8, sc3 in next st, sc9, slst in beg ch1 [20]
Rnd 15: ch1, sc1 in each st, slst in beg ch1
Rnd 16: ch1, sc9, sc3 in next st, sc10, slst in beg ch1 [22]
Rnd 17: ch1, sc1 in each st, slst in beg ch1
Fasten off.

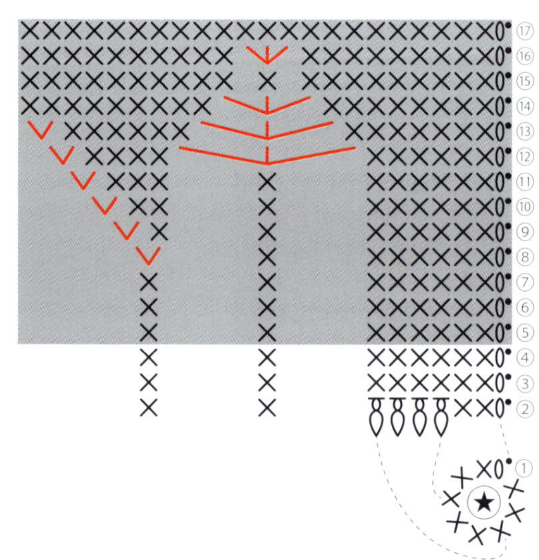

Back Legs (make 2)

With Yarn B and US 7 hook, make a magic ring.
Work as given for Front Legs to end of rnd 4 [8]
Change to Yarn A.
Rnd 5: ch1, sc1 in each st, slst in beg ch1
Rnd 6: ch1, sc7, sc2 in next st, slst in beg ch1 [9]
Rnd 7: ch1, sc1 in each st, slst in beg ch1
Rnd 8: ch1, sc1, (sc2 in next st) twice, sc3 in next st, sc5 in next st, sc3 in next st, (sc2 in next st) twice, sc1, slst in beg ch1 [21]
Rnd 9: ch1, sc10, sc5 in next st, sc10, slst in beg ch1 [25]
Rnd 10: ch1, sc12, sc5 in next st, sc12, slst in beg ch1 [29]
Rnd 11: ch1, sc14, sc3 in next st, sc14, slst in beg ch1 [31]
Rnd 12: ch1, sc15, sc3 in next st, sc15, slst in beg ch1 [33]
Rnd 13: ch1, sc16, sc3 in next st, sc16, slst in beg ch1 [35]
Rnds 14-17: ch1, sc1 in each st, slst in beg ch1 (4 rnds)
Rnd 18: ch1, sc11, sc2tog, sc2, sc2tog, sc1, sc2tog, sc2, sc2tog, sc11, slst in beg ch1 [31]
Rnd 19: ch1, sc12, sc2tog, sc3, sc2tog, sc12, slst in beg ch1 [29]
Rnd 20: ch1, sc11, sc2tog, sc3, sc2tog, sc11, slst in beg ch1 [27]
Fasten off.

Tail (make 1)

With Yarn A and US G-6 With Yarn A and US 7 hook, make a magic ring.
Rnd 1: ch1 (does not count as a st throughout), sc6 in magic ring, slst in beg ch1 [6]
Place stitch marker in first st of rnd 1 and move it up after each round
Rnd 2: ch1, (sc1, sc2 in next st) 3 times, slst in beg ch1 [9]
Rnds 3-4: ch1, sc1 in each st, slst in beg ch1 (2 rnds)
Rnd 5: ch1, (sc2, sc2 in next st) 3 times, slst in beg ch1 [12]
Rnds 6-23: ch1, sc1 in each st, slst in beg ch1 (18 rnds)
Fasten off.

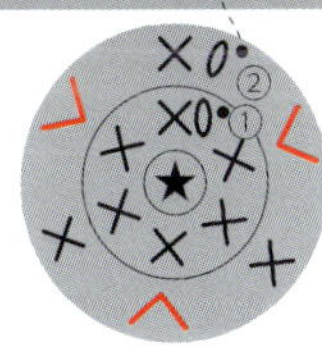

Nose (make 1)

With Yarn C and US C-2 hook, make a magic ring.
Rnd 1: ch1 (does not count as a st throughout), sc6 in magic ring, slst in beg ch1 [6]
Place stitch marker in first st of rnd 1 and move it up after each round
Rnd 2: ch1, sc1 in each st, slst in beg ch1
Slst in next 2 sts, then continue in rows.
Row 3: ch1, sc1 in next 4 sts, lengthen loop from hook and pass yarn through, pull tight to make a knot, do not turn [4]
Row 4: pass yarn across back of work, pull through beg ch1 of prev row, and rep row 3.
Row 5: pass yarn across back of work, pull through beg ch1 of prev row, ch1, sc2 in first st, sc2, sc2 in last st, lengthen loop from hook and pass yarn through, pull tight to make a knot, do not turn [6]
Row 6: pass yarn across back of work, pull through beg ch1 of prev row, change to Yarn D and ch3 (counts as dc), dc2 in first st, in Yarn C sc4, in Yarn D dc3 in last st, lengthen loop from hook and pass yarn through, pull tight to make a knot, do not turn [10]
Row 7: pass yarn across back of work, pull through top of beg ch3 of prev row, (ch3, dc2) in same st (beg ch3 counts as dc), sc2, in Yarn C sc4, in Yarn D sc2, dc3 in last st, lengthen loop from hook and pass yarn through, pull tight to make a knot [14]
Fasten off.

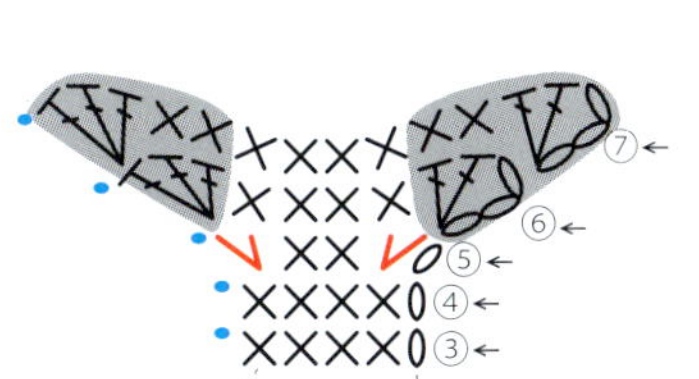

Mouth (make 1)

With Yarn C and US C-2 hook, ch10.
Rnd 1: skip first ch, sc1 in next ch, hdc1, dc2, sc1, dc2, hdc1, sc3 in last ch, rotate and work along opposite side of chain, hdc1, dc2, sc1, dc2, hdc1, sc2 in last ch, slst in skipped ch at beg of rnd [20]
Place stitch marker in first st of rnd 1 and move it up after each rnd
Rnd 2: ch1, sc4, slst in next st, sc9, slst in next st, sc5, slst in beg ch1
Rnd 3: ch1, sc12, ch2, dc4tog over next 4 sc (and skipping the slst), ch2, sc3, slst in beg ch1 [20]
Fasten off. Use the wrong side as the right side.

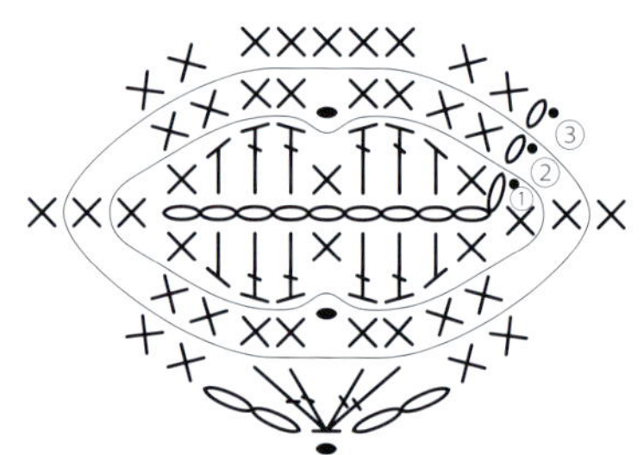

Ears

Right Ear (make 1 each of outer and inner ear)

Outer Ear

With Yarn A and US 7 hook, ch9, leaving a 12" (30 cm) tail of yarn.
Work in rows.
Row 1: dc1 in fifth ch from hook (counts as 2dc), dc1, hdc1, sc1, sc3 in last chain, rotate and work along opposite side of chain stitches, hdc2, dc2, dc2 in next ch, turn [14]
Cut a 6" (15 cm) long piece of armature wire, fold in half, position the folded area at the corner of the ear, and crochet next rnd over the wire to trap it into the sts.
Row 2: ch1 (does not count as a st throughout), sc7, sc2 in next st, sc6 [15]
Fasten off.

Inner Ear

Make inner ear in the same way with Yarn E and US C-2 hook, omitting wire.

Left Ear (make 1 each of outer and inner ear)

Outer Ear

With Yarn A and US 7 hook, ch9, leaving a 12" (30 cm) tail of yarn.
Work in rows.
Row 1: dc1 in fourth ch from hook (counts as 2dc), dc2, hdc2, sc3 in last chain, rotate and work along opposite side of chain stitches, sc1, hdc1, dc3, turn [14]
Cut a 6" (15 cm) long piece of armature wire, fold in half, position the folded area at the corner of the ear, and crochet next rnd over the wire to trap it into the sts.
Row 2: Ch1 (does not count as a st throughout), sc6, sc2 in next st, sc7 [15]
Fasten off.

Inner Ear

Make inner ear in the same way with Yarn E and US C-2 hook, omitting wire.

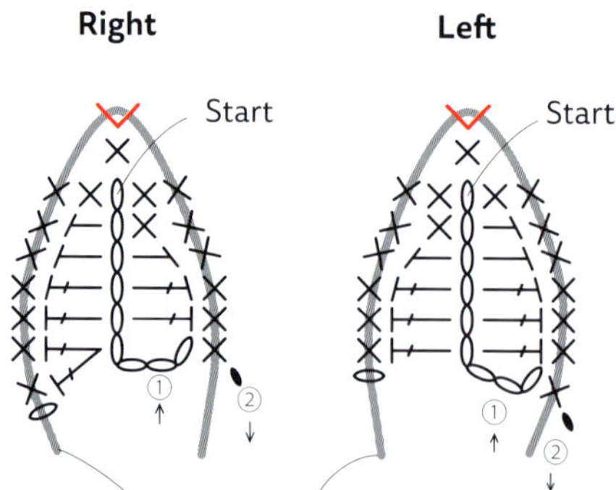

Align a 6" (15 cm) long piece of armature wire with the corner of the ear and crochet around the wire (for outer ear only)

ASSEMBLY DIAGRAM

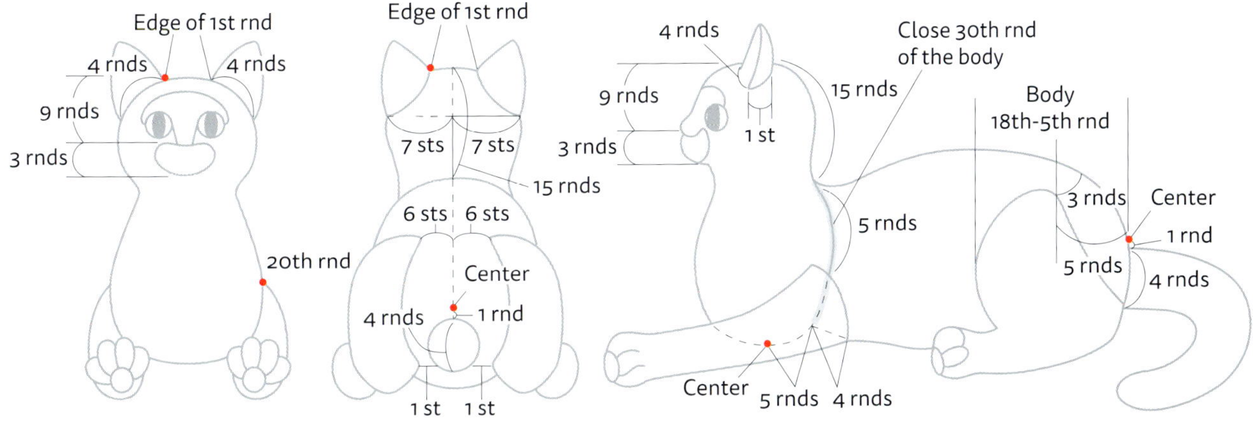

GRAFTING

Yarn Length Key

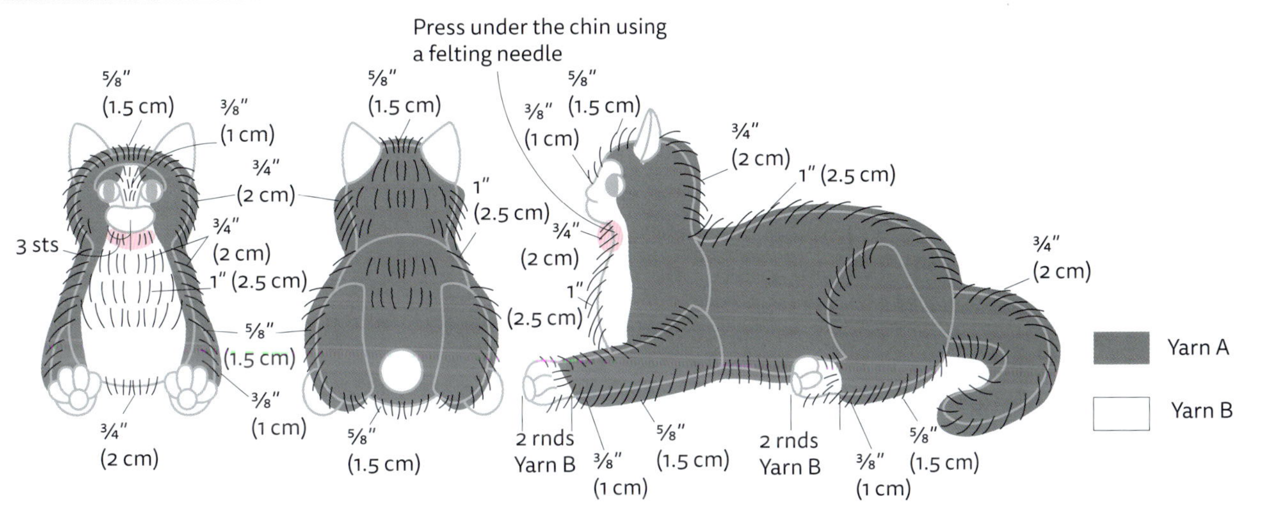

TIPS

- Do not graft ears, toes or stomach area.
- Brush the back of the ears with a slicker brush to make them fuzzy.
- If the crochet pattern is distorted, adjust the shape by using a steam iron while pulling it straight.

Somali

SHOWN ON PAGE 31

TOOLS & MATERIALS

- US 7 (4.5 mm) crochet hook
- US C-2 (2.5 mm) crochet hook
- Sport weight acrylic yarn
  - 788 yds (720 m) in golden brown
  - 79 yds (72 m) in dark brown
  - 40 yds (36 m) in off-white
- Light-fingering weight acrylic/mohair blend yarn
  - 875 yds (800 m) in brown
  - 88 yds (80 m) in dark brown
  - 44 yds (40 m) in off-white
- About 12″ (30 cm) of sport weight acrylic yarn in light pink for embroidering the nose
- About 24″ (60 cm) of sport weight acrylic yarn in dark brown for embroidering the eyes and nose
- About 12″ (30 cm) of sport weight acrylic yarn in golden brown for embroidering the mouth
- Pair of 18 mm crystal eye buttons in green
- 2¾″ (7 cm) long clear whiskers
- Polyester fiber fill toy stuffing (about 70 g)
- 2.1 yds (1.9 m) of armature wire
  - Cut two 6″ (15 cm) long pieces for the ears
  - Cut two 20″ (50 cm) long pieces for the front legs
  - Cut one 24″ (60 cm) long piece for the tail
- Stitch marker
- Yarn needle
- Felting needle
- Slicker brush

CONSTRUCTION STEPS

1. Crochet the body, head and chest, front legs, back legs, tail, nose, mouth and ears following the instructions on pages 128–132 (also see pages 37–49).
2. Stuff as required and assemble the body parts as noted in the diagram on page 133 (also refer to pages 50–56). Make sure to attach the eye buttons to the head before stuffing (refer to page 36).
3. Graft yarn as noted in the diagram on page 133. Loosen the yarn and trim the fur into shape. Embroider the facial features. Refer to pages 57–61 for general grafting instructions and use these photos as a reference.

FINISHED SIZE

Height: 13″ (33 cm)
Length: 8″ (20 cm)
Tail: 8″ (20 cm)

Front

Back

Side

YARN COMBINATION CHART

	Area	Yarn Used	Yarn Color	Strands	Total Strands	Yarn	Hook Size
Crocheting the Foundation	• Body • Head and chest • Tail • Outer ears	Sport weight acrylic	Golden brown	2	4	A	US 7 (4.5 mm)
		Light-fingering weight acrylic/mohair blend	Brown	2			
	• Front legs • Back legs Note: The front and back legs are made with Yarns A, B, and C (refer to diagrams)	Sport weight acrylic	Dark brown	2	4	B	US 7 (4.5 mm)
		Light-fingering weight acrylic/mohair blend	Dark brown	2			
		Sport weight acrylic	Golden brown	1	4	C	US 7 (4.5 mm)
		Sport weight acrylic	Dark brown	1			
		Light-fingering weight acrylic/mohair blend	Brown	1			
		Light-fingering weight acrylic/mohair blend	Dark brown	1			
	• Inner ears	Light-fingering weight acrylic/mohair blend	Brown	1*	2	E	US C-2 (2.5 mm)
	• Nose	Sport weight acrylic	Golden brown	1	2	D	US C-2 (2.5 mm)
		Light-fingering weight acrylic/mohair blend	Brown	1			
	• Mouth	Sport weight acrylic	Unbleached white	1	1	F**	US C-2 (2.5 mm)
		Sport weight acrylic	Off white	1	1		
Grafting the Fur						A***	
	Collar fur	Sport weight acrylic	Unbleached white	2	4	G	
		Light-fingering weight acrylic/mohair blend	Off white	2			
	Forehead stripes	Sport weight acrylic	Dark brown	1	2	H	
		Light-fingering weight acrylic/mohair blend	Dark brown	1			

*Use a double strand of the same yarn

**Also use Yarn D as noted in diagram

***Graft using the same yarn used to crochet the foundation

CROCHET INSTRUCTIONS

Body (make 1)

With Yarn A and US 7 hook, ch6.
Rnd 1: skip first ch, sc1 in in next ch, sc1 in next 3 ch, sc3 in last ch, rotate and work along opposite side of chain, sc1 in next 3 ch, sc2 in next ch, slst in skipped ch at beg of round [12]
Place stitch marker in first st of rnd 1 and move it up after each round
Rnd 2: ch1, sc2 in next st, sc3, (sc2 in next st) 3 times, sc3, (sc2 in next st) twice, slst in beg ch1 [18]
Rnd 3: ch1, sc1, sc2 in next st, sc4, (sc2 in next st, sc1) twice, sc2 in next st, sc4, sc2 in next st, sc1, sc2 in next st, slst in beg ch1 [24]
Rnd 4: ch1, sc2, sc2 in next st, sc5, (sc2 in next st, sc2) twice, sc2 in next st, sc5, sc2 in next st, sc2, sc2 in next st, slst in beg ch1 [30]
Rnd 5: ch1, sc3, sc2 in next st, sc6, (sc2 in next st, sc3) twice, sc2 in next st, sc6, sc2 in next st, sc3, sc2 in next st, slst in beg ch1 [36]
Rnds 6-10: ch1, sc1 in each st, slst in beg ch1 (5 rnds)
Rnd 11: ch1, sc16, sc2 in next st, sc5, sc2 in next st, sc4, sc2 in next st, sc5, sc2 in next st, sc2, slst in beg ch1 [40]
Rnds 12-13: ch1, sc1 in each st, slst in beg ch1 (2 rnds)
Rnd 14: ch1, sc16, (sc2 in next st, sc6) 3 times, sc2 in next st, sc2, slst in beg ch1 [44]
Rnds 15-25: ch1, sc1 in each st, slst in beg ch1 (11 rnds)
Rnd 26: ch1, sc16, (sc2tog, sc6) 3 times, sc2tog, sc2, slst in beginning ch1 [40]
Rnd 27: ch1, sc1 in each st, slst in beg ch1
Rnd 28: ch1, sc16, sc2tog, sc5, sc2tog, sc4, sc2tog, sc5, sc2tog, sc2, slst in beginning ch1 [36]
Rnd 29: as rnd 27
Rnd 30: ch1, (sc4, sc2tog) 6 times, slst in beg ch1 [30]
Begin to fill body with toy stuffing.
Rnd 31: ch1, (sc3, sc2tog) 6 times, slst in beg ch1 [24]
Rnd 32: ch1, (sc2, sc2tog) 6 times, slst in beg ch1 [18]
Rnd 33: ch1, (sc1, sc2tog) 6 times, slst in beg ch1 [12]
Add more toy stuffing to body before final rnd.
Rnd 34: ch1, (sc2tog) 6 times, slst in beg ch1 [6]
Fasten off.

Crochet Symbol Key

★ = magic ring
0 = ch st
• = slst
^ = sc2tog
v = sc2 in next st
sc3 in next st
sc5 in next st
• = make a knot (see page 46)

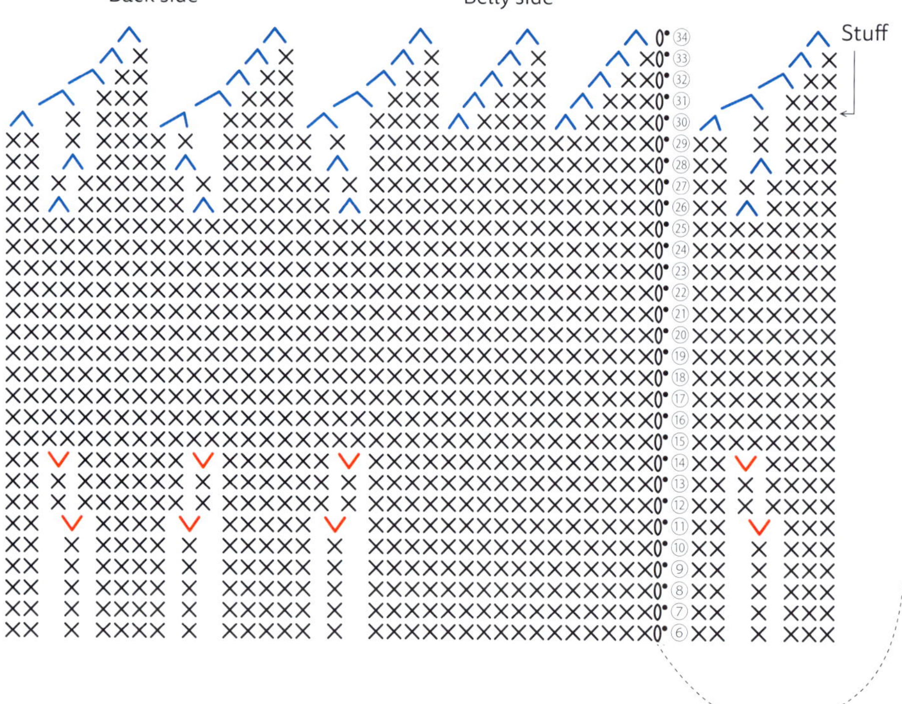

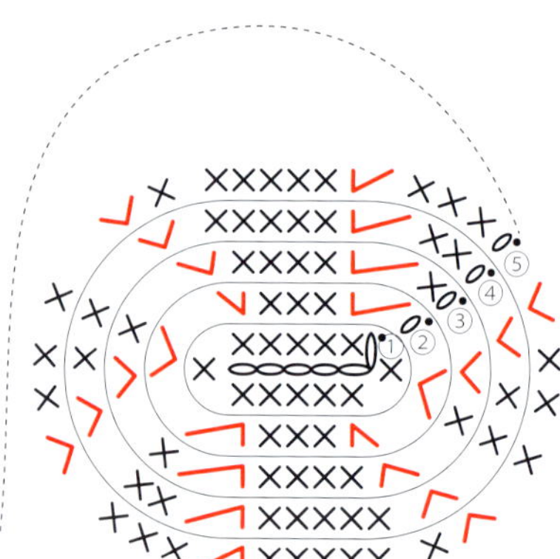

Head & Chest (make 1)

With Yarn A and US 7 hook, ch4.

Rnd 1: skip first ch, sc1 in in next ch, sc1 in next ch, sc3 in last ch, rotate and work along opposite side of chain, sc1 in next ch, sc2 in next ch, slst in skipped ch at beg of round [8]

Place stitch marker in first st of rnd 1 and move it up after each round

Rnd 2: ch1, (sc2 in next st) 8 times, slst in beg ch1 [16]

Rnd 3: ch1, sc1, sc2 in next st, sc2, sc2 in next st, sc1, (sc2 in next st) twice, sc1, sc2 in next st, sc2, sc2 in next st, sc1, (sc2 in next st) twice, slst in beg ch1 [24]

Rnd 4: ch1, sc2 in next st, sc6, sc2 in next st, sc4, sc2 in next st, sc6, sc2 in next st, sc4, slst in beg ch1 [28]

Rnd 5: ch1, sc10, sc2 in next st, sc2, sc2 in next st, sc10, sc2 in next st, sc2, sc2 in next st, slst in beg ch1 [32]

Rnds 6-10: ch1, sc1 in each st, slst in beg ch1 (5 rnds)

Rnd 11: ch1, sc17, (sc2tog, sc2) twice, sc2tog, sc5, slst in beg ch1 [29]

Rnd 12: ch1, sc3, sc2 in next st, sc6, sc2 in next st, sc4, (sc2tog, sc1) 3 times, sc2tog, sc3, slst in beg ch1 [27]

Rnds 13-14: ch1, sc1 in each st, slst in beg ch1 (2 rnds)

Rnd 15: ch1, sc17, (sc2 in next st, sc2) twice, sc2 in next st, sc3, slst in beg ch1 [30]

Rnd 16: ch1, sc3, sc2 in next st, sc9, sc2 in next st, sc3, sc2 in next st, sc8, sc2 in next st, sc3, slst in beg ch1 [34]

Rnds 17-18: ch1, sc1 in each st, slst in beg ch1 (2 rnds)

Rnd 19: ch1, sc19, sc2 in next st, sc10, sc2 in next st, sc3, slst in beg ch1 [36]

Rnd 20: ch1, sc19, sc2 in next st, sc12, sc2 in next st, sc3, slst in beg ch1 [38]

Rnds 21-27: ch1, sc1 in each st, slst in beg ch1 (7 rnds)

Rnd 28: ch1, sc18, sc2tog, sc13, sc2tog, sc3, slst in beg ch1 [36]

Rnd 29: ch1, (sc4, sc2tog) 6 times, slst in beg ch1 [30]

Begin to fill with toy stuffing.

Rnd 30: ch1, (sc3, sc2tog) 6 times, slst in beg ch1 [24]

Rnd 31: ch1, (sc2, sc2tog) 6 times, slst in beg ch1 [18]

Rnd 32: ch1, (sc1, sc2tog) 6 times, slst in beg ch1 [12]

Add more toy stuffing before final rnd.

Rnd 33: ch1, (sc2tog) 6 times, slst in beg ch1 [6]

Fasten off.

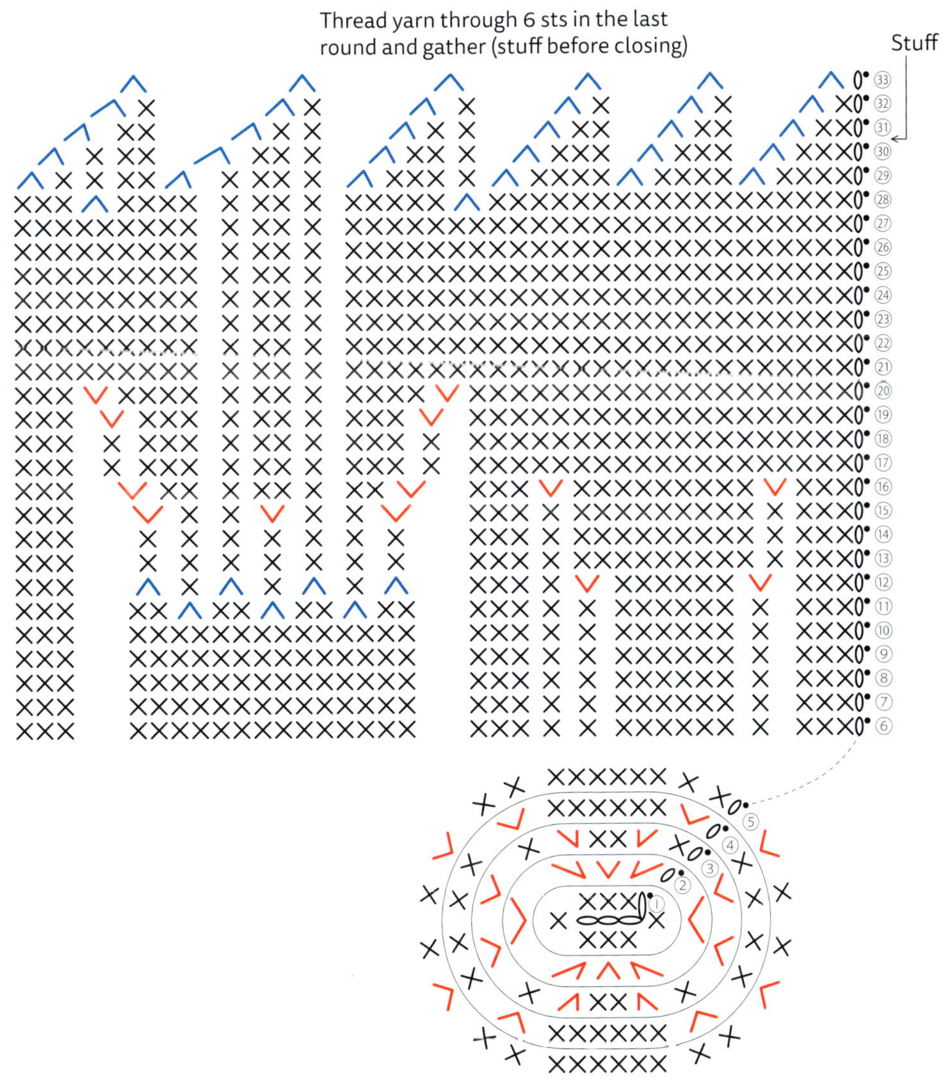

Front Legs

Left (make 1)

With Yarn B and US 7 hook, make a magic ring.
Rnd 1: ch1 (does not count as a st throughout), sc7 in magic ring, slst in beg ch1 [7]
Place stitch marker in first st of rnd 1 and move it up after each round
Rnd 2: ch1, sc1, (hdc-cl in next st) 4 times, sc2, slst in beg ch1
Rnd 3: ch1, sc1 in each st, slst in beg ch1
Change to Yarn C.
Rnds 4-6: ch1, sc1 in each st, slst in beg ch1 (3 rnds)
Change to Yarn A.
Rnd 7: ch1, sc1 in each st, slst in beg ch1
Rnd 8: ch1, sc1, sc2 in next st, sc5, slst in beg ch1 [8]
Rnd 9: ch1, sc2, sc2 in next st, sc5, slst in beg ch1 [9]
Rnd 10: ch1, sc3, sc2 in next st, sc5, slst in beg ch1 [10]
Rnd 11: ch1, sc3, sc2 in next st, sc6, slst in beg ch1 [11]
Rnd 12: ch1, sc3, sc2 in next st, sc7, slst in beg ch1 [12]
Rnd 13: ch1, sc3, sc2 in next st, sc8, slst in beg ch1 [13]
Rnd 14: ch1, sc3, sc2 in next st, sc9, slst in beg ch1 [14]
Rnd 15: ch1, sc3, hdc2 in next st, hdc1, sc9, slst in beg ch1 [15]
Rnd 16: ch1, sc3, hdc2 in next st, hdc1, sc10, slst in beg ch1 [16]
Rnd 17: ch1, sc1 in each st, slst in beg ch1.
Fasten off.

Right (make 1)

Work as given for the left front leg to the end of rnd 7.
Continue in Yarn A
Rnd 8: ch1, sc4, sc2 in next st, sc2, slst in beg ch1 [8]
Rnd 9: ch1, sc5, sc2 in next st, sc2, slst in beg ch1 [9]
Rnd 10: ch1, sc6, sc2 in next st, sc2, slst in beg ch1 [10]
Rnd 11: ch1, sc7, sc2 in next st, sc2, slst in beg ch1 [11]
Rnd 12: ch1, sc8, sc2 in next st, sc2, slst in beg ch1 [12]
Rnd 13: ch1, sc9, sc2 in next st, sc2, slst in beg ch1 [13]
Rnd 14: ch1, sc10, sc2 in next st, sc2, slst in beg ch1 [14]
Rnd 15: ch1, sc10, hdc1, hdc2 in next st, sc2, slst in beg ch1 [15]
Rnd 16: ch1, sc11, hdc1, hdc2 in next st, sc2, slst in beg ch1 [16]
Rnd 17: ch1, sc1 in each st, slst in beg ch1.
Fasten off.

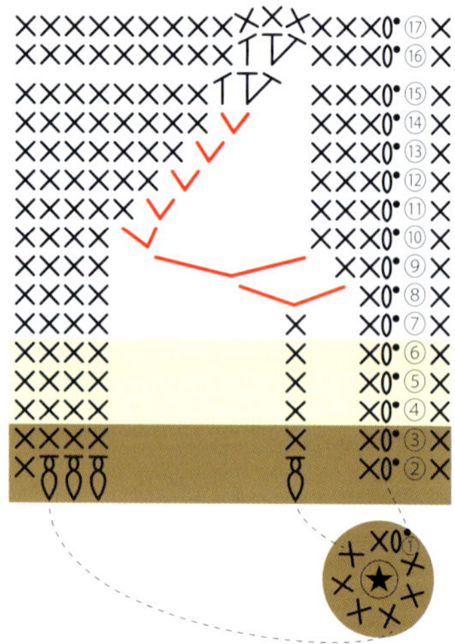

Tail (make 1)

With Yarn A and US 7 hook, make a magic ring.
Rnd 1: ch1 (does not count as a st throughout), sc6 in magic ring, slst in beg ch1 [6]
Place stitch marker in first st of rnd 1 and move it up after each round
Rnd 2: ch1, (sc1, sc2 in next st) 3 times st, slst in beg ch1 [9]
Rnds 3-4: ch1, sc1 in each st, slst in beg ch1 (2 rnds)
Rnd 5: ch1, (sc2, sc2 in next st) 3 times st, slst in beg ch1 [12]
Rnds 6-23: ch1, sc1 in each st, slst in beg ch1 (18 rnds)
Fasten off.

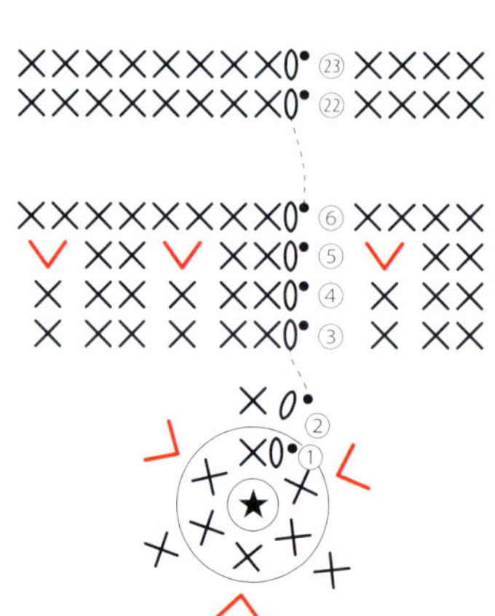

Back Legs (make 2)

With Yarn B and US 7 hook, make a magic ring.
Rnd 1: ch1 (does not count as a st throughout), sc7 in magic ring, slst in beg ch1 [7]
Place stitch marker in first st of rnd 1 and move it up after each round
Rnd 2: ch1, sc1, (hdc-cl in next st) 4 times, sc2, slst in beg ch1
Rnd 3: ch1, sc1 in each st, slst in beg ch1
Change to Yarn C.
Rnds 4-6: ch1, sc1 in each st, slst in beg ch1 (3 rnds)
Change to Yarn A.
Rnd 7: ch1, sc2 in next st, sc5, sc2 in next st, slst in beg ch1 [9]
Rnd 8: ch1, sc1, (sc2 in next st) twice, sc3 in next st, sc5 in next st, sc3 in next st, (sc2 in next st) twice, sc1, slst in beg ch1 [21]
Rnd 9: ch1, sc10, sc5 in next st, sc10, slst in beg ch1 [25]
Rnd 10: ch1, sc12, sc5 in next st, sc12, slst in beg ch1 [29]
Rnd 11: ch1, sc14, sc3 in next st, sc14, slst in beg ch1 [31]
Rnd 12: ch1, sc15, sc3 in next st, sc15, slst in beg ch1 [33]
Rnd 13: ch1, sc16, sc3 in next st, sc16, slst in beg ch1 [35]
Rnds 14-17: ch1, sc1 in each st, slst in beg ch1 (4 rnds)
Rnd 18: ch1, sc11, sc2tog, sc2, sc2tog, sc1, sc2tog, sc2, sc2tog, sc11, slst in beg ch1 [31]
Rnd 19: ch1, sc12, sc2tog, sc3, sc2tog, sc12, slst in beg ch1 [29]
Rnd 20: ch1, sc11, sc2tog, sc3, sc2tog, sc11, slst in beg ch1 [27]
Fasten off.

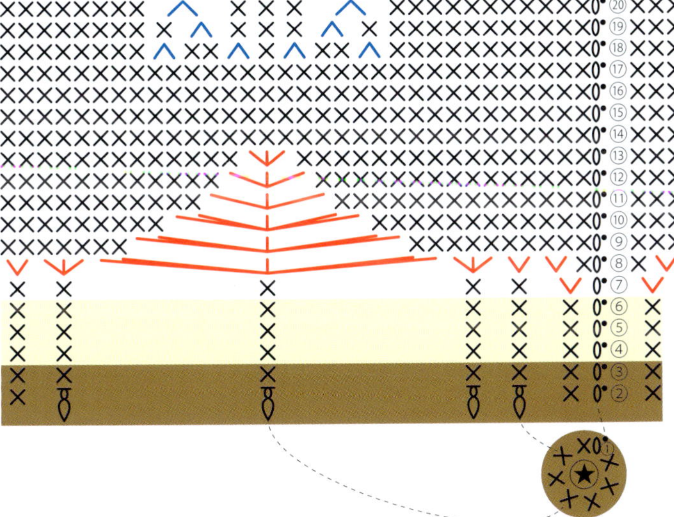

Nose (make 1)

With Yarn D and US C-2 hook, make a magic ring.
Rnd 1: ch1 (does not count as a st throughout), sc6 in magic ring, slst in beg ch1 [6]
Place stitch marker in first st of rnd 1 and move it up after each round
Rnd 2: ch1, sc1 in each st, slst in beg ch1
Slst in next 2 sts, then continue in rows.
Row 3: ch1, sc1 in next 4 sts, lengthen loop from hook and pass yarn through, pull tight to make a knot, do not turn [4]
Row 4: pass yarn across back of work, pull through beg ch1 of prev row, and rep row 3.
Row 5: pass yarn across back of work, pull through beg ch1 of prev row, ch1, sc2 in first st, sc2, sc2 in last st, lengthen loop from hook and pass yarn through, pull tight to make a knot, do not turn [6]
Row 6: pass yarn across back of work, pull through beg ch1 of prev row, ch3 (counts as dc), dc2 in first st, sc4, dc3 in last st, lengthen loop from hook and pass yarn through, pull tight to make a knot, do not turn [10]
Row 7: pass yarn across back of work, pull through top of beg ch3 of prev row, (ch3, dc2) in same st (beg ch3 counts as dc), sc8, dc3 in last st, lengthen loop from hook and pass yarn through, pull tight to make a knot [14]
Fasten off.

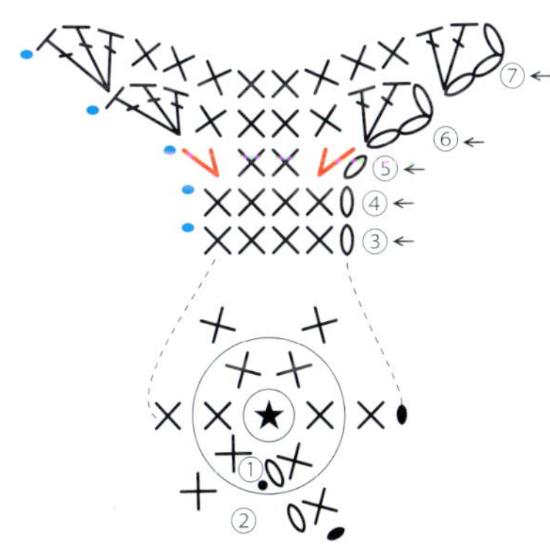

Mouth (make 1)

With Yarn F and US C-2 hook, ch10.

Rnd 1: skip first ch, sc1 in next ch, hdc1, dc2, sc1, dc2, hdc1, sc3 in last ch, rotate and work along opposite side of chain, hdc1, dc2, sc1, dc2, hdc1, sc2 in last ch, slst in skipped ch at beg of rnd [20]

Place stitch marker in first st of rnd 1 and move it up after each round

Rnd 2: ch1, sc4, slst in next st, sc9, slst in next st, sc5, slst in beg ch1

Change to Yarn D.

Rnd 3: in Yarn G ch1, sc9, change to Yarn H, sc3, ch2, dc4tog over next 4 sc (and skipping the slst), ch2, sc3, slst in beg ch1 [20]

Fasten off. Use the wrong side as the right side.

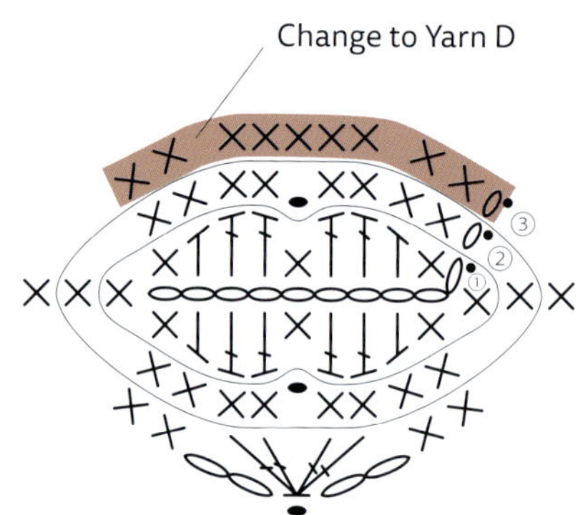

Ears

Right Ear (make 1 each of outer and inner ear)

Outer Ear

With Yarn A and US 7 hook, ch9, leaving a 12" (30 cm) tail of yarn.

Work in rows.

Row 1: dc1 in fifth ch from hook (counts as 2dc), dc1, hdc1, sc1, sc3 in last chain, rotate and work along opposite side of chain stitches, hdc2, dc2, dc2 in next ch, turn [14]

Cut a 6" (15 cm) long piece of armature wire, fold in half, position the folded area at the corner of the ear, and crochet next rnd over the wire to trap it into the sts.

Row 2: ch1 (does not count as a st throughout), sc7, sc2 in next st, sc6 [15]

Fasten off.

Inner Ear

Make inner ear in the same way with Yarn E and US C-2 hook, omitting wire.

Left Ear (make 1 each of outer and inner ear)

Outer Ear

With Yarn A and US 7 hook, ch9, leaving a 12" (30 cm) tail of yarn.

Work in rows.

Row 1: dc1 in fourth ch from hook (counts as 2dc), dc2, hdc2, sc3 in last chain, rotate and work along opposite side of chain stitches, sc1, hdc1, dc3, turn [14]

Cut a 6" (15 cm) long piece of armature wire, fold in half, position the folded area at the corner of the ear, and crochet next rnd over the wire to trap it into the sts.

Row 2: Ch1 (does not count as a st throughout), sc6, sc2 in next st, sc7 [15]

Fasten off.

Inner Ear

Make inner ear in the same way with Yarn E and US C-2 hook, omitting wire.

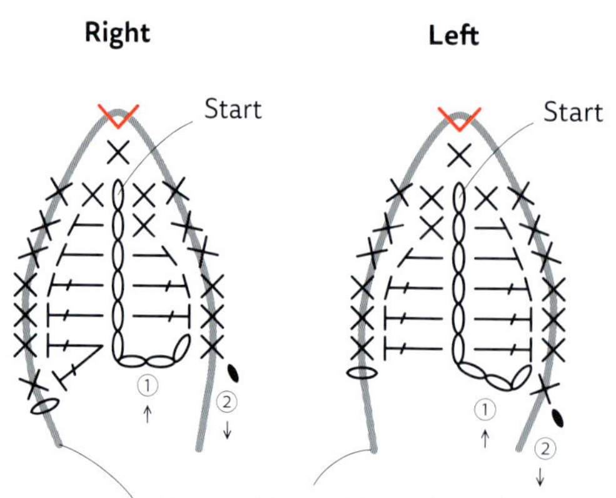

ASSEMBLY DIAGRAM

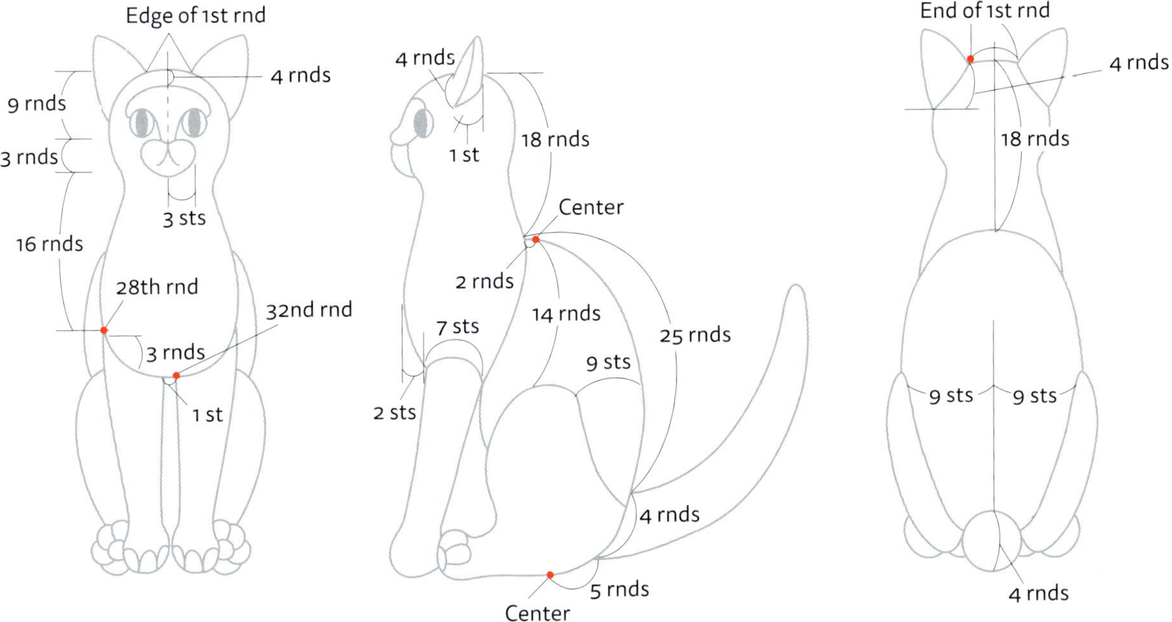

GRAFTING

Yarn Length Key

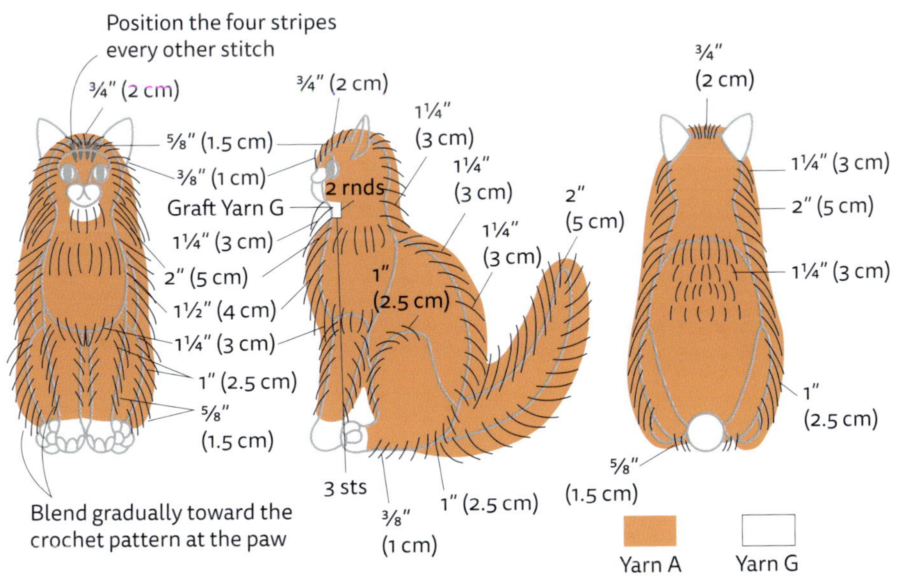

TIPS

- Do not graft ears, toes or stomach area.
- Brush the back of the ears with a slicker brush to make them fuzzy.

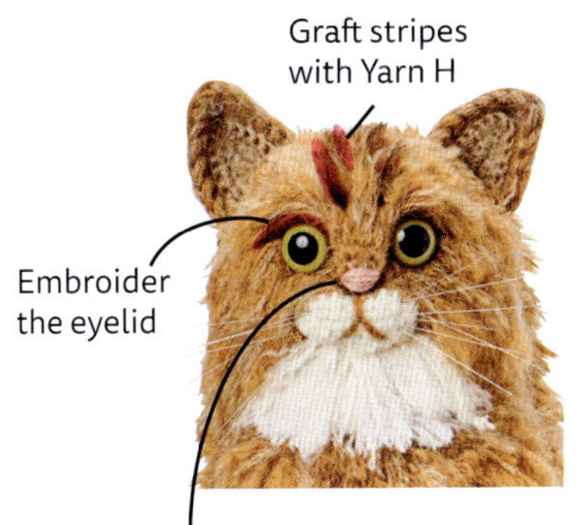

Basic Crochet Symbols & Stitches

Chain stitch: Wrap the yarn around the hook (yarn over) and pull the yarn through the loop on the hook.

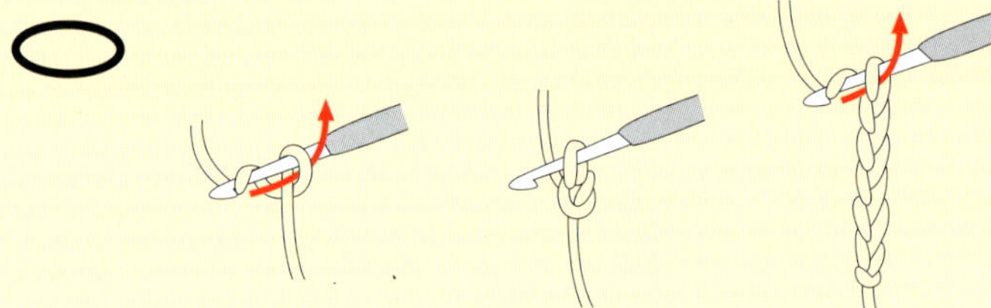

Slip stitch: Insert the hook into the stitch as instructed, yarn over, pull the yarn back through the stitch and also through the loop on the hook.

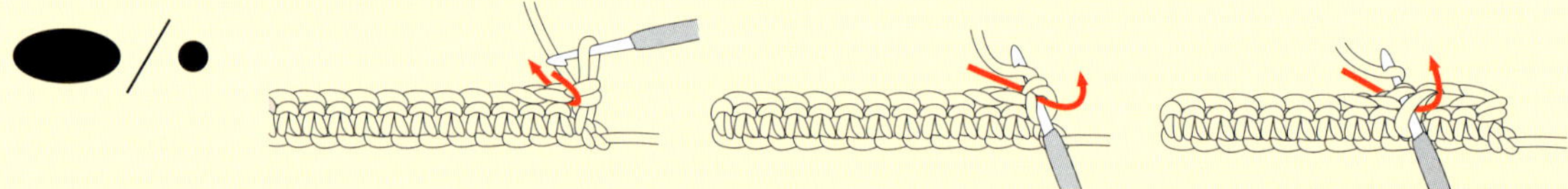

Single crochet: To work back along a line of chain stitches, skip the first chain stitch, insert the hook into the top half of the next chain stitch (the second chain stitch from the hook), yarn over, pull the yarn through the chain stitch (two loops are now on the hook), yarn over and pull through both loops.

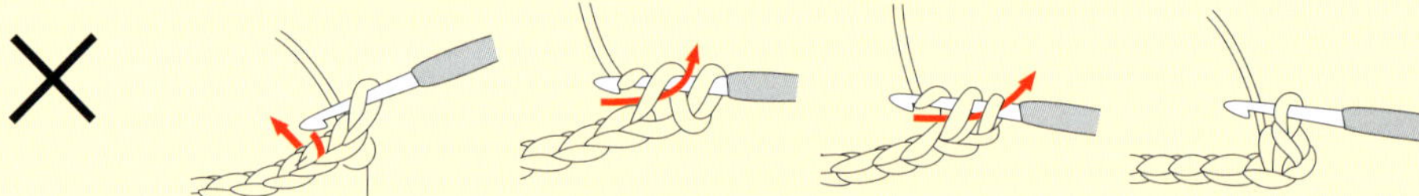

First chain stitch

When working into a row or round of single crochet stitches, you will start the row or round with a chain 1 (this does not usually count as a stitch), then you will work 1 single crochet into each stitch, always placing the hook under both loops at the top of the single crochet stitch.

2 single crochet in the next stitch: Make two single crochet in the same stitch.

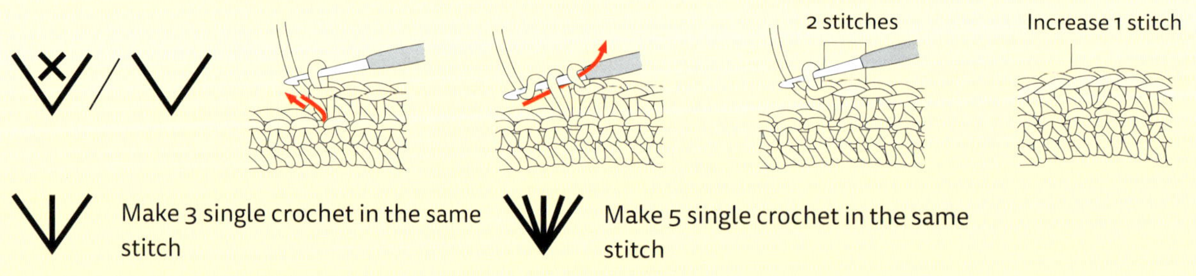

Make 3 single crochet in the same stitch

Make 5 single crochet in the same stitch

Single crochet 2 together: Decrease 1 stitch by working 2 stitches together as follows: Insert hook into next stitch, yarn over and pull loop through, insert hook into next stitch, yarn over and pull a loop through (3 loops on hook), yarn over and pull through all 3 loops.

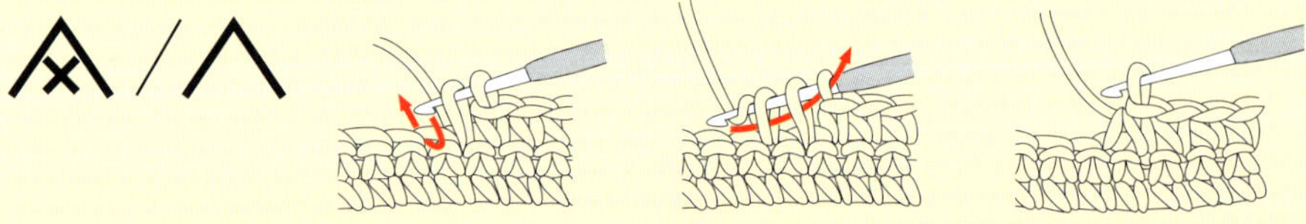

Single crochet 3 together: Decrease 2 stitches by working 3 stitches together as follows: *Insert hook into next stitch, yarn over and pull loop through* repeat from * to * in next 2 stitches (4 loops on hook), yarn over and pull through all 4 loops.

Half double crochet stitch: To work back along a line of chain stitches, skip the first 2 chains, insert the hook into the top half of the next chain stitch (the third chain stitch from the hook), yarn over, pull the yarn through the chain stitch (three loops are now on the hook), yarn over and pull through all 3 loops at once.

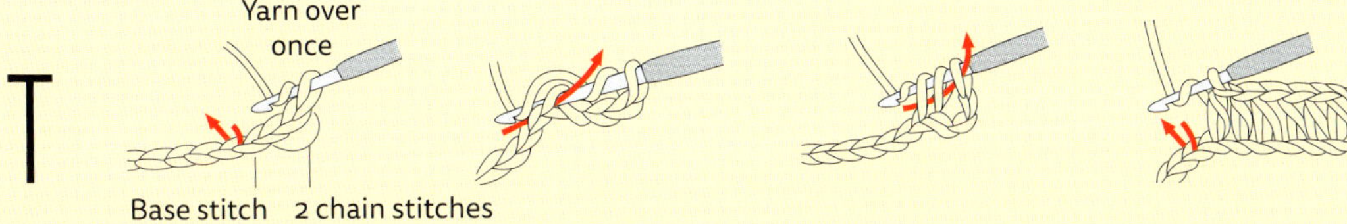

Double crochet stitch: To work back along a line of chain stitches, skip the first 3 chains, yarn over, insert hook into the top half of the next chain stitch (the fourth stitch from the hook), yarn over and pull the yarn through the chain stitch (three loops are ow on the hook), *yarn over and pull through two loops; repeat from * once more.

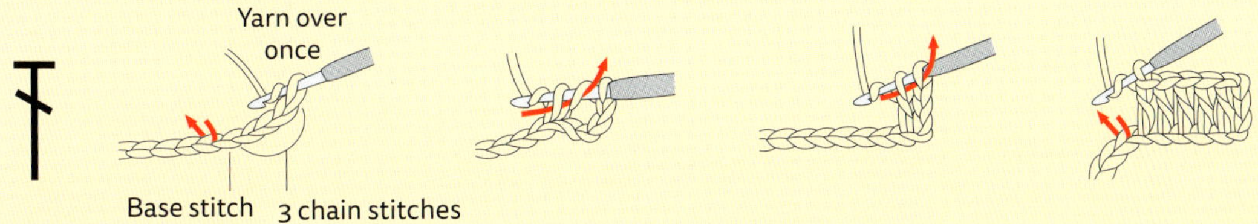

2 double crochet stitches in the next stitch: Make two double crochet stitches in the same stitch.

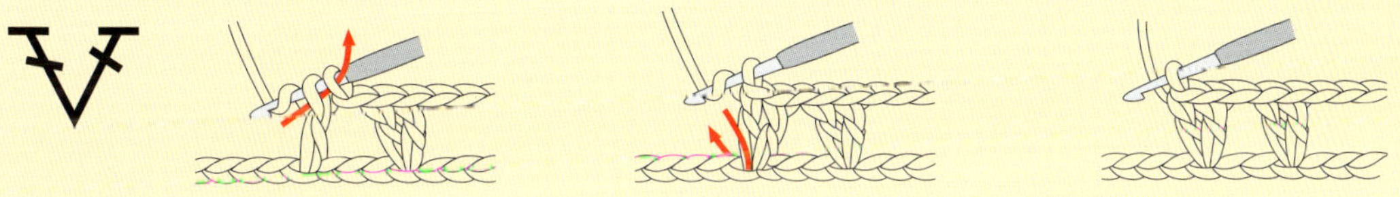

2 half double crochet stitches in the next stitch: Make two half double crochet stitches in the same stitch.

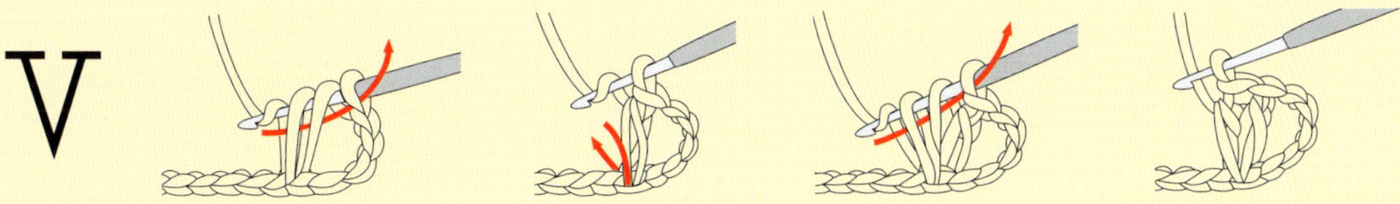

The cluster stitch variation with 2 half double crochet stitches: Make two unfinished half double crochet stitches in the same stitch, as follows: *Yarn over insert hook into stitch, yarn over and pull the yarn through; repeat from * once more in same stitch, yarn over and pull through first five loops, as shown by the arrow, yarn over and pull through remaining two loops.

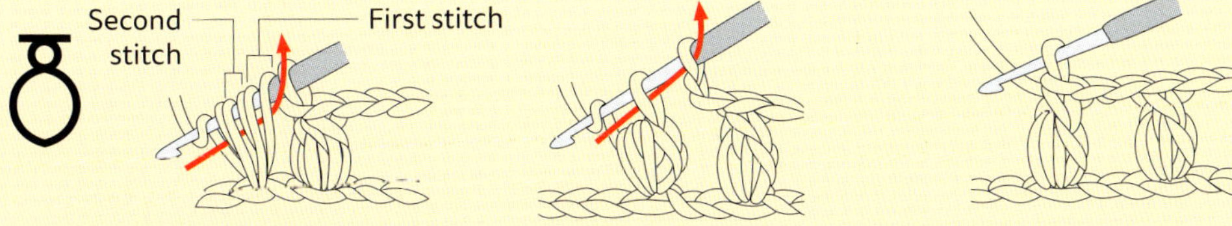

Crochet Your Own Cat
Published in 2025 by Zakka Workshop,
a division of World Book Media LLC

www.zakkaworkshop.com
134 Federal Street
Salem, MA 01970
info@zakkaworkshop.com

Original Japanese edition published by NIHONBUNGEISHA Co., Ltd. English translation rights arranged with NIHONBUNGEISHA Co., Ltd. through Japan UNI Agency, Inc., Tokyo. English language rights, translation & production by World Book Media, LLC.

Publisher: Yoshichika Yoshida
Editor: Takashi Makino
Editor: Mie Takechi
Design: Chiyomi Ito
Photography: Shimane Michimasa
Diagrams and Technical Illustrations: Midorinokuma
Translation: Kyoko Matthews
English Editor: Lindsay Fair
Technical Editor: Lynne Rowe

ISBN: 978-1-940552-93-4
Printed in China

About the Author

Mieko Shindo is a fiber artist known for her adorable animal creations. A lifelong crafter, she made her first crochet doll in 2011, which was an amigurumi version of her dog. After making an amigurumi version of her friend's pet as a gift, she started receiving orders and became addicted to making crochet animals. She loves sharing her original techniques for making these special dolls and is the author of *Crochet Your Own Dog*. Visit her website at monpuppy.com and find her on Instagram @mieko.monpuppy